Cruel Theory | Sublime Practice

CRUEL THEORY | SUBLIME PRACTICE

Toward a Revaluation of Buddhism

by

Glenn Wallis, Tom Pepper, Matthias Steingass

EyeCorner Press

© Glenn Wallis, Tom Pepper, Matthias Steingass
& EyeCorner Press | 2012

Cruel Theory | Sublime Practice
Toward a Revaluation of Buddhism

Published by EYECORNER PRESS
July 2013
Roskilde

ISBN: 978-87-92633-23-1

Cover design and layout: Camelia Elias
Image: Dazu Wheel of Reincarnation.

Printed in the US and UK

CONTENTS

Introduction
7

Part One
15

The Radical Buddhist Subject
and the Sublime Aesthetics of Truth

TOM PEPPER

Part Two
87

Speculative Non-Buddhism: X-buddhist Hallucination
and its Decimation

GLENN WALLIS

Part Three
157

Control

MATTHIAS STEINGASS

Introduction

I employ the word "cruelty" in the sense of an appetite for life, a cosmic rigor, an implacable necessity, in the gnostic sense of a living whirlwind that devours the darkness; in the sense of that pain apart from whose ineluctable necessity life could not continue...It is the consequence of an act... Everything that acts is a cruelty.

—Antonin Artaud, *The Theater and Its Double*

Whereas the beautiful is limited, the sublime is limitless, so that the mind in the presence of the sublime, attempting to imagine what it cannot, has pain in the failure but pleasure in contemplating the immensity of the attempt.

—Immanuel Kant, *Critique of Pure Reason*

Everything that acts is a cruelty. And yet the theater, the sphere of Artaud's own struggle, had devolved into a form of self-soothing diversion, creating a submissive public content to be "Peeping Toms," gawking at lives that were not their own. Artaud's sublimely impossible task was to forge this theater of complacency into an "immediate and violent" whirlwind that exposed to its viewers the raw truths of *their* lives. Only a theater that wakes up its audience "nerves and heart," he believed, can approach this goal. Such a theater must be built on cruelty—on, that is to say, "extreme action, pushed beyond all limits." If not pushed with such intentional zeal, the forces of delusion and self-satisfaction will overwhelm the vitality that is catalyzed by acts of lucid cruelty.

Everything that acts is a cruelty. What about Buddhism? Does it enable the cruel thought made possible by its sublime teaching, or does it lapse, like the theater of entertainment, into a falsely assuring aesthetics of the beautiful?

The term "Buddhism" evokes a hackneyed bifurcation. Here, we have a soft version that caters gently to the desiccated middle classes of the twenty-first century West. This version promises salvation in the form of diurnal restoration, like ease in the midst of stress or real happiness. There, we have a hard version, derived from the doctrines, practices, and institutions of Buddhism's ancient and medieval Asian past. This version advocates for a virtuosic cataclysm known as "enlightenment" or "nirvana." Both versions flourish by virtue of a curative fantasy as ancient as *Homo sapiens* ape: to emerge from life unscathed.

What use is Buddhism today? It is perpetually hoisted up as the elixir *par excellence* against the acidic tensions intrinsic to living in an ever-accelerating technological society. Its remedy? *Gelassenheit* in the midst of the infernal *samsaric* whirlwind. Is that it? Is Buddhism a modern-day Epicurean path to *eudaemonia*, a garden that "slakes the thirst with a natural cure?"

Many questions present themselves. Does Buddhism even yield useful knowledge anymore? Doesn't science provide more satisfying models of, for instance, perception and cognition, than does Buddhism? Doesn't philosophy better articulate the questions that seem to animate Buddhist discourse on meaning, language, and being? Doesn't psychology offer more effective forms and models of mental health? In short, are Buddhism's institutions and beliefs too cumbersome and unsophisticated to satisfy any but the most willing to believe?

The single most important question for us is: *Is Buddhism fit for modern life?*

The answer to that question is far from clear. Indeed, there is little evidence that it has yet to be addressed at all, and certainly not in any sustained manner. Neither those who embrace Buddhist teachings nor those who reject them are inclined toward such questioning. To the former, querying is threatening. It begets the possibility of unforeseen and undesirable transmutation, even destruction. To the latter, such questioning is irrelevant; for they have already foreclosed on Buddhism's viability. So, who does that leave? Who will ask the question?

The purpose of this book is to engage in a creative critique of Buddhism. In doing so, we neither take for granted the salubrity of Buddhist teachings for the contemporary western world nor bar the possibility of renovation and application. We see, rather, in the very process of critique an *opening*. In order to exploit this opening, however, we find it necessary to create drastically new, and buddhistically indefensible, theorems.

This book is a radical laying bare of the brutal refusal of Buddhism to honor its most basic pledge: abetment of liberation.

This is a book of heresy.

Cruel Theory | Sublime Practice consists of three parts. Each part addresses both theoretical and practical dimensions of Buddhism. Authored individually, each part nonetheless interacts with the concerns of the others. Those concerns include the formation of an autonomous subject in the face of Buddhism's concealment of its ideological force; the possibility of a practice that thus serves as a theory or science of ideology; the reconstitution of practice as an organon of authoritative structures, including controlling social-conceptual representations; and the perception of Buddhism as the subject of a historical process. Perhaps the most salient theme running throughout the book concerns the crucial necessity of transfusing anemic contemporary Buddhist discourse with the life-blood of rigorous, creative thought.

Will Buddhism in the twenty-first century West help fashion a liberated subject? Or will it continue to be a deceptive mythos spawning subjects who are content to rest at ease in the thrall of predatory capitalism? The three parts of the book share a common concern: to push Buddhism to the brink.

Glenn Wallis

Following are synopses of the book's three parts.

Part One
"The Radical Buddhist Subject and the Sublime Aesthetics of Truth"
By Tom Pepper

Pepper proposes to bring Buddhist thought into conversation with modern western thought, in order to create an approach to Buddhist practice that can produce socially engaged and truly radical subjects in a late-capitalist world. His intention is to strip away western Buddhism's tendency to produce illusions of mystical bliss or quietist contentment, and to leave behind only the (perhaps unpleasant) truth that we can actually be liberated.

Buddhist thought has been mapped onto just about every modern philosophical approach, from Kant to Derrida. In this section, Pepper proposes that producing such analogies is never useful and is usually merely reductive and misleading; instead he attempts to bring concepts from the Pali Canon and from Nagarjuna into a conversation with modern thought, particularly the thought of Badiou, Bhaskar, Lacan, and Althusser. His suggestion is not that these modern thinkers are saying the same thing as Buddhist thinkers, but that these Buddhist texts reveal truths that are absent from contemporary discourses. Badiou insists that a Truth is always available, that no truth is confined to a culture or historical moment; however, a Truth can only ever appear in a specific World, and so must always appear in the form of that World. It is Pepper's argument that there are concepts available in modern thought to enable us to bring the Truth of Buddhism into our World.

Pepper's focus is on two related concepts: the concept of the non-atomistic, socially-constructed Mind; and Althusser's productive concept of ideology as the real relations to our relations of production. These concepts can help us to make sense of the centrally important Buddhist concepts of emptiness, dependent arising, and non-self. Pepper argues that Buddhism is primarily a theory of ideology—of how it is produced and of how we can change it. Western Buddhists have mostly taken Buddhism to *be* an ideology; Pepper's argument is that it is better understood as a *theory of* ideology. More specifically, the truth discovered in Buddhist thought is the insight that we must always live in ideology, and our ideologies are always produced in aesthetic practices. We cannot neatly map the concepts of Buddhist thought onto any western thinker, because they contribute something new that can take us beyond the familiar impasses of our philosophical thought. We can, however, come to understand the Truth of Buddhism only in thought, and not in a retreat into the mystical, the ineffable, or the illusion of "pure experience."

Finally, the goal of "The Radical Buddhist Subject and the Sublime Aesthetics of Truth" is not to produce a new philosophy of Buddhism, a new conceptual system to reflect the world as it is or simply reinforce its weakest joists. Buddhism is a theory of ideological production, and can only be of use if we find practices in which to make use of these insights. It is an old cliché that we "feel" what our parents thought. While gravity was once, for Newton, a merely intellectual, mathematical model of the movement of bodies, we can now "feel" its pull as naturally as we can the warmth of a fire. In order to change our experience of the world, to remake, in Lacanian terms, our imaginary register, new concepts will need to precede and guide experience of the world. In the true sense of aesthetics, as the negotiation between the abstract idea and the felt bodily world,

Buddhist thought suggests that we can rationally and consciously choose and construct our ideologies with a sublime aesthetic practice. Pepper gives some suggestions about what that practice could look like for us today—and argues that it need not resemble the practices that may have worked for other subjects in other Worlds.

Pepper asserts that the origin of Buddhism was a "Truth Event," in Badiou's sense, and that "Buddha" can best be understood in terms of Badiou's concept of the subject of truth. This subject, incorporating many individual bodies over the course of many centuries, was able to break the grip of reproduction of the existing relations of production, to become a radical subject of change. The history of Buddhism, Pepper suggests, is a long dialectic of struggle between this subject of truth and the reactionary subjects that seek to contain the radical implications of Buddhist thought; most of Western Buddhism so far has been the Buddhism of the reactionary subject. As Buddhism moves to the West, and into a new millennium, we have the capacity to make it a radical force for liberation, to resurrect the radical Buddhist subject of truth. A Buddhist aesthetics of the sublime can be the practice in which this truth can reappear in our world.

Part Two
"Speculative Non-Buddhism: X-buddhist Hallucination and its Decimation"
By Glenn Wallis

Part Two of *Cruel Theory|Sublime Practice* presents a practical theory of Buddhism in two sections, "Critique" and "Performance." It should be said at the outset that the purpose of the theory that Wallis calls "speculative non-buddhism" is *not* to move cumbersomely through the morass of the Buddhist canon making proclamations *apropos* of this or that ancient doctrine. His ambition is both more limited and farther reaching than that. The theory is concerned with Western cultural criticism in the present. As such, it is being designed with three primary functions in mind: (i) to uncover Buddhism's syntactical structure; (ii) to serve as a means of inquiry into the *force* of Buddhist propositions; and (iii) to operate as a check on the tendency of *all* contemporary formulations of Buddhism—whether of the traditional, religious, progressive or secular variety—toward ideological blindness. Speculative non-buddhism creates the conditions for revisiting Buddhist sources—*conceptually and creatively*, not philologically or genealogically—and to do so unburdened by tradition's concealing and coercive tessellation.

The second section of the book offers a heuristic. This heuristic is performative in two senses of the term. First, it constitutes an act of *decimation.* This term is intended both metaphorically and literally. Metaphorically, it refers to a procedure in digital sound processing whereby the sampling rate of a signal is reduced via filtering. In practice, this reduction often requires discarding, or "downsampling" extraneous data. The result is decimated data, which means: reduced cost, eliminated distortion, destruction of excess signal. Again, the purpose of the heuristic is not to perform intricate philological surgery on the Buddhist "text" or, indeed, even to explicate its meaning. The purpose is to allow performance in a second, more literal sense: to create a subject who regards the decimated Buddhist material alongside of "radical immanence"—reality stripped of its buddhistic representations.

"Radical immanence" is a term coined by the contemporary French thinker François Laruelle. Wallis's idea for the interpretive strategy that will permit this analysis—speculative non-buddhism—was initially inspired by Laruelle's recent work in non-philosophy. Wallis does not see speculative non-buddhism, however, as a mere transposition of Laruelle's non-philosophical procedures for understanding the nature of philosophy over to a study of Buddhism. Given the specific Buddhist discourse-related issues that this approach uncovers, an entirely new theory is required. The insights of Laruelle nonetheless figure in Wallis's work.

Part Three
"Control"
By Matthias Steingass

This text is about history. It shows how a certain kind of Buddhism today in the modern day world can adapt and develop while at the same time ignoring the multitude of conditioning influences it is exposed to. Steingass shows how a tradition incorporates cultural artifacts from a new environment without being aware that the sheer act of integrating these new strands leads to its own change, thereby remaining oblivious to its own historicity. The text shows that this kind of Buddhism, as an example, instead of being aware of its historicity, uses a certain distorted picture of its history as an image cultivation for the pretension that it is one of the foremost harbingers of peace on earth. Western Buddhism wants to teach us that the *evil ego* is the central delusion of the human. This is a message sold to the public by a compliant publishing industry with books titled *No Self No Problem* and the like. But contrary to this simplistic popular view, what comes into sight, when one lurks under the surface, is ample evidence that the *evil ego* sits at the very core of Buddhism itself. In fact we will see that Western Buddhism, with its constant aggressive anti-ego polemics, possibly constitutes an act of repression. But, as we will see, too, the repressed resurfaces in Western Buddhism's dream of omnipotence.

The omnipotence dream is a desire to build a life and a world under perfect control. Neo-Buddhism, as the Buddhism under investigation will be named, dreams this dream by fantasizing a perfect past which only has to be rebuilt again. But yet again, an unwelcome truth resurfaces. The past isn't paradise. It is war, a war fought by holy Buddhist men killing each other mercilessly.

While this first consideration aims to show the reader the social side of the conditioning of a religious entity, and by the same token the conditioning of its believers, a further part of the investigation intends to show the role that the cognitive system of the human might have to play in creating the impression of religious experience. There is evidence today for the hypothesis that religious experience in general, and the phenomenon of the charismatic leader in particular, is a phenomenon that can be in part explained elegantly by phylogenetic cognitive structures. With both parts taken into account, the social and the cognitive side, the picture of contemporary Buddhism changes to that of an entity that is a result of effects in the historical process like any other social institution. Moreover it is shown that this Buddhism cannot demand for itself the claim to educate anybody anyway. All this might be seen as examples of *aporetic inquiry* and *aporetic dissonance* and may help lead to *ancoric loss* (cf. Wallis's heuristic, §§ 21-23).

Finally, Steingass explicates the particular historic setting in which all this takes place. This setting is characterized by the fact that capitalism is able today to integrate even the most adverse forces into its own structure and to its own avail. And not only this. An example is given that shows that even human emotion is subject to this commodification. It is important to see the development of Buddhism in the West in this context. If Buddhism is not aware of its own historicity, then this is already a tragedy. But if Buddhism as a self-declared "master of awareness" is not cognizant of the ongoing ubiquity of commodification of the whole human, regarding not only his workforce but also every aspect of his intellectual and emotional life, then the conclusion is that Buddhism is entirely useless, and even dangerous, as a social institution.

PART ONE

The Radical Buddhist Subject and the Sublime Aesthetics of Truth

TOM PEPPER

Preface

Over the past few years, I have often found myself asking (and asked) the question "Why Buddhism?" When so many Western Buddhists want a Buddhism stripped of its uncomfortable beliefs, one made compatible with science and secularism, brought in line with Western philosophy, psychology, even with capitalist economics, I find myself asking: why not just turn to Western thought? What is added by labeling this particular selection of Western values "Buddhist"? Is it just for the new-age décor, the incense, and the zafus?

This essay is an attempt to answer this question for myself. Is there anything particular to Buddhism that exceeds what could already be found in thoroughly Western thought, and which is useful and worth keeping, however unfamiliar and uncomfortable it might be? In putting Buddhist concepts into dialogue with Western thought, I am trying to discover what is excluded from our conceptual World. In what way can a practice shaped by Buddhist thought help us to re-make our World, to become better able to see truth, and become more active agents instead of just bearers of the structures that determine us?

My answer is that there are important core concepts in Buddhist thought that occur very rarely and only on the margins of Western thought. A correct understanding of concepts like no-self, karma, and conventional truth, concepts which are inseparably interrelated, can help us awaken from our ideological daze. My hope is that someday they can become so thoroughly integrated into our World, that we no longer need the label Buddhism at all, and can simply call it the practice of awakening.

I am not a scholar of Buddhism, and this is not meant as a scholarly work in the field of Buddhist studies. I am a teacher of British Literature, and a practicing Shin Buddhist. I am not seeking to uncover what the early Buddhists must have understood their texts to mean, or how Buddhism was really practiced by ancient cultures. To my mind, this would be like trying to discover how a contemporary of Spinoza would have understood his *Tractatus*; an interesting and perhaps important thing to do in the history of ideas, but not the most important thing to do with Spinoza's text. My interest, then, is in trying to uncover what true and useful concepts we can find in Buddhist texts, to treat them as the writings of intelligent and useful thinkers in the same way I would treat the writings of Hume or Althusser. The goal is neither to recover a complete and coherent system, nor to insist that these thinkers were always right, but to discover what they allow us to think, and so to do.

I have attempted to write in a way that will be accessible to anyone who has some knowledge of Buddhist thought and a college education. I have tried, therefore, to indicate what I take various thinkers and texts to be saying, rather than assume any specific knowledge of these texts or any shared interpretation of them. I may not have always succeeded in my attempts at clarity, but I hope I have been clear enough to at least raise some questions in the collective Mind of readers.

None of the ideas presented here are completely new. I make no claim to originality in any particular concept. The only uniqueness in this essay is in its assemblage of concepts and discourses that are usually quite disparate. It is my peculiar karma (in the sense in which I will define the term) to have brought together these strands of thought in a manner that, I hope, suggests their radical potential. Now if only someone, with greater facility at the practical matters of organizing and motivating people than I have ever had, could be inspired by this essay to attempt new forms of practice and bring some glimmer of enlightenment to our tenebrous times.

Introduction: Buddhism, Aesthetics, and Anti-Intellectualism

Buddhism must be understood as a practice and theory of aesthetics.

To most readers this will likely seem, initially, an ethnocentric, anachronistic, or simply incomprehensible assertion. At best, it is likely to sound absurdly reductive and insultingly dismissive, given the common meaning of the term "aesthetic" today. So perhaps I should begin by defining my terms.

I use the term in an increasingly uncommon philosophical sense, to refer to that category of human thought and practice which negotiates the relationship between the universal and the particular, in its many versions: the general and the specific, the abstract and the concrete, the mind and the body, the idea and the sensory perception. Since the eighteenth century this has been called the aesthetic, and although the study of aesthetics has often focused on art, the concerns of aesthetics clearly far exceed this limited range of human activity.

Hegel famously defined the aesthetically beautiful as the "sensory manifestation of the idea," a perfect correspondence of thought and sensation, of mind and body. In an increasingly secular, temporal world, the problem of the relationship between the mind and body clearly posed a new kind of problem. Rather than conceiving the body as profane, fallen, and in opposition to the divine soul, human beings were faced with the problem of the nature of the relationship between our thoughts and our sensory experience of the world. Do all ideas originate from perceptions, as Locke and the empiricists would have it, or are there ideas already in the mind that shape our perception of the world? How do our sensations shape our thoughts? To what extent can our thoughts function to control our bodies, shape our perceptions, and manage our emotions?

The issue is clearly one of social stability. If our bodily experience of the world is the primary source of motivational force, how can we contain and shape the unruly sensual desires? Can thought, specifically reason, function to restrain and guide our bodily impulses? On the other hand, how can we be sure that our ideas in any way correspond with the world? Isn't there always the danger that we might produce a philosophical construal of the world which has no correspondence with material reality? Hadn't it been done for centuries, in Aristotelian physics and the Ptolemaic description of the cosmos? How can we ensure that we don't get carried away by our ideas, without sinking into an animalistic sensualism? For the eighteenth century, the solution was the category of the aesthetic. Burke, in his *Enquiry into the Origins of Our Ideas of the Sublime and the*

Beautiful, attempts to demonstrate how aesthetic experience, bodily and emotional responses to particular sensuous forms, can shape our moral actions in the world. For Kant, the gulf separating the mind from the noumenal object can be bridged by the aesthetic; we have sensory experiences of the world, and a cognitive faculty, but only aesthetic judgment can guarantee that our concepts actually correspond to the external physical world. The only way we know we are not deluding ourselves in our ideas, and misperceiving the noumenal world too drastically, is by the guarantee provided by a universal faculty of aesthetic judgment. When we perceive the beauty in nature aesthetically, Kant assures us, we know that our thoughts and sensation are both functioning properly, and properly aligned.

The highest form of aesthetic practice, for Kant, was poetry. In literature, we experience the balance of the general and the particular most perfectly suited to guide our everyday beliefs and actions in the world, to avoid the dangers of excessive critical thought likely to occur in more abstract uses of language, or the dangers of hedonism that can result from the more thoroughly sensory art forms. The poem, play, or novel can be perfectly enjoyable in purely "aesthetic" terms, judged only by its formal perfection, and can thus provide proper conceptual content and emotional motivation without allowing the consumer of the aesthetic object to question the universality of these particular values, beliefs, attitudes, and tastes.

That this functions as a powerful form of social control should be evident. If one has the proper taste to enjoy a Wordsworth poem or a Jane Austen novel, to find it self-evidently "good" and pleasurable in the proper intensity, then one will obviously possess the proper morals, beliefs, politics, and sensibilities to be a good member of bourgeois society. As Wordsworth assures us in his famous "Preface to *Lyrical Ballads*," if we do not enjoy his poems it is because we are in an unhealthy mental state. If we do enjoy them, they will automatically produce in us the proper moral sensibility to survive the horrors of urbanization and industrialization. At the time when population increase, urbanization, industrialization, and increased literacy were producing dangerous revolutions in France and America, Wordsworth set out to establish poetry as the practice which would inculcate properly conservative values, and make it possible for people to accept the "uniformity of their occupations," their poverty, overcrowding, and forced removal from a familiar agricultural way of life, without stirring up rebellious thoughts or the craving for "gross and violent stimulants" (176-177). The beautiful work of literature should gently shape our attitudes and beliefs, and motivate us to proper moral action, without our even noticing.

There is, of course, the problem of the universality of tastes to deal with. Or perhaps a better way to put it: the notorious variability of tastes. As Paul de Man has pointed out, although aesthetics has always been with us, the fact that this particular practice was "left nameless until the end of the eighteenth century is a sign of its overwhelming presence rather than of its nonexistence" (92). We only named a category of social practice aesthetic, and proceeded to insist it must remain in splendid isolation from politics and science in the triumvirate of the true, the good, and the beautiful, once it became disturbingly clear that our social practices produce our tastes, and so our most deeply held truths are in fact open to change. In the realm of Literature, there has been a pronounced move toward rejecting the social determination of taste, denying the politics of literary canon formation, and insisting that aesthetic "qualities" are "far more fundamental structures" than ideology or politics or economics (Lamarque, 8); in his introduction to Frank Kermode's lectures on "the aesthetics of the canon," Robert Alter gleefully celebrates the fact that Kermode eschews "polemically engaging the ideological definition of the canon," preferring instead to focus on "intrinsic qualities" of work which give "pleasure" universally, and relegating canonical change to the category of "chance"(3-5). This is the strategy that aesthetics has taken for the last couple of centuries, because it is crucial that the point of intersection between our concrete bodily experience of the world and our abstract theoretical understanding must remain unexamined, must be an ineffable, mystical and timeless quality at the level of intuition or feeling. The alternative is that we may be able to change the social system in which we experience the world; *pace* Kant, the aesthetic sense that the world corresponds perfectly to thought is not a guarantee of correctness, but a socially produced experience functioning to reify and naturalize our ideologies.

Of course, as de Man implies, we have been seeking a negotiation between general concepts and particular experiences as long as there has been human thought and language. However, we have not always tried to bring this negotiation to a sudden halt with a purportedly transcendent set of "qualities" and ineffable emotional experiences. This is not to say that there have never been *any* attempts to foreclose this negotiation until the aestheticization of art in the modern era; there have been many strategies to stop the progress of social formations, to reify and naturalize the existing situation. It may even be that the very nature of the human animal requires this foreclosure, that its occurrence is a condition of any progress in our social productive powers. Etienne Balibar has suggested that one of Marx's fundamental insights is the realization that what I have been calling aesthetics is at the core of all human society:

> Marx did not produce a theory of 'class consciousness,' in the sense of a system of ideas which might be said, consciously or otherwise, to express the 'aims' of a particular class. He produced, rather, a theory of the class character of consciousness, i.e., of the limits of its intellectual horizon which reflect or reproduce the limits of communications imposed by the division of society into classes (or nations, etc.). The basis of the explanation is the obstacle to universality inscribed in the conditions of material life, beyond which it is only possible to think in imagination. . . . Ideological consciousness is, first, the dream of an impossible universality. . . . The universalization of particularity is the compensation for the constitution of the State, a fictive community whose power of abstraction compensates for the real lack of community in relations between individuals. (Balibar, *Marx* 48)

Human beings can produce our basic necessities more effectively, effectively enough to escape the limitations of our animal existence in nature, only through collective effort, but this collectivity always comes at a price. Balibar argues that it is another aspect of Marx's great insight that what follows from this aesthetic negotiation of universal and particular is almost always the division between bodily and intellectual labor; further, it is paradoxically only once we become thoroughly convinced that thought, often referred to derogatorily in terms like *mere theorizing* or *overthinking* or *intellectualizing*, has no potential to effect change in the real, that we witness an "astonishing conversion of impotence into domination"(*Marx* 46-47); the conviction that thought is pointless and unreal mental activity divorced from the bodily real is exactly what enables the reification and naturalization of existing ideologies, and the oppressive impossibility of real action guided by reason, of *praxis*. The belief in the impotence of thought can then allow one particular kind of thought—uncritical ideological belief—to have absolute power over us, controlling us completely.

In the realm of the aesthetic, we have the insistence that rational thought cannot grasp the ineffable mystery of aesthetic beauty. But there are other strategies as well, and in an age in which the power of art is rapidly fading, one of the most common is perhaps a kind of sophisticated anti-intellectualism which those still interested in thinking refer to as postmodernism. It will be part of the argument of this essay that Western Buddhism is poised to become a religion of global capitalism, the ultimate cosmopolitan anti-intellectual aesthetic practice which can teach us to eschew thought and become thoroughly indifferent to those merely worldly things which are exactly the things we *can* and *should* be working to change. My concern, then, will be to suggest that Buddhism has a long history of precisely *refusing* to halt the aesthetic negotiation, and that there is an alternative to the postmodern anti-intellectualism that is actually no more than a reactionary aesthetics of the beautiful.

The pervasive hostility to philosophical thought, at Buddhist retreats, in popular Buddhist books and magazines, and sometimes even in scholarly works, is particularly puzzling in light of the long tradition of sophisticated and rigorous Buddhist philosophy. In the last couple thousand years, there has been enormous intellectual work in many different schools of Buddhism, but American Buddhists are adamant that any such efforts be labeled "clinging to views" or "ego." Why, I have often wondered, adopt Buddhism at all if one is so opposed to rigorous thought? Of course, there are some easy answers about the myth of the exotic east and spiritual snobbery; however, I have come to think that there is a more subtle, and less dismissive, answer to this puzzle. Perhaps instead of just putting this down to the general American stupidity, we can explore why this anti-intellectualism is so compelling, and what, exactly, is so terribly anxiety-producing about thought?

I would suggest that the particular kind of anti-intellectualism found among Buddhists (who are often more educated and intelligent than average) is a reaction to the desolate landscape of postmodern thought; it is, I will suggest, not the only possible reaction, and there is another alternative, which I think is more in line with the history of Buddhist thought. That alternative is not a retreat from thought into pure experience, but the willingness to think our way out of this bleak intellectual wasteland. In short, while many Buddhists have been trying to escape the trap of post-modernity by retreating down into the thought-free depths of the body, a more useful (and, I will argue, more Buddhist) response is to escape up, into the limits of philosophical rigor.

To begin, I want to delineate the particular kind of anti-intellectualism that has permeated popular forms of Western Buddhism. Now, in mentioning only a handful of Buddhist teachers, I don't want to suggest that they are solely responsible for this anti-intellectualism, or that this represents the entire function of their work as a whole. I am simply picking a few examples, to clarify the kind of resistance to thought I see as being most prevalent; these examples are certainly not exhaustive, nor are they the entire story of Western Buddhism. There are some Buddhist thinkers today (I will mention only a few of them, as well) who are very explicitly not in the anti-intellectual camp. My goal here is simply to suggest one reason why anti-intellectualism is so popular a position for a group of people who are, more often than not, well-educated, intelligent, and politically progressive—all descriptors with which the term "anti-intellectual" would not seem to pair well.

I have often heard it suggested that the suspicion of thought is the result of Zen being the first form of Buddhism widely introduced to Western audiences. I wonder, however, if it might have been the other way around—that Zen was attractive because it is so easy to portray it as eschewing thought. In fact, it is also possible to see the practice of koans as exactly demanding that the practitioner take his conceptual framework to the limits and transcend it, not escaping to pure thoughtless sensation but advancing the possibilities of thought. I'll come back to this suggestion later. For now, I want to start with some popular presentations of Zen, and their rejection of conceptual or philosophical thought.

D.T. Suzuki, in *An Introduction to Zen Buddhism*, declared that "Zen has nothing to teach us in the way of intellectual analysis," and that the sutras are "mere waste paper whose utility consist in wiping off the dirt of the intellect and nothing more" (8-9). The goal is "absolute peace of mind," and this is only attained by eliminating the "reasoning faculty," which only "hinders the mind from coming into the directest communication with itself" (14). We must seek a state in which we eliminate logic and even words from our minds, and live in direct, sensory experience, understood to be the deepest truth. On this understanding, our senses are a pure apprehension of a primal reality, which have been screened from us by thought; now, I'll set aside critiquing this position for the time being, and simply note that it would strike most philosophers today, and I believe many Buddhists throughout history, as startlingly naive to think that our sense perceptions aren't always already structured by culture and language.

More recently, Thich Nhat Hanh has followed a similar approach. One could open almost any of his books and find a statement about the futility of thought, or the vanity of "philosophy," or a statement that true enlightenment is full enjoyment of a cup of tea or the beauty of a flower. We must never examine the history of imperialism that is the condition of our enjoying this cup of tea, or the cultural privileging of the temporary, of the extravagant ability to devote resources to the useless, which are the cause of our pleasure in the flower. That would be thought, and so delusion: enlightenment is just insisting that the culturally produced experiences we enjoy the most are a contact with the timeless reality of "interbeing." In *Understanding Our Mind*, perhaps Thich Nhat Hanh's most explicitly anti-intellectual book, he explains that in the first stage of the bodhisattva path, the bodhisattva must remove the "obstacles of knowledge and affliction," and then "experience" reality directly as a "state of being refreshed" (117). Note that these are not obstacles *to* knowledge—knowledge itself is the obstacle to experiencing reality: "Before ideation, before the mind begins to construct, the mind touches the ultimate dimension, the realm of suchness" (128). The only way back to this mystical suchness is eliminating thought and fully enjoying our sensory present.

It is not only the Zen Buddhists in the West who have embraced this belief in an experiential truth to be found beneath the layers of conceptual thought. Stephen Batchelor is but one example of a Buddhist trained in the Tibetan tradition who has become quite popular by teaching this understanding of Buddhism. Nearly thirty years ago, in his book *Alone With Others*, he presented his "existential approach to Buddhism" as a rejection of the Mahayana "preoccupation with speculative metaphysics" (125), which led, in his view, to a neglect of the "existential experience" that he believes can lead us to see through the attachments produced in reaction to our primal anxiety in the face of emptiness. In *Confession of a Buddhist Atheist*, he explains how he became dissatisfied with his Buddhist teachers once he discovered Heidegger, as a reaction to the abstraction of philosophical thought: "Heidegger believed that the entire project of Western thought that began with Plato had come to an end. It was necessary to start all over again, to embark on a new way of thinking, which he called *besinnliches Denken*: contemplative thinking" (51). This "contemplative thinking," according to a common reading of Heidegger which Batchelor seems to have accepted, is a form of access to the autochthonous, the primitive and primal experience before rational and scientific thought separated us from this deep reality, and is, for Heidegger, accessible in the authentic purity of the true German language, and in the timeless greatness of the true German poets. The alienation of modernity is seen as the result, not of capitalism, industrialism, fascism, but of too much abstract thought and too much scientific progress. The return to the primitive experience of Dasein can restore us to "authenticity." Among self-styled "secular Buddhists," this justification for rejecting the demands of rigorous thought seems to be very appealing; it might be worth remembering where it led Heidegger.

In the period between the two World Wars, in the great capitalist crisis of the twentieth century, when the bourgeoisie was stuck in its attempt to throw off the yoke of the *ancien régime* without accidentally launching a worldwide communist revolution, this Heideggerian retreat from thought perhaps makes some sense. Modernity was sapping the meaning from the world, and it was either make a bid for the imaginary plenitude of Dasein while sitting on a cushion, or goose-step in line. Or, of course, to do the unthinkable: turn Red. In our time, the meaninglessness of the world is supplemented by the meaninglessness of thought, with philosophy reduced to a postmodern language game. Accepting the radical division between the meaningless material world accessible to science and the thoroughly relativist world of humanity which no scientific thought can reach, a view most commonly going by the name of Rorty, the postmodern world is left with only two choices: accept the absolute reduction of all human experience to the working of the neurons in the brain, or retreat into a mystical ideal of pure experience, with the (misguided) belief that we can access perceptions that are not tainted by the world of language and conceptual thought. Thought becomes "fixed views" or "intellectualizing" because in the present tyranny of absolute freedom of opinion, no position can be argued for; to make an argument is to deny that all opinions are equally valid in the purely relativist world of human thought. In this extreme relativism, we have reached the absurd state in which at least one popular Buddhist teacher, with the proper credentials of years spent in the exotic East, can quite seriously suggest that we could even walk up walls if we just believed that we could!

The anti-intellectualism is perhaps understandable, then, as a retreat from the arrant nonsense of so much popular postmodernism. One way of understanding the history of philosophy is as a series of containments of radicalism. There is a sense in which Kantian transcendental idealism functions to contain the radical potential of the enlightenment, and a sense in which Heideggerian phenomenology contains the radical potential of Nietzsche, Marx and Freud, and today the postmodern "linguistic turn" can contain any potential for radical thought by simply insisting that all thought is a language game that constructs the reality it purports to describe. In the current state of Western culture, it is perhaps understandable that when people are dissatisfied, when they have a felt sense that there are things excluded, left unthinkable in the language games of philosophy and the tyranny of free opinion, they look to find that excluded something in an experience that they are told is "purified" of all thought, a return to the primal unity with "suchness." That they don't find it there is perhaps the reason that so many Western Buddhists move on, after a year or two, to the next New Age fad.

There is, however, an alternative to this defeat of thought. And, what is most important, it is one that is more compatible with the history of Buddhist philosophy than the attempt to retreat into mindless experience of a cup of tea or a flower. For if Buddhism has always insisted on the limitations of conceptual thought, it has also always insisted that our experience is never free of those very same limitations. Every gut-level intuition is shot through with the structure of ideology; our very sensory perceptions are active structuring of the world, not passive reception of stimuli. When we stop thinking, we do not escape ideology, but become fully enslaved by it at the level of the body.

We can seek the limitations of thought not by sinking down into the realm of the purely physical, but by accepting the challenge of rigorous thought. In the words of Alain Badiou:

> in order to think, always take as your starting point the restrictive exception of truths and not the freedom of opinion. This is a worker's principle in the sense that thought is here a matter of labour and not of self-expression. Process, production, constraint and discipline are what it seeks; not nonchalant consent to what a world proposes. (*Second Manifesto,* 25)

Badiou is only one example, but I think a very good one, of what thought could do if we accept realism, instead of either a relativist idealism in which consciousness creates the world or a reductive materialism in which thought becomes a useless epiphenomenon. For Badiou there is a truth external to anything we may think, a reality which is true whether we know of it or not—Badiou makes a distinction, then, between truth and knowledge. Our thought will always run up against the limits of what our conceptual system cannot include, what is unthinkable. This aporia produces the potential for rigorous thought, for the insistence on including what we can think as true but which cannot be proven or formalized in any existing paradigm of knowledge. And it is in this excess of truth over knowledge that the subject arises, as the embodiment of an idea that is produced by the network of causes and conditions having pushed the current paradigm of thought to its limits; it is not the subject, as individual genius, that produces the idea, but the new idea that produces a subject. Badiou's term for this is "ideation:" "that which, in the individual undergoing incorporation within the process of a truth, is responsible for binding together the component of this trajectory... it is that through which a human life is universalized" (115-116). For Badiou, thought does not endlessly reach the same inevitable impasse, because the subject is not an autonomous, atomistic self in dualistic relation to an objective world; instead, the subject is purely an effect of a structure, of a set of discourses and knowledge practices that are an endless dialectical process of excess and containment. This structure is not fixed and limited, but can endlessly gain more and better knowledge, can endlessly decrease the realm of what must be excluded from the symbolic order. I will return to Badiou's thought, and the alternative it presents, shortly. First, I want to briefly indicate some alternatives to the rejection of thought that have been proposed by Buddhist thinkers over the last couple thousand years.

The Beautiful and the Sublime in Buddhist Thought and Practice

To return, then, to the world of Buddhism: I would like to suggest that there is a long tradition in Buddhism of attempting to transcend the limits of knowledge by means of more rigorous thought. That enlightenment demands we pursue thought to its (upward) limits is at least one possible reading of Nagarjuna. Instead of seeing Nagarjuna, as Richard Hayes does, as a sophist who conflates two meanings of the term *svabhāva* and so produces an illogical argument, we can see him as a thinker who pushes to the limit the conceptual network of his time, a conceptual system in which it is not yet possible to think the distinctions between the two meanings of *svabhāva* that Hayes argues are conflated ("identity" and "causal independence;" see Hayes, 316-322). We can see Nagarjuna as a philosopher who, in the words of Jay Garfield and Graham Priest, "does not try to avoid the contradiction at the limit of thought" (4), and whose "extirpation of the myth of the deep" may turn out to be his "greatest contribution to Western philosophy" (16). Similarly, on one way of understanding Vasubandhu's *Yogācārin* thought, what is most important is that it is not a form of idealism in which the mind creates reality, but an attempt to understand the causes and conditions of the mind itself. As Dan Lusthaus puts it, for *Yogācāra* "mind is not the solution but the problem," and every attempt to escape consciousness is itself "nothing

but a projection of consciousness" (5-6). Vasubandhu's way of practicing Buddhism is to discover, in rigorous philosophical thought, in what way and to what
ends our mind produces phenomena from an actually existing reality external to
it. Like Spinoza (but unlike many phenomenologists) the *Yogācārins* believed
this knowledge was obtainable, and could enable better and more complete
ideas of reality. In Spinozist terms, we are only as free as our ideas of reality are
correct and complete; if our ideas are inherently incomplete, we can only pursue
liberation if we pursue liberation of all sentient beings—because each individual
subject is no more than an effect of the entirety of sentience.

In his recent book *Brains, Buddhas, and Believing*, Dan Arnold has demonstrated, I think quite convincingly, that the problem we have called the aesthetic
for the last two hundred and fifty years is the same problem that Buddhist
thought addressed for millennia. The Buddhist thinkers of the first millennium
may have come up with different terms in which to address this problem, approaches to the negotiation of the abstract and the concrete that have no precise cognate in Western thought, but the core of the issue remains the same. As
Arnold explains it:

> Dharmakīrti influentially argued—with his predecessor Dignāga, and as would commonly
> be held by Buddhist writing subsequently—that only perception (*pratyakṣa*) and inference
> (*anumāna*) have the status of *pramāna* [an epistemological warrant, or guarantee of truth];
> all other ways of arriving at knowledge are reducible to one of these criteria. These two
> kinds of cognition have as their respective objects the only two *kinds* of things (on one way
> of dividing up the world) that exist: unique particulars (*svalakṣaṇa*) and such abstractions or
> universals (*sāmānyalakṣaṇa*) as concept and complex wholes. Since the kinds of things that
> figure in conceptual content are not particulars, to say that perception apprehends only
> unique particulars is thus to be committed (as in fact Dignāga and Dharmakīrti commonly
> were) to the view that perception is constitutively nonconceptual; as these thinkers put the
> point, perception is *kalpanāpoḍha*, "devoid of conception." (20-21)

Arnold's argument is that this commitment leads Dharmakirti to the same
kind of intractable problems faced by eliminative materialists and cognitive science today, and that this is the source of disagreement between Dharmakirti
and the *Madhyamaka* school of Buddhism founded by Nagarjuna. Importantly,
Dharmakirti's insistence on an absolute distinction between the concrete-partic-
ular perception and the abstract-universal concept forces him to be "ever at
pains to bridge the gap between these" (121). This is, we can clearly see, an aesthetic problem in the philosophical sense, and the particular solution one pro-

poses to this problem has far reaching consequences. Dharmakirti, like the Western philosophers Locke, Hume, and Kant with whom Arnold puts the Buddhist thinker in dialogue, wants to insist on the need for an absolute correspondence between thought and sense, between universal and particular, but cannot find a way to guarantee this correspondence without rejecting the causal power of thought completely; and, as Arnold shows, this does not really solve the problem for Dharmakirti any more than it has for post-Kantian thought in the West. (The solution to this problem, I will suggest later on, is to understand thought as a tool with which to act in the world, and not an attempt to map the world).

We are left with the logic of the aesthetics of the beautiful, in which our thought-free contemplation of a mystical and ineffable experience can stabilize our experience of the world, but only by denying us any capacity to change it for the better. Western Buddhism has adopted exactly this solution, in its insistence on a realm of experience that transcends thought *and* the world, but which can produce only a thoughtless, emotional acceptance of things as they are, equanimity understood as the retreat from engagement with the world, into some core self which remains untouched by earthly events, and will achieve its bliss in the afterlife (or in the infinity of the present moment). Nothing, it seems to me, could be further from the history of Buddhist thought than such rejection of philosophical rigor and assumption of the existence of an abiding and world-transcending consciousness.

My suggestion here is that Western Buddhist anti-intellectualism is perhaps understandable, given the current state of the situation. If thought demands of us hard work, a kind of faithful labor, but we are constantly told that there is no point in it because there is no "correct" thought, there is just the majority opinion, well, then of course we may be reluctant to put in the effort. This rejection of the rigors of thought has not been the response of Buddhism for most of its history, and is not the only possible response to the dismal failure of Western intellectual activity. If we find that the work of intellectuals is beating a reactionary retreat at a time of crisis, and giving us no help at all, we don't need to return to our teacups and flower gardens. We can find what the present limits of thought leaves as unthinkable, not in our pure experience, but in thinking the limits of emptiness.

This need not be as terrifying as many Western Buddhists might think. It does not necessarily mean that Buddhism would be reserved for those with the greatest capacity for abstract or philosophical thought. Anyone can make the attempt to transcend the limits of their own conceptual framework. Indeed, until every-one does, there will be no single subject capable of moving forward beyond an outer limit, because every subject is an effect of the structure of all subject posi-tions. To put this somewhat more concretely, when the calculus was discovered, very few could grasp it; to reach the stage at which the subject had sufficient *a priori* knowledge for Fermat's last theorem to be solved, we had to reach the stage at which an understanding of calculus could be expected of school chil-dren. For any of us to make progress toward awakening, the entire structure which produces our subjective "mind" must move beyond the current limita-tions of conceptual thought. There is no elite, there is only a structure, so there is no value in leaving anybody behind.

I will try to outline ways in which we can break free of the impasse of the aesthetic problem that has left us completely unable to effectively shape a world seemingly doomed to economic and ecological catastrophe. My suggestions will require a recovery of the concept of ideology from the philosophical trash bin to which it has been resigned. It will also require a somewhat radical new conception of the Buddhist concept of non-self (*anatman*), but one I will argue is new only for us in the West and radical only in the sense of recovering the full implications this concept has had in the past and can have for us today. To get to that point, though, what is required is a shift from the aesthetics of the beautiful to the aesthetics of the sublime, and it is to this that I will now turn.

For if the aesthetics of the beautiful is a guarantee of stability, freezing in place the structure of our thought and the practices they inform by means of an ineffable emotional experience, leading to anti-intellectualism and philosophi-cal dead-ends, the sublime is instead an aesthetics of instability, openness, and change. Whereas the beautiful seeks to assure us of an absolute correspondence between the abstraction of our reason and our perceptual experience, the sub-lime demonstrates the non-correspondence of universals and particulars, their incompatibility, the impossibility of lining up universals with particulars in our existing construal of the world. As Hegel put it:

> The sublime in general is the attempt to express the infinite, without finding in the sphere of phenomena an object which proves adequate for this representation. Precisely because the infinite is set apart from the entire complex of objectivity as explicitly an invisible mean-ing devoid of shape and is made inner, it remains, in accordance with infinity, unutterable and sublime above any expression through the finite.

> Now the first content which the meaning gains here is this, that in contrast to the totality of appearance it is the inherently substantial *unity* which itself, as a pure thought, can be apprehended only by pure thought...this essentially expresses the fact of substance's elevation above individual phenomena as such, and above their totality, with the logical result that the positive relation is transposed into a negative one in which the substance is purified from everything apparent and particular and therefore from what fades away in it and is inadequate to it. (Vol. I, 363)

If we can bear with Hegel's idealist terminology here, we can see the necessity of the sublime in any attempt to allow for real change in our construal of the world. If the beautiful remains beyond explanation only so long as we refuse to examine the social practices that make it aesthetically pleasing, the sublime is much less comforting, and resists explanation in an altogether different way—exactly by demanding of us thought and action. The sublime indicates to us those parts of our "world" which remain invisible in the existing system of knowledge, and those places where thought begins to exceed a clear, formal presentation, where we "know" something to be true (either perceptually or conceptually) but cannot yet "prove" it. We may come across some occurrence which defies explanation in all existing discourses, or we may conceive some idea which our material practices allow us no opportunity of demonstrating.

Let me offer some examples, by way of illustration. We are all familiar with the tragic mass shootings that have occurred at schools in recent years. The one thing we consistently hear is that they are unthinkable, unfathomable, that they cannot be explained. These are exactly sublime moments, opportunities for us to realize that our existing discourses exclude certain causes, cannot see or name them; they must remain invisible from within our present construal of the world. Similarly, the insistence by American economists that the workings of the economy are beyond prediction or explanation is an instance of the sublime, revealing a place where our thought remains inadequate to the phenomena we can no longer ignore. In both of these cases, we tend to insist that the world is "too complex" to be explained or understood, that there is some incomprehensible and mysterious "human factor" that must always escape explanation or understanding. This is a case of the concrete exceeding the abstract, of the ineluctable phenomenal reality forcing us to go to great lengths to avoid admitting the aporia in our present conceptual construal of our world.

There is also another form of the sublime, in which thought exceeds the capacity of our practices to manifest. This occurs, for instance, in theoretical physics, when extending a conceptual structure to its logical limit suggests the existence of a phenomenon we cannot yet detect. The pursuit of the God Particle, then, would count as a sublime aesthetic practice, the particle collider at CERN being the most expensive aesthetic object yet constructed. Such sublime moments may lead us to extend our capacity for detection, to find things that were right in front of us all along but undetected because they were invisible in our discourses, and so remained unnoticed, or perhaps counted only as error or artifact or background noise. Or, these sublime extensions of thought may take the form of a deconstructive critique, demonstrating the limits or aporia in our conceptual system, demonstrating the need to reconfigure the system completely.

The twofold division of the sublime has a long history; it is found in Kant's *Critique of Judgment* and Hegel's *Aesthetics*. Either there is an excess of idea over sensory manifestation, as in the sublimity of the concept of the infinite, or an excess of sense over idea, as occurs in the sublime of incomprehensible phenomena (those observable events which we cannot avoid noticing, but for which we have no adequate explanation). I would suggest, though, a third category of the sublime, in which what is absent is exactly the mediating discourse which could successfully unite our intuition and our experience. Consider, for instance, the case of Fermat's Last Theorem, which was a baffling mathematical puzzle for over three hundred and fifty years, until it was finally proven in 1995. The concept seems simple enough: there can be no solution to the equation $a^n + b^n = c^n$ where a, b, c and n are integers, and n>2. Fermat knew it to be true, said he had a "simple" proof, which was never found, and for hundreds of years mathematicians worked to prove the theorem. Intuitively, it seemed it *must* be true; experientially, nobody could find a specific instance in which it is not true; yet there was no formal mathematical proof of its truth. What needed to change, in this case, was neither the perception of particulars nor the intuitive "knowledge," but the discourse of mathematics itself, the most formal language in which we seek to manage the negotiation between the abstract and the particular. This problem, as a sublime moment, helped drive the advance of mathematical discourse for centuries.

Now it is time to come to terms with the element I have been somewhat fudging over the last couple of pages. If the sublime is the aesthetic mode in which change occurs, what exactly is it that is being changed? I have used the term discourse, but that is not completely right. I have also used the term construal, but that is only partial as well. To explain what is actually being changed, and how the change occurs, we will have to introduce another concept, one that has a troubled history in philosophy, the concept of ideology. I have used the term in passing, but much like the term aesthetics I am using it in a particular sense that is not at all the common use of the term. I will proceed, then, to a more thorough consideration of the concept of ideology, because if Buddhism is a theory and practice of the aesthetic, it is also inherently a theory and practice of the aesthetic production of ideologies. It will be my argument in the next section that one cause of enormous difficulties in interpreting ancient Buddhist thought is a failure to recognize the distinction between what we might today call ideology and science, a distinction that seems not to have even needed mentioning for early Buddhist thinkers because the reality of the realm of ideology was, for them, a given. Many problems in Buddhist thought can, I will argue, be cleared away once we understand that much of the time what is at stake is not a description of a mind-independent (or mind-created) reality, but a theory of the production of proper ideologies.

Buddhism as a Theory of Ideology

"Philosophy," Etienne Balibar points out, "has never forgiven Marx for *ideology*. It is constantly at pains to show that this is a badly constructed concept, which has no unambiguous meaning...[y]et philosophy comes back endlessly to this same point: as though, by the very fact of introducing this term, Marx had set it the problem it must master" (43). Why is ideology so troubling for philosophy? What exactly is ideology in marxist theory? Moreover, is it conceivable that Marx and the Buddha were in any way working toward the *same* concept?

I intend to show that, in fact, Buddhist thought has long engaged in the problem of ideology, but that just like Marx's concept of ideology it has remained extremely disturbing, repeatedly misunderstood or pushed aside, because the full implications of this category of human thought and practice are quite profound. My suggestion will be that what Marx and the Buddha both realized is that we are ideological animals by nature, that it is always and only in ideology that we live our lives, and that awareness of this inexorable truth can help us to reduce suffering. I want to suggest that Buddhist concepts such as those usually translated as "views" and "conventional truth" are best understood as being about how we live in ideology, and how our practice can serve to help us construct better, more useful, ideologies. That is, I am hoping to produce a kind of comparative philosophical investigation here, in which we can use a modern, Western concept to help us better get a handle on the value that Buddhist thought and practice can still have for us today. To that end, I will first attempt to explain exactly what I take the marxist concept of ideology to be, focusing on the theorist I take to be its most important and insightful proponent, Louis Althusser.

Althusser's most famous, most anthologized, most cited, most widely read work is, I would argue, almost never understood. "Ideology and Ideological State Apparatuses: Notes Towards an Investigation" (hereafter, the ISA essay), has generated thousands of pages of commentary, more often than not attempting to argue against the existence of such a thing as ideology. So, despite the fact that the essay is so well known that almost any graduate of a halfway-decent college probably believes she already knows what it says, I am going to briefly recount its most important claim here.

Ideology is not an illusion, a false consciousness, or a deception. It is not a mistaken understanding of reality, because it is not primarily an understanding of reality at all. The most important insight in Althusser's essay is that ideology does not represent reality in some distorted form, in order to deceive us into accepting our oppression. Instead, ideology is that set of practices in which we reproduce our *relations to the relations of production.* Our ideological beliefs always exist in a material practice—if they do not, if our beliefs are not productive of and reproduced by some concrete behavior, then they are not our actual ideology, and we do not in fact believe them at all (although we may believe in the need to *claim* we believe in them). There is nothing necessarily false or distorting about ideology; it may include some distortions, some falsehoods, but it does not need to do so. In the essay cited at the beginning of this section, Balibar attempts to explain why Marx drops the term ideology in his later work, shifting his focus to an analysis of "fetishism." He sees this "suppression of the very concept of ideology" (55) as troubling, as an "aporia" in Marx's thought; I would suggest it is perhaps simply a shift in emphasis, an attempt to avoid the mistaken assumption that ideology itself must be eliminated. Instead, under the concept of "fetish," Marx attempts to isolate only those particular ideologies which do require some distortion or falsehood.

What ideology *must* include is a set of beliefs-in-practices which function to *reproduce* the existing relations of production, the material and economic system in which we are living. These beliefs are primarily on the order of morals, values, tastes, emotions—not beliefs about mind-independent reality, although certain conceptions of what is real may be entailed. Ideologies then are not mere illusions, unnecessary epiphenomena, the ornament or drapery of life which we could do without. They are the very real practices with which we reproduce our social formations, passing on knowledge and facilitating the more efficient organization of work, so that every individual need not start human culture from scratch, learning how to make a fire or grow crops all over again with each generation. The existence of ideologies is unavoidable, and a useful thing, but they do sometimes become rigid and reified, locking us into ways of organizing our world that are unproductive, or that benefit the few at the expense of the many. What we need to eliminate is not ideology, but the mistaking of ideologies for natural and inevitable truths. On the other hand, there is a tendency to assume that if ideologies can be changed, then they are not "real" and have no importance, that they are mere illusions; this mistake must also be avoided. The fact that something is socially constructed, a practice produced by human invention, does not mean it is any less real, or that it does not have causal powers. As we will see, this is very similar to the common misunderstanding of the *Madhyamaka* concept of "conventional truth," the assumption that since it is convention and not ultimately real the truly enlightened should do without it. We do not need to think that *either* there is a mind-independent reality and we should eliminate all human conventions *or* there is a humanly-created reality and so no external reality exists. We must always inhabit both.

This seems to be tremendously difficult for most readers of Althusser to fully grasp, to *think* and not just "understand." We do not represent our mode of production in our ideology, any more than we represent the physical universe there. Instead, what ideology does is to produce a set of beliefs and values *connected to practices*, all of which function to enable the reproduction of our existing social formations. Ideology does not give us a blueprint of the building we live in; instead, ideology consists of the set of tools with which we keep that building in repair. We could always devise better tools, the ones we have are not the only kind possible, but that does not mean they are therefore "mere illusions" and we can do without them. The educational system serves as Althusser's central example in the ISA essay, so perhaps we can use that example here. There is clearly a sense in which education requires a conception of the mind-independent world, a depiction of both the physical universe and human social formations. However, the specifically *ideological* function of education is in its reproduction of the existing means of production and social relations. Without education, we could not reproduce our current relations of production—we need individuals with specific technical skills to keep things running, and need to sort individuals into specific social functions, and education is the system we have produced to do this training and sorting.

Let me try to clarify this with a metaphor. What Althusser would call "scientific" knowledge functions to describe reality, both the natural world and humanly created social formations. It functions, in a sense, like a map: scientific knowledge attempts to give a useful model of the world, and can be more or less accurate. Our maps may be wrong, may be imprecise, and can be corrected and refined. Ideology does not function to map the world, but to enable us to get around in it; so, metaphorically, ideology functions more like the mode of transportation. The mode of transportation and the map are, of course, related. If our mode of transportation is an automobile, we are most interested in road maps; road maps are not "incorrect," they are not (usually) deceptive or illusory, but they are of limited use if we decide we want to go for a hike in the forest. The difficulty of ideology is that we tend to believe that our existing mode of transportation is the only one possible, that it is natural, universal, and cannot be modified or changed, so that it becomes inconceivable to do such a thing as go for a hike. Instead, we focus on changing the map of the world, paving the forest to make it accessible.

Keep in mind that this is only a metaphor, and like all metaphors it is limited. Ideology functions to enable us to keep the world running, but it also produces much of our motivation and investment it the world. We need to educate new individuals in our existing technology, to produce new technology, and to organize the world in such a way that individuals are sorted into functional roles. In order to do this, we need to value technological change, hard work at tedious tasks, financial success, an understanding of higher education that emphasizes technical training over critical thought. Our ideologies are, for Althusser, how we reproduce the existing relations of production; they are not an image of those relations of production, not an image of the world. "Hard work at tedious tasks" is not a thing out in the mind-independent world, it is a thing we *do*. Education clearly enables the reproduction of relations of production, but so do other ideological practices. We believe in love, so we court, marry, reproduce, and support our families: love and the nuclear family are essential ideological formations in the reproduction of the exiting relations of production, assuring that there will be new individuals interpellated into all the existing roles in society, into each socio-economic strata, in a way that appears to us fully "natural." For an American today, what could be more "natural" than the nuclear family as the primary unit of social organization? These ideological formations are not false or delusory, are not imaginary in the ordinary sense of the term—people really do feel romantic love, really are attached to their children—but they can become problems when we mistake a socially produced practice for a natural and necessary one. We will always need some ideology, but we need to know that that is what it is, and be able to change it when it is no longer a useful way to produce human happiness. If it should become desirable or necessary to go into the forest, we need to realize that we can get out of the car. If we decide we want to live in skyscrapers, we must stop trying to build them with the tools we used to build log cabins.

And for Althusser, this is entirely possible: "As is well known, the accusation of being in ideology only applies to others, never to oneself (*unless one is really a Spinozist or a Marxist, which, in this matter, is to be exactly the same thing*)" (ISA, 175; my emphasis). What he is saying here is not that the Spinozist or the marxist has no ideology, but that she is *aware that she does have one.* We are, as Althusser puts it, an ideological animal by nature: we produce practices invested with meaning which enable us to reproduce and transform our relations to the natural world, so that we can escape the constraints of natural history. And we do transform our ideologies all the time (metaphorically, we produce new–and sometimes better–modes of transportation with every passing generation), but too often we do it without conscious awareness. Our ideologies, that is, begin to reproduce themselves, and we simply go along for the ride. What must not be missed, but often is, is that we are also a species of animal capable of gaining conscious awareness of our ideologies.

Althusser's theory of ideology has come in for quite a bit of criticism, not least from marxists who see it as leaving the subject completely trapped in the realm of illusion. This is, I would argue, a misunderstanding of the profound insight of Althusser's essay. The usual argument against Althusser goes something like this: on Althusser's account of ideology, only subjects can take action in the world, and subjects are always only functioning as supports for social structures (they are subjects *of* an ideology); theoretical practice can produce objective knowledge of the world, but is powerless to motivate action, since action can only be taken in an ideology by a subject. We are left, the argument goes, with the choice of knowing what changes to make but being unable to make them, or being active subjects in the world but with no objective knowledge of the effects of our actions and so blindly reproducing the existing social formation. All objections to Althusser's theory of ideology I have ever encountered ultimately boil down to this same problem. But this is a misunderstanding of Althusser, which ignores the importance to his theory of those subjects (Spinozist or marxist) who can know their own ideology. The ISA essay does present an overwhelmingly claustrophobic picture of the pervasiveness of ideology, but this must be understood to function as Ernest Mandel has suggested Marx's third volume of *Capital* does: it is meant to explain how such a system is so often able to work at all, not to argue that it is inexorable. We have powerful attachments to our ideologies. Certain degrees of transformation are already built into the system of reproduction. We mistake our humanly created social formations for inexorable natural occurrences. And so, ideology keeps us going round in circles, reproducing our subject positions and filling the vacancies in the structure with new individuals interpellated as subjects. For Althusser, we can escape this endless going round in circles, and there are practices which will make it more likely that we can do so. *It will be my argument that certain kinds of Buddhist practice can serve this purpose.* They can do so, I will argue, because Buddhism has always operated in the register of the ideological. It can function to produce another kind of subject aware of its ideology and able to use this knowledge of its own ideological practices to transform the social formation. It seems to me that the production of just such a subject, one which, like Althusser's "Marxist or Spinozist," can remain aware of the ideology it inhabits and consciously work to transform its world, is a potentially radical project made possible by the practice of Buddhism. Just as philosophy cannot forgive Marx for ideology, however, the world cannot forgive Buddhism for producing the threat of such a subject position; the repeated refusal to see this potential in Buddhist thought has led to endless problems of interpretation and doctrinal argument, most of which dissolve once we look at Buddhism as a theory and practice of ideology.

I want to demonstrate this proposition by responding to a collection of essays by a group of scholars of Buddhist studies who call themselves, collectively, "The Cowherds." Their book *Moonshadows: Conventional Truth in Buddhist Philosophy* takes up the question of the epistemological and ontological status of the Buddhist philosophical concept of the "two truths." They are attempting, as the title of the second essay in the book puts it, to take conventional truth seriously. The concern is precisely the problem with the concept of ideology; because, if conventional truth is put in opposition to ultimate truth, we can easily assume that we want only the latter, and that conventional truth, being *merely* conventional, is purely relative and we need not concern ourselves with it. The problem seems to be that for the *Madhyamaka* school of Buddhism, there has been a persistent concern that we take this conventional truth seriously, that it is not mere illusion or error, and that it is subject to correct understanding and not open to relativism. To perhaps oversimplify, conventional truth is like a chair: it has no *ultimate* existence, it is impermanent, and it only has the capacity to serve its function in the presence of beings that bend at the hip and sit on their buttocks; but it is, nonetheless, very real, and we can be correct about its proper use and produce true knowledge about how good a chair it is. As the Cowherds put it in the introduction, their concern is, in part, to suggest ways that "a Mādhyamika can espouse emptiness and yet avoid having to accept extreme conventionalism"(19). What particular suggestions the various contributors arrive at will depend on how exactly they take conventional truth to be *real*, and on why exactly we cannot simply do without it. My argument will be that what is being discussed here as conventional truth is what I, following Marx and Althusser, have been calling ideology, and that once we grasp this, once we understand that the theory of conventional truth is a theory of ideology, some of the apparently paradoxical and troublesome passages of *Madhyamaka* Buddhist philosophy become much more transparent—although they then impose on us a task that is far from easy to undertake.

As Jay Garfield puts it in his only solo contribution to the volume: "One of the Buddha's deepest insights was that there are two truths and that they are very different from one another" (37). One way to think of these two truths is along the lines of the Althusserian division between science and ideology: there is truth that is an effort to describe mind-independent reality as it actually is, and there is the truth of real and causally efficacious humanly-produced social practices. Both are really existent, which is one definition of the term *satya* that the Cowherds typically translate as "truth," but they are really existent in different ways. The very fact that *satya* means both "true" and "really existing" would seem to suggest that the distinctions between ephemeral, powerless thought and real, causal matter were not even operative for the early Buddhist thinkers. Their texts are perhaps difficult for us because we need to work so hard to get beyond distinctions that they never conceived of making.

The various "meanings" for which the *Madhyamaka* philosopher Candrakirti employs the term *samvrti*, ordinarily translated as "conventional," can illustrate how close his concept is to what, in my modern idiom, I refer to as ideology. In the introduction to *Moonshadows*, the Cowherds delineate three meanings for this term:

> Candrakirti's three usages of the term *saṃvṛti* are instructive regarding the formidable task facing the commentator who wishes to account both for the use of this term and its Sanskrit etymology. In his *Prasannapadā* he tells us that one usage of *saṃvṛti* is to refer to *ignorance*, whereby one takes as true what is not, thus concealing the actual way things are. Another usage is as dependent arising (*pratityasamutpāda*), more exactly as "mutual dependence" (*parasparasaṃbhavana*), and hence means things that lack intrinsic nature (*svabhāva*). The third usage is to mean agreements governing the use of signs, that is, *sa The*, as well as the various worldly practices, or more accurately, worldly *transactions* (*lokavyavahāra*). Included here are both agreed-upon linguistic expressions (*abhidhāna*) and objects of expressions (*abhidheya*), as well as cognitions (*jñāna*) and their objects (*jñeya*). (12-13)

I give this long passage because it so well illustrates that this concept for Candrakirti covers the same philosophical terrain as the concept of ideology. To take the third meaning first, the conventional takes in the use of language, the relationship between signs (words) and signifieds (the objects referred to, i.e., concepts or abstractions), as well as the realm of human practice and interaction. These practices, including language, are true in the sense that they really are existent and have real causal powers; they do not, however, have "intrinsic nature," in the sense that they are not part of a mind-independent reality (the second usage of the term). If there were no more conscious beings, the entire register or realm of ideology would cease to exist. Finally, the first definition returns us to the problem Marx set out to solve: why do we insist that certain practices are "natural" and inevitable when clearly they are socially constructed and not in our best interest to continue participating in? Ideology often does serve this function of obfuscation and distortion, but, as I have been arguing, it does not always or necessarily do so. Avoiding the tendency to think that if ideology *ever* presents an erroneous picture of reality it must *always and only* do so is one reason Marx stopped using the term, and developed a different term for the concept of ideology that serves this distorting function.

We can see Candrakirti, then, as attempting to sort out the nature and function of ideology, to remind us of the Buddha's "deepest insight" that there are two truths, two kinds of things that really exist, and they really exist differently. Considered in this way, we can avoid the trap of relativism. The humanly constructed practices which shape our lives are real, and have real causal power, but they are conventionally real in that they are not the only possible way we could structure our inhabitance of the earth. The educational system we have produced functions to reproduce certain kinds of knowledge and foreclose other kinds; the family structure in which we reproduce helps facilitate the distribution of individuals into different kinds of work and different social and economic roles. These practices have real causal powers, they shape the kind of world we inhabit, and simply knowing that they are humanly constructed, that they are *merely conventional*, does nothing to diminish their power. This is why it is crucial to become aware of these practices, of how they shape our understanding of and interaction with the world. If we don't gain this kind of awareness, we will either assume that our conventions are timeless and inevitable, or assume that we can be "free" of them simply by recognizing that they are not natural kinds but human constructions.

The importance of this level of awareness was also suggested by Aristotle and, as with our difficulty making sense of Buddhist thought, we have been troubled for centuries by our inability to make sense of this seminal Western thinker, and for the same reason. Unable to recognize that Aristotle thinks of our ideological formations as having a different ontological and epistemological status than the mind-independent world, we have been troubled by some apparently incomprehensible passages in his works. On the typical reading of the *Nichomachean Ethics*, Aristotle is said to propose that character is produced by making virtuous action habitual, and then to propose that the highest form of the good life is the life of pure contemplation. To caricature this reading of Aristotle somewhat, it is as if he is suggesting that we train ourselves to be mindlessly well behaved by mere habit so that we can occupy our minds completely with abstract thought. The problem, for most philosophers, is that this hardly seems like anything we might want to call a good life.

An alternative to this troubling understanding is offered by Joe Sachs, in the wonderful introductory essay to his translation of *Nichomachean Ethics*. He points out that the term that has come to be translated commonly as "habit" has a quite different meaning in the original Greek:

A *hexis* is not only not the same as a habit, but is almost exactly its opposite....The verb *echein* means to have something in [an] effortful way, or to be something in an enduring and active way, and its corresponding noun is *hexis*. By choosing that word, Aristotle says that a moral virtue is an active state or conditon....Virtue manifests itself in action, but only when one acts while holding oneself in a certain way. In Greek, the phrase "holding oneself in a certain way" is *pôs echôn*, and the noun equivalent to it is *hexis*. How must one hold oneself, if one's act is to be worthy of the name virtue? Aristotle's first and most general description of this active state is that in it one holds oneself in a stable equilibrium of the soul, in order to choose the action knowingly and for its own sake. (xii-xiii)

What is at stake for Aristotle is the conscious production of ideology, the highest life being one in which we choose, through contemplation (Greek: *theoria*) the actions we will accustom ourselves to. The ethical "mean," Sachs explains, is not some "point on the dial we need to fiddle up and down," but is the ability to produce a space "free from both the tyranny of desire, and the forcible restraint of desire" in order to "judge what seems most truly pleasant and painful" (xix). For Aristotle, thought is not some useless and causally inert realm in which we try to escape the body; contemplation has important causal powers, as does the realm of virtue or ideology. Aristotle's famous "middle state," much like the Buddhist "middle way," is not the midpoint between two (ideological) opposites, but the production of a theoretical knowledge of what ideological practices would be best to participate in. The highest good, then, is not to escape ideology, but to consciously choose what ideology we want to produce. I am suggesting that the difficulty we have long had in understanding Aristotle is quite similar to the difficulty we have in understanding Buddhism. Our own inability to grasp what ancient thinkers seem to have taken as a given, that ideology is humanly constructed yet has very real causal powers and that we can and should consciously choose our ideologies, has led to endless debates about apparent paradoxes, inconsistencies, or incoherence in ancient texts.

We make our own ideologies, but we cannot make them exactly as we choose. We need to consider the question of how, and how much, we can change our ideology, and also the problem of how we might know that the change we intend to make is for the better. If ideology is of a different epistemological and ontological status than the mind-independent world, what kinds of guarantees can we have that we are producing the right practices and beliefs, the ones that will minimize suffering and increase happiness?

To respond to this issue, I want to return to the Cowherds, because this is exactly one of the questions they take up in their examinations of conventional truths. In particular, Tom Tillemans's essay "How Far Can a Madhyamika Buddhist Reform Conventional Truth?" addresses the issue of the dangers of "an extreme conservativism that nothing the world ever endorsed could be criticized or rejected and that, on the conventional at least, a Madhyamika's principle task was just to passively acquiesce and duplicate" (152). This quietism of pure acceptance and absolute relativism does seem to be the reigning ideology of Western Buddhism, but is there an alternative? Tillemans points out that this has been a concern for Buddhist epistemologists all along, and cites Kamalasila's concern that the *Madhyamaka* position "eschews epistemic instruments (*pramāṇa*) that can confirm or correct the world's beliefs" (155). But is this really the case? Tillemans takes Candrakirti to be arguing that since we cannot reform conventional truth by appeal to how things really are ontologically, all reform is worthless and futile. However, there seems to be an implicit collapse, in Tillemans argument, of all levels of reality to one. If we do not understand conventional reality as true for the ordinary folk, while ultimate reality is the truth the enlightened see, the problem seems to dissolve. That is, we can take Candrakirti as working under the *assumption* that conventional truth is still true for the enlightened, but that they *know* it is conventional, they recognize the line of divide between mind-independent reality and ideological reality. The *Madhyamaka* concern, then, is not to reject all epistemic instruments, but to insist that those which will work to reform our understanding of the mind-independent world will not be the same as those which will work to reform our ideologies. It is not the case, then, as Tillemans seems to fear, that for Candrakirti "*all sophisticated explanation is lumped together and that sophistication is itself to be ruled out*" (160, emphasis in the original). Tillemans uses the example of explaining why rice can be used to grow more rice, but not to grow barley; for Candrakirti, a complex metaphysical explanation is not needed at the level of ideology—it is enough to say that this is just the way it is. But Tillemans assumes that this argument extends to the realm of the sciences and it simply will not do to tell a biologist that this is just the way things are. At this point, I would suggest, Candrakirti would likely agree; because the whole point is that we do have sophisticated epistemological instruments that work perfectly well in improving our description of the mind-independent world, but the error comes when we try to use them to refine our ideologies.

Ideologies require a very different set of epistemological instruments, but this does not rule out the possibility of improving them. The major difficulty is that conventional truth is not falsifiable, and so there is not necessarily a single best one; however, this need not rule out solid grounds on which to improve our conventional reality. The legal system, for instance, or the emotion of romantic love, cannot be dismissed as not "real" so long as we enforce the laws and engage in practices of courtship that produce this particular emotion; we could, however, decide that these particular conventional truths are not the best ones, that they do not produce human happiness for most people. It is one thing to scientifically improve the quality and yield of crops, quite another to improve the social structure which teaches people the skills needed to grow surplus crops and motivates them to work hard to do so. To return to my map metaphor, we can improve our maps by making them more accurate and more inclusive, more "sophisticated," but this does nothing to change the way we get around. No matter how careful we are to include the hiking trails in addition to the roads, encouraging people to get out of their cars and walk is not a matter of complexity or greater detail.

There is, clearly, an interaction between improving our understanding of the mind-independent world, and improving our ideological capacity to act in the world. The problem, though, comes when we conflate or confuse these two levels of reality. And this is, it seems, an ancient and persistent tendency. If, as Garfield suggests, the Buddha's great insight was that there are two truths, he also suggests that "Nagarjuna's deepest insight was that, despite the vast difference between the two truths in one sense, they are, in an equally important sense, identical" (37). What is the similarity, and how can we avoid allowing it to impede attempts to improve our ideologies?

Let me illustrate with the example of a recent "discovery" in the discipline of physics. Physics is clearly a human social practice designed to map mind-independent reality. So, when we do this mapping, we need to be sure we are not producing a map that functions only to support and promote the currently existing mode of transportation.

The Higgs boson particle is, according to the popular media, that magical final cause that somehow gives form and mass to the universe, that provides the underlying structure of our material existence. It is the final piece of the puzzle, unfortunately, but perhaps aptly, named the "God Particle" by the physicist Leon Lederman about twenty years ago. I say aptly, because the particle is often talked about as if it had intent and causal power, as if it were the transcendent "mind" that shapes creation. Even among physicists, it is often assumed that the existence of the Higgs boson will enable us to finally engrave our map in stone, to decide once and for all that the "standard model" of particle physics, with all its quantum probability, is the correct picture, which can be refined, but not fundamentally changed. Most importantly, the god particle serves as the "deepest" strata of reality, relieving us of the need to search for new levels of causal mechanisms which can explain phenomena in such a way as to cut out the element of probability. Is such a final, causal essence even possible?

It is a commonplace in academic philosophy and eighteenth-century studies to say that David Hume argues that there is no such thing as causation, that there is only constant conjunction, and we mistakenly attribute causal power when we encounter such repeated conjunctions of events. This, the argument goes, is the origin of all our error: we mistake our misattribution of causal powers for a really existing entity, and delusions proliferate from there, because in actuality we are only justified in speaking of conjunctions we have actually witnessed as events occurring closely in time and space. Now, this isn't, I think, completely accurate as an account of what Hume says. His claim is, ultimately, that there in fact is causal regularity in the universe, that a specific set of conditions really will lead to another predictable set of conditions, and we in fact can *know* that this will happen. If I let go of this book, it will fall to the ground. Every time. Not only in the instance in which I have witnessed it, but in every instance, even those that have yet to occur. What Hume claims is that we make an error when we reify our *explanation* of *why* this happens. We say it happens because of an invisible universal force called "gravity," when in fact we have no perceptual experience of that force, and only a mathematical model which works to predict what would happen if that force in fact *did* exist; or, more precisely, the concept of gravity serves only as a model which serves to predict what always happens in the world we can actually perceive. Hume's point is that we think in metaphors, creating models to explain and predict, and what is most important is that we not forget that these models are always *only* models, that we not mistakenly convince ourselves that we can perceive these metaphorical explanatory constructs. Our description of the world, then, will always be open to greater refinement. We will be able to explain and predict events better and better, but only if we remember that we are using conceptual models, metaphors—only, that is, if we avoid reification.

The similarity of this position to Nagarjuna's discussion of causality in the first chapter of his *Mulamadhyamakakarika* is significant. As Jay Garfield explains, for Nagarjuna "carving out particular phenomena for explanation or for use in explanations depends more on our explanatory interests and language than on joints nature presents to us" (113). The assumption that there is a causal power inherent in a thing, separate from its conditions, is a fundamental error: "phenomena arise as consequences of the collocation of those conditions" (110). We are, if we think in terms of causes, stuck with "a vicious, explanatory regress, for then one has to explain how the powers to act are themselves brought about by the conditions" (113). But this "explanatory regress" is only a problem if we insist that there must actually *be* some final, transcendent, ultimate cause, some "prime mover" of the universe. If we are content to accept that everything is the result of conditions, and that our explanation will never be final, our knowledge never complete, then we have not a problem but an opportunity. The Higgs boson is desperately needed because we want the final answer, we want to know we have reached the ultimate level of explanation. But for Nagarjuna, as indeed for Hume, to think that this particle is finally the one in which causal powers inhere, that its capacity to give structure to the world is its essence, and *not* a result of its "collocation of conditions," would be an epistemological error, bringing our description of the world to a stop, and preventing us from further refining our explanations and predictions.

Now it may be that we don't, for any practical reason, need to get any finer in our predictions than the Higgs boson would allow for. If we were to stop there, and simply say we should fill in the picture a bit before we go any further, smaller, deeper (pick your metaphor), that would not be a problem; we would be considering this particle as part of the descriptive, metaphorical model that allows us to interact more extensively with the world. If, however, we say it is the final level of explanation, we must imbue it with intention and essence.

And this is where the question of ideology enters the picture. Because our model of the world, even though it is always only a conceptual model, is *not* ideological so long as we remember that it is a model, and so long as we are describing an actual state of affairs in the world, about which the model *could* possibly be imprecise or incorrect. This is the register of science, that category of human thought and practice which seeks to map out the intransitive dimension, the world as it is regardless of what intentions or desires we may have. Ideology, to continue the mapping metaphor, would be our mode of getting around in the world we have mapped out: where do we want to go, and what's the best way to get there? Ideology, then, is not falsifiable in the same way as science; we *can*, perhaps, be wrong about where we really want to go, but this is a different kind of wrongness than being wrong about whether or not that location exists. Sometimes, science and ideology will impact one another—they are not completely isolated categories. We may cut off scientific investigation at a certain point for ideological reasons, for instance if to go further, to know more, would destabilize our social system; we don't want to know that all races are biologically equal if we have a slave mode of production. Clearly, scientific knowledge would impact our ideologies, because knowing what the world is like is bound to influence what we want to do in it, what we think we *can* do in it. Nevertheless, we need to maintain the distinction between the two. We don't want to invest the Higgs boson with godlike qualities simply because we are uncomfortable with too much detail in the map we are drawing; and we cannot assume that nature of the universe can tell us anything about what kind of social formations will provide the most human happiness. We need ideology, because it structures how we can get around in the world, and we can produce an ideology that helps us do that with a minimum of suffering.

This, I would suggest, is where Nagarjuna parts ways with Hume. Hume is consistently puzzled by the existence of things like customs, morals, tastes; he always collapses science and ideology into one category of knowledge, and so cannot quite make sense of where our "habits of thought" come from, or why we might need them. Nagarjuna, in contrast, ends his *Mulamadhyamakakarika* with a chapter on the formation of the subject, the central concern in the register of ideology. Although Garfield implies it is a bit anticlimactic after the crucial arguments of chapters XXIV and XXV, for me the chapter on "Views" is the pinnacle of the argument. Here, Nagarjuna addresses the question of the nature of the self. Just as Hume argued that there is some "secret connection" that unites our past, present and future experiences, producing a kind of bundle of phenomena, Nagarjuna addresses the existence of an "appropriator" which *has* the experiences; both find this hidden, appropriating, connecting principle to be logically flawed and experientially non-existent. For Hume, this is a defeat, and he abandons all hope of solving this problem. For Nagarjuna, however, this is not a problem at all: "There is no self without appropriation. But it is not true that it does not exist. To say 'in the past I wasn't' would not be tenable. This person is not different from whoever existed in previous times" (MMK XXVII 8-9; Garfield, 346).

The "appropriator," for Nagarjuna, is conventionally existent, similar to a physical phenomenon in that it is also a "collocation of conditions." Yet it does exist, so long as the conditions persist. Hume's atomistic concept of the mind will not allow him to consider that the "secret connection" exists in ideology, and his atheism will not allow him recourse to a soul, so he finds the problem impossible. For Nagarjuna, the construction of a (conventional, non-essential, impermanent) "self" by human social conventions is not troubling at all. Our ideology then becomes something that is just as open to infinite improvement as is our scientific knowledge of the world. For Nagarjuna, not having a permanent, abiding, transcendent self is the condition for having a self that can improve its world: "If anyone had come from anyplace and were then to go someplace, it would then follow that cyclic existence was beginningless" (XXVII 19). If we had an essential self, we would never be able to escape our present *samsaric* existence, our ideology would be ontology, and suffering would never cease.

This new scientific discovery, then, doesn't serve to support any ancient mystical wisdom. Instead, it can serve as an opportunity to put some of these concepts to use. Why is the Higgs boson particle so popular? What makes it so much more appealing than the various "Higgsless" models of the universe? Are we going to reify our metaphorical model just because we so desperately need a final answer? And do we need that final answer because without it we face the possibility that our own autonomous, abiding, transcendent selves are just "collocations of conditions"? Are we interested in science, or ideology?

Finding the Higgs boson may say more about our "interests and languages," to borrow Garfield's phrase, than it does about the natural structure of the universe. We do science to get a better map of the world, to explain and predict, to aid our interactions with our environment. What explanations and predictions are aided by this discovery? That is its scientific value. However, to the degree that we are seeking this particle to validate our "interests and languages," to convince ourselves that the way we choose to interact with our world is meaningful and important and inevitable, that there is a "god particle" that explains it all, well, that is its ideological function. When ideology masquerades as science, it never seems to turn out well.

If one of Nagarjuna's great insights is that there is a similarity between the levels of truth, the similarity is that both are infinitely corrigible. It does not follow, though, that both are infinitely malleable, that we can shape them any which way we choose. The truth about the intransitive dimension is constrained by the way mind-independent reality actually is, regardless of how we want it to be. The constraints on conventional reality are somewhat different, always partly internal and partly external to ideology. We cannot produce an ideology which requires that physically impossible things happen, and we cannot produce an ideology that fails to take into account the natural needs of the human animal. Beyond that, our attempts to change our ideology depend to a certain degree on choice. It is conceivable that someone may argue that an ideology which causes suffering for the majority of human beings is perfectly acceptable, because of the benefits it brings to the minority. There is no ontological fact to contradict such a conclusion. If, however, we want to begin with the premise that one goal of ideology is to minimize human suffering overall, then we are left with a different question: which of our needs and desires are naturally occurring, and need to be accommodated in our ideological formations, and which are in fact ideologically produced? Can we make such distinctions, if we are always within some ideology? How can we be objective about our subjectivity?

Another way of asking this is: Can there be a science of ideology? Is it possible to produce knowledge of our humanly created practices which has the same kind of objectivity as our knowledge of mind-independent reality? Roy Bhaskar, in his book *The Possibility of Naturalism*, makes a very strong case that this is in fact possible. The important thing is to keep in mind that the object of study is of a different kind, and so the method of investigation must be completely different. As Bhaskar puts it, we must "debunk the claims to scientificity made by practices which merely ape the image of science" (17), such as economics and psychology. Once we set aside the silly attempt to study ideology with the same method we use to study biology, we can begin to constitute a real science.

The fact that our ideologies will always shape our practices, will in fact shape what kinds of human social practices we choose to produce scientific knowledge of, need not be the problem that postmodern epistemology pretends it is, so long as we avoid the error of collapsing the two kinds of reality into one level. As Bhaskar explains, we must keep in mind that "social forms are necessary conditions for any intentional act, that their *pre-existence* establishes their autonomy as possible objects of scientific investigation and that their *causal* power establishes their *reality*" (25). That is, it is exactly *because* our ideologies shape our reactions and our perceptions, and do so in relatively consistent and persistent ways, that we can study those ideologies objectively, even if we do so for subjective (ideological) reasons. In Bhaskar's critical-realist understanding of epistemology, we must understand that "human beings, like any other empirically given object, are fields of effects (though of course none the less real for that)" (111). The fields of effect that we are have the power to "creatively manipulate symbols" (81) in ways that serve as beliefs about the world, symbols that exist in practices (linguistic and other), and so can serve as causes of future actions. For this reason, Bhaskar argues that the science of psychology would need to focus on explanation, not prediction, and could never hope to succeed in explaining anything if it attempts to produce experimental "closed systems" where all variables are "controlled." The one "variable" that constitutes persons is the ability to gain knew symbolic information about the world, and this acquisition by definition cannot be "controlled" for, or it would fail to *be* new information.

In producing a science of ideology, then, we must consider the substantial difference in the object of study and in the goal. For a science of ideology would not aim to describe things that already exist, but to produce things that do not yet exist, and it would aim to do this both by describing existing and past ideological systems and the processes which enable them to change and also by determining what the current ideology *lacks*. While scientific method, in trying to accurately map the intransitive world, is concerned with what exists, a science of conventional reality would also have to consider what fails to exist. We would have to consider what are the non-ideological, relatively enduring capacities, needs, and tendencies of human beings (the intransitively human), and determine the degree to which our ideologies fail to accommodate these.

It would be essential to bear in mind that ideology is always an open system, that no classically scientific "experiment" could be conducted, because "the objects of study of social scientific inquiry . . . only ever manifest themselves in open systems," and as a result, "theories in social science must be *explanatory and non-predictive*" (Bhaskar, 45-46). Bhaskar suggests that although this "*may* affect the subjective confidence with which beliefs are held, if a social scientific theory or hypothesis has been *independently* validated (on explanatory grounds) then one is in principle just as warranted in applying it transfactually as a natural scientific one" (46). In the register of the ideological, the question is not whether or not to engage in an ideological practice, as such engagement is inevitable, but *which* ideological practice should be preferred, and explanatory evidence is the best, if perhaps not an infallible, guide to this situation.

Such a science of ideology, then, is inevitably tied to a practice which can produce ideology, and it is my overall suggestion in this essay that Buddhism has been such a theory and practice, and can give us a useful starting place in how to construct one in the present. Ideology is always essentially aesthetic, negotiating the relationship between abstract, universal concepts and concrete, particular practices. If we can begin with an aesthetics of the sublime, with an epistemology that endlessly seeks non-correspondence between these two poles instead of seeking to lock them in place, then we can produce a theory and practice of ideology open to endless transformation, allowing us to transform the world to reduce suffering, instead of adjusting our "selves" to learn to better endure it. A thoroughly naturalized version of Buddhism could give us a model for producing this kind of practice. I am using the term naturalized, here, only in the sense that we must find an understanding of Buddhism which includes all of its concepts, including rebirth and karma, without recourse to a belief in the supernatural or any process or entity that can transcend the natural, phenomenal world in which we live.

In order to explain how this is possible, I will want to have recourse to many of the concepts produced in the thought of Alain Badiou. So, to make the leap from the Althusserian theory of ideology to my reconstitution of Buddhist concepts, I will need to detour through a brief reading of Badiou's project, in which I will make what may seem, to those familiar with continental philosophy, an unlikely claim.

Alain Badiou's Continuation of the Althusserian Project

It is my contention that, perhaps even contrary to his own claims, Badiou's entire body of work is in fact a continuation of the project begun by Althusser's ISA essay. In the seventies, Badiou wrote a book with François Balmes largely devoted to the rejection of Althusser's theory, entitled *De L'ideologie*. Their argument there was that as an "image of an image, ideology has no referent," with the effect that "consciousness of our exploitation and revolt against exploitation are unthinkable, with no possibility of objective knowledge of class relationships having any effect" (30; translations from this work are my own). His concern was that "if the 'young Hegelians' struggled against the illusions of consciousness, our 'young Marxists' have gained no ground at all if they are only using their knowledge to incite the 'subjected' masses to struggle with all their hearts against the *unconscious*" (21). Badiou is clearly concerned that Althusser's theory will lead to a kind of postmodern relativism, in which all we can do is blindly struggle to change our ideological cathexes, with no guarantee that the change will be for the better, and no real need to develop a practice in which to change the social formation.

This is a valid concern; there is always the danger that Althusser's theory could be misunderstood (in fact, it very often *has* been misunderstood) to suggest that we need only change our thoughts to eliminate our oppression. This is clearly not the intention of the ISA essay, however, which is motivated by the events of 1968 and is an argument that change will require a reconstruction of our material institutions (specifically, that there can be no change in the ideology or the subject until there is a reorganization of the material practices of the educational system). Althusser's goal is to enable the production of a subject that *can* go out and change the social formation. This, I would argue, is what the ISA essay calls for, but does not fully realize; Badiou's theory of the subject, of "Worlds," and of the relationship these have to truth, makes enormous progress toward producing the kind of subject Althusser suggests is possible.

In *Theory of the Subject*, Badiou had suggested that the subject be understood very differently from the Althusserian subject of an ideology. While Althusser understood *all* individuals to be interpellated as subjects, Badiou wanted to reserve the term subject for the subject of a truth, free of the limitations of its ideology and able to force the acceptance of a truth foreclosed by the ideology of its time and place. When we get to *Logics of Worlds*, however, the role of the subject has become more complex, with multiple possible relations to truth and ideology. Badiou now considers it possible for the subject of truth to be opposed by the reactionary subject, intent on denying the truth, or the obscurantist subject, intent on mystifying it. Badiou has replaced the Althusserian concept of ideology with his concept of "World," but the function is much the same. Worlds, in Badiou's theory, are the structuring of a particular appearance or construal of reality, and reality can only ever appear in a particular World. There is truth, but it must always appear in a World, and every World, in allowing a certain reality to "appear," necessarily excludes from appearance other parts of or construals of reality. Badiou's concepts of truth procedures and Worlds may be more subtle and sophisticated, may be a useful advance in thought, but they are still in line with the Althusserian division of science and ideology, which always shape and limit one another, but operate in different registers.

The advantage of the concept of Worlds is the ability to analyze the interrelations between ideologies, concepts of mind-independent reality, and the structures of subjectivity, in order to determine what would be a useful and significant change and what kinds of practices might bring about such a change. For my purposes here, one of the most useful features of the practices and processes of change is that they always seem to be dependent on an aesthetics of the sublime. As Christopher Norris puts it, "Badiou's central thesis," at least in *Being and Event*, is "one that goes clean against the anti-realist grain—concerning not only the recognition-transcendent character of certain truths in the formal sciences but also the capacity of thought to register such truths, so to speak, *in absentia* through their disturbing or anomaly-inducing effect on the discourse of present knowledge" (253). Since the eighteenth century, this is how the sublime has been described, as a paradoxical combination of excess and absence, in which a perception is both irresistibly and overwhelmingly present and at the same time incomprehensibly inaccessible to our mental faculties. Our discourse cannot make sense of the anomalies we run up against, and for that very reason they take on an enormous but troubling "meaning."

In *Logics of Worlds* Badiou discusses this sublime presence of truth in terms of the "transcendental" which structures the World. Somewhat analogous to the Lacanian *point de capiton*, the transcendental is an organizing concept or practice which assigns meaning to all elements in the World, attributing their worth, their relation, and even the recognition of their existence. There is always the possibility that a World may be so effective at foreclosing what it must exclude that a truth "might remain purely and simply unthinkable" (360). However, "it can happen that multiple-being, which is ordinarily the support for objects, rises 'in person' to the surface of objectivity. A mixture of pure being and appearing may take place. For this to happen, it is enough that a multiple lays claim to appearing in such a way that it refers to itself, to its own transcendental indexing"(360). The point here is that there can be those occurrences, which Badiou calls "sites," at which what is excluded from the construal of the World, from its discourses or systems of knowledge, becomes unavoidably present and forces a change in the World sufficient to allow it to appear. Change, new truths, the escape from our ideology, then, always function in a kind of sublime experience:

An event ... is a pure cut in becoming made by an object of the world, through that object's auto-appearance; but it is also the supplementing of appearing through the upsurge of a trace: the old inexistent which has become an intense existence.

With regard to the continuum in the becomings of the world, there is both a lack (impossibility of auto-appearance without interrupting the authority of the mathematical laws of being and the logical laws of appearing) and an excess (impossibility of the upsurge of a maximal intensity of existence). 'Event' names the conjunction of this lack and this excess. (384)

We can change our World to some extent, and with some degree of awareness of the structures we inhabit, because of the inevitable occurrence of these sublime events. It becomes imperative, then, to attend to the sublime, and avoid trying to squash the emergence of troubling truths under the soft and comforting pillow of an aesthetics of the beautiful.

Worlds, for Badiou, are produced by a structuring principle which determines what appears, and what remains unthinkable. Like Nagarjuna's concept of "conventional truths," Worlds are all we have to work with, we cannot step outside of them, and they are always limiting, subjective, socially produced—but, they are nonetheless capable of presenting truths. To clarify at the risk of oversimplifying, we can think of a mind-independent truth such as the occurrence of the evolution of species. This can only ever be known in a World, in a conventional construal of reality, and so, for us, will always necessarily include some value judgments functioning to shape how we experience our selves. In some Worlds, this truth may be completely foreclosed, but it remains a truth; in other Worlds, in which it appears, it may take on different *meanings,* different significance, different importance. We could imagine, for instance, a World in which we referred to the "adaptation" of species, without the implicit teleology and anthropomorphism of the term "evolution." The process, however, as a mind-independent truth about reality, would still be the same. Moreover, truth can also be truth about the effects of a humanly produced social system; such truths exist even if they remain obscured by the social system itself—as in the case of the fetish of exchange value functioning to obscure inherently exploitative social relations behind an illusion of the "free exchange" of labor and wages. The appropriation of surplus value occurs in the capitalist social formation even if nobody is aware that it is going on, even if there is no clear conceptualization of the workings of the economy. This truth can only become "known" in some World, in some ideological practice which produces the knowledge. One could, for instance, conceive of this truth making an appearance in a World with absolutely no radical communist value being attached to it. If there were a World in which only those who benefit from the extraction of surplus value could participate in the study of economics, we could imagine this truth being incorporated by the discipline without any concern that it might promote radical sentiments; one would simply assume that this is the way things are, and that such knowledge is useful to more efficiently extract the maximum surplus value from the uneducated workers.

The subject of a truth, then, is the subject which functions to force the truth into appearance in a World which forecloses it. The subject is not identical with the biological individual, cannot be mapped onto a brain, but exists in the human socially produced symbolic/imaginary system (the influence of Lacan's thought on Badiou is quite clear). To overstate the matter somewhat (only slightly), *the mind is not in the brain but in systems of symbolic communication, which must always take place between multiple individuals.* This is perhaps the most important concept in all of Badiou's, Lacan's *or* Buddhist thought, and is certainly the most important concept to my argument. I will repeat it. Take a moment to consider how important this concept is:

The mind is not in the brain but in systems of symbolic communication, which must always take place between multiple individuals.

We do not have a mind, which then attaches to a symbolic system; instead, there is a symbolic system that makes use of individual biological organisms. This is an inherently ideological and aesthetic process, constructing our conventional realities in which we reproduce our systems of acting within mind-independent reality, and do so by negotiating the relationship between our bodily sensations and the symbolic abstractions in which we communicate. It is in a sublime aesthetic practice, in which truth remains obscure or unthinkable in the prevailing system of knowledge, that we can produce change and recognize truth foreclosed by our World.

It is also crucial to understand that a subject may be a political party, a couple, an entire school of thought. This subject, then, transcends the individual bodily being, and can be reborn, brought back to life, by new individuals in a new World. The actions of each individual's life will affect the subject, of which it is part, far beyond its bodily death—because the subject can and often does continue, even "unappear" and "reappear" in Worlds, far beyond a bodily life. As Badiou puts it: "Several times in its brief existence, every human animal is granted the chance to incorporate itself into the subjective present of a truth. The grace of living for an Idea, that is of *living as such*, is accorded to everyone" (*Logics of Worlds*, 514; my emphasis). If we are able to become the subject of that truth, we have the chance "to live . . . 'as an immortal'" (*Logics of Worlds*, 40).

We must not forget the significance of what Badiou calls, in *Ethics*, "interest." Our motivating cathexes, attachments, sources of pleasure, which we cannot and should not fully renounce, may at times, in ideal situations, align with the demands of the truth procedure, and "disinterested-interest might be representable as interest pure and simple" (*Ethics*, 55); this is possible, but it might always turn out that the alignment is less than perfect, and we will need some form of thought and practice which can enable us to persevere in the truth. And pursuit of truth is always going to be a struggle, because there is a tendency for any truth in any World to produce a reactionary subject, fighting against the emergence of that truth. Worlds will tend to reproduce themselves in an endless circle of blind determination, oppression, and suffering. And a World, it seems, always will produce a degree of suffering, because despite his objections to Spinoza, Badiou is quite Spinozist on this point: the source of joy for the subject is in its ability to move towards the greater appearance of truths in its World. Depriving us of this ability, attachment to a World blocks our *conatus*, and produces suffering.

If Badiou is wary of Althusser's concept of ideology, this is not because he wants to collapse all reality into the intransitive, mind-independent dimension. Rather, it is because he wants to focus almost exclusively on how our ideology, our World in Badiou's terminology, is by far the most essential register of the real. For if there are truths about mind-independent reality that do not appear in a particular given World, they can nevertheless always only appear to us, as human beings, in *some* World. If the given state of things, the World we inhabit, is an attempt to quilt together our concepts and perceptions—our languages and bodies, in Badiou's preferred idiom—then the question Badiou poses and attempts to solve is how we can break free of this World, in which "freedom" appears to be only the right to do as we choose with our own bodies in private, never to interact with the world fully and expand the realm of what appears in it. His solution is a kind of epistemology of the sublime:

> It is a matter of knowing if and how a body participates, through languages, in the exception of a truth. We can put it like this: being free does not pertain to the register of relation (between bodies and languages) but directly to that of incorporation (to a truth). This means that freedom presupposes that a new body appear in the world. The subjective forms of incorporation made possible by this unprecedented body—itself articulated upon a break, or causing a break—define the nuances of freedom. (*Logics of Worlds*, 34)

What is at stake is how we can construct an ideology that functions always on the logic of the sublime, and never on the logic of the beautiful. The sublime assumes a lack or emptiness, a gap in our World, our ideology, and also assumes the emptiness of conventional truth. As Badiou puts it, "Without the void there is no world. ...Ultimately, man is the animal that desires the worldly ubiquity of the void. It is—as a logical power—the *voided* animal" (*Logics of Worlds*, 114).

Much of Badiou's work, then, is an attempt to determine what kinds of practices are truth procedures, capable of producing subjects which will force the appearance of truths in the world. My suggestion is that, in Althusserian terms, this is an aesthetic project, because for Althusser the aesthetic is the practice of producing a distance from our ideology. In "'The Piccolo Teatro': Bertolazzi and Brecht," Althusser argues that, like Brecht's epic theatre, the production of Bertolazzi's play produces an alienation of ideology which "is really the production of a new spectator, an actor who starts where the performance ends, who only starts so as to complete it, but in life" (151). The danger is that the aesthetic object may be captured by what Althusser calls an "aesthetics of consumption," in which it produces only comforting pleasure that subtly reinforces our existing ideologies—as happens when we read a novel like Upton Sinclair's *The Jungle* as a moving love story and family drama, warmly reassuring us of our progress over the distant past of industrial production and reinforcing our belief that what is truly important is not labor politics but family togetherness. To ensure the aesthetics of distantiation requires a certain prescriptive practice and a conceptual framework for the aesthetic experience. This theoretical apparatus would consist of a theory of ideology and the subject, and also a theory of the strategies of containment by which the distantiating effect is managed in various literary genres, according to what ideology is being distanced and what alternative ideology is being produced in its wake.

If Badiou's project is a step forward in producing the subject that is aware of its ideology, this is because it advances the theoretical knowledge of ideology, subjects, and strategies of containment. To return to my metaphor of the map, the subject of truth is more capable of choosing the best mode of transportation for any part of the map it seeks to explore. We can stop reproducing Worlds, and start remapping them. And we can remap them in ways that allow us to make use of all of our human potential for interaction with the world—because the source of suffering is not, ultimately, the need to make an effort in the world, but in the inability to make productive effort. And joy will not be found in some passive state of physical comfort, but in full engagement with reality. Reducing suffering, then, will require a subject that can find enjoyment in effortful engagement with mind-independent reality. The next section of this essay, then, will suggest that the production of this form of subjectivity has always been one possible use of Buddhist concepts; the production of the reactionary subject seeking to reproduce the existing World is perhaps the unavoidable consequence of this. Nevertheless, if we can recover a naturalized account of a Buddhist theory and practice of ideology, we can then proceed to suggest some possible new forms of practice, and in the penultimate section of this essay I hope to offer some concrete examples of what such a practice might look like.

Naturalizing Buddhist Concepts Without Being Reductive

My claim, in this section, is that we can thoroughly "naturalize" Buddhism, eliminating all supernatural and otherworldly notions from its profound philosophical insights, only if we see it as operating in the register of the ideological. That is, Buddhism has nothing useful to tell us about the neurological processes underlying contentment, or about ontology or the natural world. Its domain is the realm of humanly produced Lacanian symbolic and imaginary systems, of Althusserian ideology, or Badiou's "logics of Worlds." It can teach us a great deal about how we produce Worlds, and about how we can more consciously transform them.

The historical emergence of Buddhism, what we might in Badiou's terms call the Buddha Event, occurred at a time when the stagnation of the social system was becoming particularly difficult to maintain. The existing World of the ruling class sought to fix the social system, by insisting on the existence of a pure divine language in which truth existed, and through the repetition of formal ritual. The truth that appeared in the world was the rejection of the Brahmanical ideology, the recognition of the socially produced nature of social formations, the chance to break out of stagnation and open up new possibilities for the exercise of human productive and creative potential. Buddhism, in short, is an attempt to produce a new social practice that enables a subject capable of escaping the endless circle of the reproduction of the existing relations of production—a primarily agricultural form of production and a "sacrificial" form of distribution and exchange. The history of Buddhism ever since can be seen as a struggle between the reactionary, obscurantist, and faithful subject, the dialectic of radical forcing of truth and mystical or institutional strategies of containment.

I offer here a partial glossary of naturalized Buddhist terminology, then, as an illustration of how Buddhist concepts can be coherent and useful once we reject the reactionary denial, and the obscurantist mystification, of the truth of the Buddha Event:

Samsara becomes simply the endless self-reproduction of a World, which always requires the closing off of the appearance of something new, the foreclosure of some truths, and so is always a source of suffering. Reproducing our existing ideologies, as if they were the goal instead of the means, is the source of the suffering of subjects. Here is how Thanissaro Bhikkhu explains the concept of *samsara*:

> Samsara literally means "wandering-on." Many people think of it as the Buddhist name for the place where we currently live — the place we leave when we go to nibbana. But in the early Buddhist texts, it's the answer, not to the question, "Where are we?" but to the question, "What are we doing?" Instead of a place, it's a process: the tendency to keep creating worlds and then moving into them. As one world falls apart, you create another one and go there. At the same time, you bump into other people who are creating their own worlds, too. (Thanissaro Bhikkhu, "Samsara." *Access to Insight*)

What we must do to escape *samsara* is not to stop producing Worlds but stop reifying them. We should, certainly, hold very strongly to our values and ideas, but we should bear in mind that they are humanly created values, that our descriptions of reality are metaphors. There is a tendency in Western Buddhism to shout "Clinging To Views!" whenever someone advances an argument; the most important thing we must remember is that we should always hold strongly to our ideologies, because that is the only thing that makes them functional, but we must never "cling" to them in the sense of reifying them, of forgetting that they *are* ideologies. This is not to suggest that any old ideology will do, of course, and there is no point debating them—the whole point is to remember to *always argue about ideologies*, to never accept absolute relativism, because that can only lead to the kind of quietism or even asceticism into which the reactionary subject has so often attempted to transform Buddhism. *Samsara*, then, is not the entire phenomenal reality; it is only our ideology to the extent that we mistake it for an eternal and naturally occurring truth. On one hand, escaping *samsara* is not difficult at all, requires no special capacity or lengthy practice; on the other hand, it is exactly the most difficult thing of all to do, because for almost all of us, our ideology is usually as hard to notice as the air we breathe or the language we speak.

Karma can be understood as the structures of our reality, including both ideological formations and the relations of production. Karma has always referred to both intentional actions and the effects of those actions. In my reconstitution, then, we can see karma as a thoroughly natural concept, referring to both the ideologically shaped actions we take in the world and their ongoing effects in shaping the possible actions of subjects in the future. We reproduce our world by acting with "intention" in our ideologies, and will bear the effects of these actions as subjects long after our individual bodies are gone. We can, then, escape our karma, not by being freed from some magical force, but by coming to see the constraints on our actions produced by our ideologies, which exist in structures that have been built up by the actions of countless generations. As Marx said, we can make our own history, but we cannot make it exactly as we choose. We escape our karma once we can see the constraints within which we can act, and the degree to which we can change the structures we bear instead of merely reinforcing them. Karma, then, exists and operates at multiple levels: it is the existing productive capacity of the human race, but it is also the current social construction of the form and content of our conscious and unconscious minds. We are bearers of structures—linguistic, economic, educational, familial, and others—and our actions re-produce those structures (both replicate and remake them); what we can do is limited by the karma produced by the collective mind in past generations, and our current actions will influence the collective mind in the future.

Let's consider a couple of the key Pali sutras which discuss the concept of karma.

Here is Thanissaro Bhikkhu's translation of the *Kamma Sutta* from the *Samyutta Nikaya*:

> "Monks, I will teach you new & old kamma, the cessation of kamma, and the path of practice leading to the cessation of kamma. Listen and pay close attention. I will speak.
>
> "Now what, monks, is old kamma? The eye is to be seen as old kamma, fabricated & willed, capable of being felt. The ear... The nose... The tongue... The body... The intellect is to be seen as old kamma, fabricated & willed, capable of being felt. This is called old kamma.
>
> "And what is new kamma? Whatever kamma one does now with the body, with speech, or with the intellect: This is called new kamma.
>
> "And what is the cessation of kamma? Whoever touches the release that comes from the cessation of bodily kamma, verbal kamma, & mental kamma: This is called the cessation of kamma.
>
> "And what is the path of practice leading to the cessation of kamma? Just this noble eightfold path: right view, right resolve, right speech, right action, right livelihood, right effort, right mindfulness, right concentration. This is called the path of practice leading to the cessation of kamma.
>
> "So, monks, I have taught you new & old kamma, the cessation of kamma, and the path of practice leading to the cessation of kamma. Whatever a teacher should do — seeking the welfare of his disciples, out of sympathy for them — that have I done for you. Over there are the roots of trees; over there, empty dwellings. Practice jhana, monks. Don't be heedless. Don't later fall into regret. This is our message to you."

There might seem to be some difficulty here, unless we are meant to understand the goal of Buddhism to be a kind of transcendence of the world. In what sense is the cessation of all bodily and mental effort achieved exactly by diligent and strenuous effort, unless the cessation to be sought is in some otherworldly bliss? Moreover, such cessation might seem to conflict with other sutra passages which suggest that karma is limitless, such as this passage from the *Culakammavibhanga Sutta* (Ñanamoli Thera, Trans.):

> Beings are owners of kammas, student, heirs of kammas, they have kammas as their progenitor, kammas as their kin, kammas as their homing-place. It is kammas that differentiate beings according to inferiority and superiority.

However, there is not necessarily a conflict, and karma need not be seen as some supernatural force we cannot grasp and must break free of. Instead, we can understand karma as our conventional reality, as our ideological formations, in which we all must live, and which have very real causal powers, however difficult to detect and to fully explain these turn out to be. The cessation of karma, then, turns out to be very much like Sachs's reading of Aristotle's concept of "the mean" discussed earlier: we are in some sense free of karma when we become free from both the tyranny of desire and the need for forcible restraint of desire, and can choose our actions consciously, can choose those "habits" we wish to cultivate.

Punabbhava (rebirth) is possible, then, because there is no soul to be reborn, no world-transcendent entity that leaps from body to body. Instead, the mind, which exists only in the socially produced symbolic and imaginary system, can interpellate new concrete individuals to participate in a subject position. As Roy Bhaskar puts it in *From East to West: Odyssey of a Soul*: "If the soul is regarded as a disposition to be embodied, then traditional Buddhist objections to a realist rendition of it are overcome" (p. 92). The reborn "soul" is nothing but a disposition or tendency in the symbolic/imaginary structure to reproduce a certain kind of subject by interpellating new bodily individuals. Our attempt to change our karma, to transform the structures we bear, can lead to better rebirth, to dispositions to produce subjects less prone to suffering.

I want to emphasize here that this is not a matter of taking what was once understood literally and now understanding it metaphorically. I am suggesting that we quite really and literally are "reborn" or reproduced in the socially produced symbolic/imaginary system of our ideologies. Rather than being a shift from the literal to the metaphorical, this is a shift in the *inherently* metaphorical model we use to explain the causal mechanism of that reproduction. That is to say, all explanatory models are metaphorical to some degree; our contemporary explanation of the causal mechanism of this rebirth is just as metaphorical as any ancient one, but the phenomena it explains is still just as real.

Bodhi (enlightenment, awakening) then need not be a supernatural state we must humbly deny having reached; instead, it can be a quite real state of being the Buddhist/Spinozist/Marxist subject which is aware of its ideology and better able to change it. It is, in Badiou's terms, the subject faithful to a truth, and engaged in changing its World to force the appearance of this truth. We can be awakened without claiming grand supernatural powers or even perfection as human beings: we can be awakened only as subjects, not as individuals, and no subject can be awakened except in relation to some truth. *Bodhi* can be far more common than the reactionary or obscurantist subject of Buddhism would have us believe, and to claim its achievement is not to make a claim about one's individual, personal worth but about a truth procedure to which one remains faithful.

Finally, the concepts of **sunyata, anatman, pratityasamutpada**: we can see that once we grasp these as attempts to theorize the particular immanence of a truth in a World, the mystery and incomprehensibility disappears. Nagarjuna becomes much more comprehensible once we grasp that he is arguing that there is certainly a truth, but it can always only appear in a World. There is no single form in which a truth must appear (it can potentially, if it is a truth, appear in every conceivable World, and will always take the form necessary to that World); there is no abiding self, because the subject is always only a socially constructed symbolic/imaginary system, which transcends the bodily individual but is clearly not other-worldly or immortal; everything is always dependently arisen, even a universal truth, because it can only ever exist in a particular World, and to change any subject requires a change in the entire social structure which it inhabits. To claim, in postmodern fashion, that all we can change and all we need to change is our minds, is absurd if we understand that the mind is a product of, dependently arisen from, the structures it inhabits. *Pace* Gandhi, we cannot be the change we want to see in the world; we cannot begin to transform the structures we inhabit by *first* transforming our (individual) consciousness. To change our mind, we must change our World.

The only question, then, is: how is change possible? If our mind is the socially produced symbolic/imaginary system, where is the Archimedean vantage point from which to force a change? This is where we must reject the radical disconnection Badiou argues exists in Althusser's thought between ideology and objective truth (the argument is echoed in the Anglophone world by Althusser's major expositors: Eagleton, Elliot, and Benton). To suggest that there is no clear way out of the prison of ideology fails to see that the solution lies precisely *within* the register of ideology, not in a move into a realm of pure truth. Ultimately, Althusser remains a realist, and our ideology is not so perfectly sealed-off as it might appear to be when it is working successfully. There is a mind-independent world, which does not yield to our conceptual reconstrual of it. Occasionally, we are going to drive our car into a tree. There will be catastrophic failures of the economic system, for instance, which cannot make any sense in the current state of knowledge. Our ideologies may just break down. Eagleton suggested that Althusser has "produced an ideology of the ego, rather than one of the human subject" (*Ideology: An Introduction*, 144), and this is true to an extent: to the degree that ideology works seamlessly and smoothly, it works like the ego—but it never does work completely seamlessly and smoothly; there is always the problem of the unconscious, of the superego. If Althusser seems to have produced and "ideology of the ego" this is only because he is trying to explain how it is ever possible that something so certain to produce error and suffering is so powerfully persistent.

There is always the possibility that, even without crashing head-on into reality, we can gain the capacity to alter our World. It is important to remember that there are always multiple Worlds, that there is no single, monolithic ideological position, that there are always multiple subjects. We need not worry about the problem of solipsism, because there is no possibility of a private, personal and untranslatable symbolic system, and we need not worry about being trapped in a single ideological vision because we can always see another person's ideology, and point it out to them, and they can, hopefully, see ours. Just as there are limits to the possibility of psychoanalyzing oneself, there are limits on an individual's ability to escape her ideology; however, we can serve as one another's analysts, and bring to consciousness what is unconscious.

There are some difficult implications of all of this. We cannot, for instance, simply "live and let live." The current obsession with "tolerance" and "multiculturalism" would need to be rejected, because we cannot gain our own freedom from *samsara* without forcing a change in the World. Our mind is a social construction, and so I cannot change "my" mind without changing "yours." When, for instance, the peasants decide to stop believing that birth conveys power and wealth, this decision will force a change in the mind of the aristocratic subject; and, when the mass of unemployed and underemployed citizens of capitalism decide that they have the right to work and improve their quality of life regardless of whether their effort produces profit for the capitalist, this decisions will force an unpleasant change in the mind of those who assume that wealth and ownership of private property can control who gets to live as a human being and who does not. We must not accept the quietist insistence on learning to accept the world as it is, because the world as it is constructs our mind; we must demand the right to change the World, to insist that others see truths they don't like, because we are not atomistic individuals.

There is also the likelihood that the "interest" of the individual, in Badiou's sense, may trump the desire to see the truth. There may be so much material benefit, so much comfort, so much attachment, that seeing the truth would require a kind of asceticism, an abandonment of individual cathexes, that is unlikely to be successful. As I mentioned earlier, Badiou suggests that in the ideal state the individual interests and the interest of the subject faithful to the truth will so coincide that there is no feeling of ascetic renunciation, no need for great effort; however, this ideal state is unlikely to often occur. What, then, can take its place?

For Althusser, the aesthetic is the practice that can produce a motivational attachment to changing our ideologies, and the world. I would argue that Buddhist practice can become such an aesthetic practice. Because the best way to produce an investment in change is to actually experience the truth that the mind is not an atomistic entity but a collective and socially produced effect of a symbolic/imaginary system. We can become subjects faithful to a truth, even a truth that opposes the interest of our own individual bodily existence, once we experience the truth of what a subject is. Experiencing the existence of our mind in the trans-individual symbolic/imaginary system could motivate us to place the interest of the entire system above the interest of our individual bodily selves. The difficulty and importance of this experience can easily be seen in many works of and on Buddhism. To take just one particularly explicit example, Sue Hamilton, in her book *Early Buddhism: A New Approach*, attempts to reconceive Buddhist concepts in modern philosophical terms. The book is interesting, provocative, erudite and insightful, but ultimately Hamilton's understanding of Buddhism is limited by her insistence that one simply cannot "experience that one has no self . . . in any context outside of a madhouse" (21). For all her knowledge of Buddhist thought, and that is quite a bit, she cannot access an experience which would allow *anatman* to make sense to her. Much like psychoanalysis, in which simply accepting the truth of the offered interpretation does nothing to alleviate our symptoms, a purely intellectual agreement with this theoretical position can do little to produce change. Perhaps only engaging in a material practice, which must involve multiple individuals, and which is designed to allow the experiencing of the constructedness of the mind, can produce subjects faithful to the truth of the Buddha Event.

The history of Buddhism has been a dialectic of emergence and containments of truth, of faithful subjects being endlessly absorbed into reactionary or obscurantist subjects. When meditation seeks to stop all thought, to insist on a world-transcendent experience of pure consciousness outside of language, it is functioning to strengthen the hold of our ideological formations, to shore up the walls of our World, by insisting on the timeless universality of our purportedly "pure" perceptions. What we need, instead, is a framework for Buddhist practice that is faithful to the truths of *samsara, sunyata, anatman, karma, punabbhava*, and *bodhi*. We can produce subjects capable of stepping out of the car and walking.

My suggestion, though, is that we can do this only if we grasp that Buddhist concepts can be understood in a completely naturalist way, with no need to accept any world-transcendent or mystical beings or forces. Further, we need to grasp that Buddhism operates completely in the register of the ideological, its truths are transcendent truths of human ideological practices; Buddhism includes no truths of physical reality external to the existence of human social structures. We may be able to produce such truths, we may even need to do so, but we would be better able to do so as subjects aware of our own ideologies, and able to change them in productive ways guided by rigorous thought.

The Buddha's great insight was that humans are ideological animals; in Althusser's terms, it was a production of a theory of, or truth about, "ideology in general." This insight enables us to escape *samsara*, to be freed of our karma, and to create our own World. Unfortunately, it requires us to break free of our ideology, to take responsibility for the structures we bear, and to remake our World. The price of awakening is eternal diligence.

But the benefit is the ability to enjoy effortful and productive interaction with the world, to work with all the joy of a child hard at play.

Some Suggestions for a Modern Buddhist Practice

Many Westerners approach Buddhist practice looking for smells-and-bells Buddhism, for the incense and singing bowls and all the mystical-sounding chants and sitting on cushions that give us the experience of something exotic. What they are looking for, in the terms I've been using, is an aesthetic experience to give comfort and assurance. The last thing they want from their Buddhism is to be challenged to think hard thoughts and become socially engaged; they want, and will sometimes angrily insist on, a Buddhism that assures them that the only real way to change the world for the better is to increase one's own personal, psychological and physical comfort. A Buddhist book should be like a nice bedtime story, a retreat like a sentimental Broadway musical.

I doubt anyone who has made it this far through this essay is interested in this kind of practice. But we have seen that there is another kind of aesthetic experience, one that does not serve to ossify our ideologies with ineffable experiences and comforting illusions. The aesthetics of the sublime can serve, as Althusser suggests, to produce the spectator who is motivated to complete the play, but in real life. It can distantiate our ideologies sufficiently to allow us to achieve that Aristotelian mean in which we can consciously, in *theoria*, choose to act, while still producing sufficient psychological motivation to cause real action. Such a practice is never, of course, dependent on the captivating power of a work of art; any aesthetic effect depends on the practice, not the object. Such practice need not be unpleasant, any more than physical effort or thought is necessarily unpleasant. Certainly alienated labor and mindless bookkeeping tasks are unpleasant, but playing soccer, dancing, and solving mathematical puzzles can be pleasant activity, and we could even learn to enjoy productive labor like growing food or building things, writing and reading, designing a building. What I want to offer here is an example of an aesthetic practice of the sublime, one which demands effort of us but still need not be unpleasant, and can help us work toward the highest form of enlightenment there is, a life of contemplation, a life in which we fully know what we are doing when we do it, awareness of our ideology right down to the very core of our unconscious.

Such practice need not depend on silent, sitting meditation. This is only one practice among many in the history of Buddhism, a relatively rare one at that. The current obsession with meditation as the cessation of all thought has no real warrant from the Pali canon, for instance, where meditation most often is said to involve intense concentration on the causes and conditions, as well as the potential effects, of our thoughts, actions and perceptions. Such meditation is meant to guide us to exactly the kind of insight Hume claims to have had through simple introspection: "when I enter most intimately into what I call *myself*, I always stumble upon some particular perception or other, of heat or cold, light or shade, love or hatred, pain or pleasure. I never can catch *myself* at any time without a perception, and never can observe anything but the perception" (*Treatise*, 165). Compare this to the description of "no self" in Rupert Gethin's *The Foundations of Buddhism*: "The gist of the Buddhist critique of the notion of 'self' is then this… What we find when we introspect, the Buddha suggests, is always some particular sense datum, some particular feeling, some particular idea, some particular wish or desire…I never actually directly come across or experience the 'I' that is having experiences" (138). One of the core goals of Buddhist meditation would seem to be achievable by means not necessarily passed down from the ancient East.

As I have been arguing, Buddhist practices are always a particular type of aesthetic practice, with a particular relationship to ideology. The ideology we wish to distantiate would, I would argue, be a better guide than tradition is to the practice we should undertake. Buddhist practices no doubt function to distantiate or reinforce the Worlds they were invented in. Now, if we undertake to distantiate our own ideology, can we be guided by a *theoretical* knowledge of Buddhist concepts and their goal, instead of attachment to traditional *practices*?

What I'm going to suggest here is that we begin with a practice that engages with what we already take to be aesthetics. Meditation practice is clearly a renegotiation of the relationship between mind and body, but one that we can easily fail to understand as such, and so can produce an aesthetics of the beautiful, and strengthen our ideological reification, against our attention. Reading works of literature, watching films, looking at paintings or photographs, are all consciously aesthetic practices, and perhaps the best place for us, today, to begin the shift from the logic of the beautiful to the logic of the sublime. I'll begin with an example of reading a poem, one many people will probably be familiar with, and I will try to suggest a way to read it that takes us beyond a comforting reassurance of our existing beliefs.

Ode on Melancholy
By John Keats

No, no, go not to Lethe, neither twist
    Wolf's-bane, tight-rooted, for its poisonous wine;
Nor suffer thy pale forehead to be kiss'd
    By nightshade, ruby grape of Proserpine;
        Make not your rosary of yew-berries,

Nor let the beetle, nor the death-moth be
    Your mournful Psyche, nor the downy owl
A partner in your sorrow's mysteries;
    For shade to shade will come too drowsily,
        And drown the wakeful anguish of the soul.

But when the melancholy fit shall fall
    Sudden from heaven like a weeping cloud,
That fosters the droop-headed flowers all,
    And hides the green hill in an April shroud;
Then glut thy sorrow on a morning rose,
    Or on the rainbow of the salt sand-wave,
        Or on the wealth of globed peonies;
Or if thy mistress some rich anger shows,
    Emprison her soft hand, and let her rave,
        And feed deep, deep upon her peerless eyes.

She dwells with Beauty—Beauty that must die;
    And Joy, whose hand is ever at his lips
Bidding adieu; and aching Pleasure nigh,
    Turning to poison while the bee-mouth sips:
Ay, in the very temple of Delight
    Veil'd Melancholy has her sovran shrine,
        Though seen of none save him whose strenuous tongue
    Can burst Joy's grape against his palate fine;
His soul shalt taste the sadness of her might,
        And be among her cloudy trophies hung.

One can imagine a kind of Western Buddhist response which sees this poem as giving us the very definition of *dukkha*. And in one sense, of course, it does. Keats urges us to accept the inevitability of dissatisfaction, the truth that every pleasure is temporary and leads to the sadness of loss and impermanence. He asks us not to sink into nihilistic despair, but meet our melancholy moods head on, allowing the intensity of the feeling to stand out in sharp contrast to the fleeting joys. Only one who can feel intensely both pleasures and pains, who can mix beauty, joy, delight and pleasure with sadness, can truly experience the fullness of life. The demand that we openly accept both good and bad with equanimity is one of the trite platitudes of new-age Buddhism. But is this really what Keats is trying to show us? Is it really what we should want to do?

In all the ancient Greek allusions and personifications, doesn't the poem seek to keep us sufficiently surrounded by abstract universals to prevent any concrete and powerful emotional or sensory experience? Keats offers us the aesthetics of the beautiful in a poem that refuses to investigate the causes of suffering just as much as it refuses to investigate why only temporary sensory pleasures can possibly be pleasurable. If Wordsworth offers us his poems as compensation for urbanization and industrialization, as our only respite from social alienation as well as the alienation of labor, Keats offers us the poem as a guarantee that we can, through the practice of the aesthetics of the beautiful, construct for ourselves a soul which experiences the delights and sorrows of the world at a remove, in proper aesthetic balance. We need not do anything to change this world, simply learn to construct the illusion of an autonomous and abiding soul blissfully separated from it.

To the degree that we love this poem and believe the truths, or truisms, it offers us, we participate in creating the most powerful delusion to which humans are prone. We forget to question why *joy* must be defined as a momentary sensory experience. Why couldn't we instead define joy as Spinoza did, as the increasing or assisting of our capacities for acting and thinking? In this sense, joy can be an effortful and ongoing process, not a fleeting moment of bodily pleasure. What is at stake in using poetry as a practice to produce this particular construal of the world and the human subject?

In the Romantic period in England, the most advanced capitalist economy in the world at the time, the production of a hegemonic ideology was of the utmost importance. While the Romantics ostensibly reject the crass commercialism and utilitarianism of the industrial economy, they do so in such a fashion as to thoroughly naturalize the fundamental structure of capitalist ideology. The form in which the aesthetic is negotiated in the economic sphere is the relationship between exchange value, the abstract pure value of gold or money, and use value, the particular and impermanent commodities produced and consumed. It is imperative to reach a privileging of the abstract, and to naturalize it as something thoroughly uncreated by humans. Exchange value is the illusion of the one timeless, unchanging value that can be put to any use, which, like a magic wand, can serve to supply any need or desire if only we have enough of it. Use value, on the other hand, is the merely temporary satisfaction of needs and desires, consumed in the use while money is re-circulated to be used again and again, or invested to magically grow on its own. In one sense, only exchange value is real and natural, the invisible hand of the ineffable economy which directs all human actions, obscuring the truth that our social systems are humanly created: we must take our economic and social practices as necessary responses to the transcendentally "real" power of money. Yet, at the same time, only the bodily, impermanent and particular is real—we cannot eat or wear or keep warm in our cash—but it is constantly elusive, out of our control, given or taken from us at the whim of the capricious god, economy. Our solution to this impossible paradox is the aesthetics of the beautiful, where we are offered the infantile imaginary plenitude, instant (if imaginary) gratification for our every whim, in place of the power to actively satisfy our needs ourselves, materially. The transcendent soul, or consciousness, or self which appreciates this imaginary pleasure is, of course, ideologically very real, and reproduced every time we enjoy an aesthetic object like this poem, every time we are reassured and comforted by the aesthetics of the beautiful.

Prior to the Romantic period, poetry, literature was almost always understood to have some motivational function. Dryden, the great poet of the Restoration period, could write a poem attempting to prompt a response to the Exclusion Crisis, *Absalom and Achitophel*, and it was not only accepted as real literature but is still in the canon today. After the Romantic period, literature must only move our emotions, never move us to action. We go to literature for thought-free escape, much like we do television, or like many people do Buddhism.

What I am asking, then, is that we consider this practice of reading a kind of Buddhist practice. Like any Buddhist practice, it is best done in a group, because the mind is always collective, and attempting to think our way free of our ideology alone is generally fruitless. We must always bear in mind that we can only think clearly what we can say to other individuals, and the progress of our thought is therefore always limited by their ability and willingness to comprehend. To cultivate a collective practice of this kind is essential, because thinking things through to their underlying causes, even things like the source of our enjoyment of a beautiful poem, is a practice capable of changing the very structure of our collective mind, capable of naturalizing this tendency to push toward rational understanding instead of retreat into comforting feelings.

I chose this particular poem merely for illustrative purposes, but such a practice should focus on aesthetic objects found powerfully appealing and engaging by members of the group. This is where a group is vitally important, because we are most likely to be blind to the ideological reifications at work in our own personal enjoyment. This is not to suggest we must necessarily give up all aesthetic practices; on the contrary, my suggestion is that in an important sense all ideologies, which is to say all conventional truths, are aesthetic, and we can learn to enjoy them without reification. We can also learn to cultivate enjoyment of those practices which produce more useful ideologies, ones that produce less suffering and greater capacity to interact with the world.

For many years, teaching an introduction to literature class for students who were not English majors, I would assign, as their final paper, the task of identifying the ideology of an aesthetic object, then determining whether the text, and the reading practice in which it was consumed, functioned to inculcate or distance that ideology. Students always wanted to choose a favorite work, something they found so gripping and seductive it felt effortless to read it; inevitably, the more they loved the work they chose, the harder it was to see the ideology it was producing or reinforcing for them. Often, our ideologies are beliefs-in-practices which have been so thoroughly naturalized we fail to even notice their existence, like the air we breathe or speaking our native language, we can't attend to them easily unless they suddenly fail us. This is one part of the importance of practicing this in a group, and a group eclectic enough to have some variety of ideological positions and aesthetic practices.

Let me illustrate, with some aesthetic objects frequently chosen by my students, the kinds of ideological reinforcement that can powerfully reinforce our ideologies while we think we are being harmlessly entertained.

One favorite for years was *Harry Potter*, which many of my students had read during their middle-school and high-school years. To many readers, this book seems completely devoid of ideology; in fact, because the author is a woman even the sexist gender ideology tends to go unremarked. How could a silly fantasy about a boy wizard possibly be producing ideology at all? Let's consider Zizek's explanation of the workings of fantasy:

> The most elementary matrix of fantasy, of its temporal loop, is that of the "impossible" gaze by means of which the subject is present at the act of his/her own conception. What is at stake in it is the enigma of the Other's desire: by means of the fantasy-formation, the sub-

ject provides an answer to the question, "What am I for my parents, for their desire?" and thus endeavours to arrive at the "deeper meaning" of his or her existence, to discern the Fate involved in it. The reassuring lesson of fantasy is that "I was brought about with a special purpose." Consequently, when, at the end of psychoanalytic treatment, I "traverse my fundamental fantasy," the point of it is not that, instead of being bothered by the enigma of the Other's desire, of what I am for the others, I "subjectivize" my fate in the sense of its symbolization, of recognizing myself in a symbolic network or narrative for which I am fully responsible, but rather that I fully assume the uttermost contingency of my being. The subject becomes "cause of itself" in the sense of no longer looking for a guarantee of his or her existence in another's desire. ("Love Beyond Law")

Clearly, anyone who has read *Harry Potter* or even seen the movie can recognize how well it maps onto this Lacanian matrix. Harry must be "brought about for a special purpose" in order to deny the radical contingency of his existence, and this purpose includes Harry's entrance into the permanent state of imaginary plenitude. Imaginary plenitude is perhaps, in our post-theistic age, the nearest our ideologies can come to a world-transcendent state, and so such fantasies are the most powerful means available to reify and naturalize our ideologies. Simply put, imaginary plenitude is the assumed state of the infant before entrance into the symbolic order, when it can still fully perceive all sensations and its every whim is met with pleasurable satisfaction. This never occurs, of course, but it becomes the state we fantasize we can return to when we obtain full possession of the phallus (or, for Western Buddhists, when we achieve a state of enduring "mindfulness"). As Zizek indicates, the mature position would escape this reassuring fantasy, but Harry Potter becomes our fantasy other, complete with a host of symbols that read like they could have been taken straight out of *The Interpretation of Dreams*: the magic wand, the flying broom, the train that passes magically through walls, the cloak of invisibility. Even the narrative point of view functions as the position of the "impossible gaze" of the ideal mother able to see one's every thought and approve it, express it, and fulfill its demand for recognition.

The point here is that this novel serves to reinforce a subject position in which we find our enjoyment only in passive fulfillment of our every psychosexual desire—thus, the novel never motivates us to do anything in the world except to read the next installment in the series. This kind of fantasy, like the cult of mindfulness in Western Buddhism, serves as a blissful retreat from and compensation for a world we must always accept exactly as it is. Where once our fantasy could be a wish for unalienated labor, for the capacity to have meaningful work to do in the world (think of old boyhood fantasies in which herding cattle or hunting whales could be depicted as fulfilling activities), now we can only fantasize a retreat into infancy. If we read these novels critically, seeking to explain the ideological function, they might lose some of their appeal; reading them in this way can itself be a practice capable of producing a very different kind of subject. They may, as my students have told me, lose some of their thrilling appeal, but this in itself opens up the capacity to cultivate pleasure in consciously chosen ideological practices.

A recent favorite example is the movie *Avatar*. In fact, shortly after this movie came out I was spending a weekend at a Zen monastery, and the movie was discussed approvingly as having a wonderfully "Buddhist" message. Hundreds of millions of people saw the movie, and approved of its ecological and multicultural themes. But what *is* the ideology of this movie? Can any movie which devotes so much time to expensive and violent battle scenes possibly have a "Buddhist" message in any sense?

Much like *Harry Potter*, the form of this movie's ideology depends on the fantasy of achieving imaginary plenitude, of achieving a state in which the body *is* rather than *has* the phallus, and can effortlessly do incredible things with thought alone, like playing an elaborate video game, while lying in some high-tech incubator. There are all the same kinds of dream symbols for sexual fulfillment, the same insistence that we reach bliss only in fantasy, as compensation for tolerating our miserable and meaningless lives. This movie, however, functions just a bit differently from *Harry Potter* because it does actually motivate us to do something beyond wait for the sequel. The actual practice which *Avatar* encourages, which is therefore its real ideology, turns out to be the exact opposite of its ostensible message: the source of real bliss is not a return to an organic union with nature, but the purchase of more and better high-tech devices on which to enjoy such new, insanely expensive forms of entertainment. What remains invisible and unthinkable in such a movie is any form of productive and unalienated labor. The only alternative to destruction and violence remains the pure fantasy of imaginary plenitude.

If one is caught up in the enjoyment of such aesthetic objects, it can be difficult to see the ideology into which they are interpellating us; a collective practice of reading such works against the grain, of reading beautiful aesthetic objects with a sublime aesthetic practice, can cultivate the conscious awareness of our ideologies, can teach us that we can learn to take pleasure in activities that turn out to be better for us, like acquiring a taste for vegetables. Surely anybody who has ever built their own furniture or grown their own food can bear witness that working hard to transform the world in productive ways can be just as pleasurable as, perhaps more pleasurable than, fantasizing about playing Quidditch or sitting in front of a 3-D television. Since the ideology, and the collective subject, is in the social practice, not in the content of the aesthetic object, then we could potentially produce a new form of subjectivity, a sublime subject if you will, which could make real change in our World possible.

Aesthetic objects need not be the only way we distantiate our ideologies. They are a good way to start, but there are other practices we can use. When we get that familiar road rage, we can examine why we accept as inevitable the most environmentally destructive and needlessly expensive mode of transportation ever invented; we think we freely *choose* to drive, but did the elimination of the railway result from consumer choice, or from corporate profitability? About six hundred people die each week in automobile accidents in the U.S. If a disease killed that many people, there would be a dozen grass roots organizations seeking to eliminate it. Why not spend a fraction of the money we spend on cars and insurance and gas and highways on a system of public transportation? Why not make your practice the attempt to stamp out automobiles, instead of the attempt to use "mindfulness" to control your anger while you drive?

Relationships are a constant source of suffering in our world; why not investigate the social construction of the modern concept and practice of romantic love? Lacan has shown us that romantic love is the desire to be desired by the other: we fall in love with someone who somehow represents that Other for whom we wish to be the object of desire. Perhaps it is looks, voice, job, money, style, tastes—something about them convinces us that if they desired us we would be assured that we have that special purpose in life, that we have fulfilled the deeper meaning of our existence; we imagine this romantic other to inhabit the impossible position of the gaze, which can grant us imaginary plenitude. Then, we are surprised that it doesn't work out. What if we chose to define "love" not as a fated meeting of soulmates, ineffable and pure emotion, but as a consciously chosen relationship in which people can support and assist one another's increased capacity to interact with the world? Or consider the mystery of money. In the film *The Examined Life*, the philosopher Peter Singer questions the ethical value of buying a pair of expensive shoes when that money, donated to the proper charity, could save dozens of lives. Can one morally justify buying a pair of Dolce&Gabbana shoes, instead of simply buying a hundred-dollar pair of Rockports and donating the other five hundred dollars to buy medicine that will save a dozen lives? This might seem obvious, but what Singer cannot even consider questioning is the very existence of money, of exchange value itself, which surely since Marx we can see is the very cause of the unequal distribution of wealth Singer is bothered by. As long as we have money, the symbol of pure abstract value which is as close as we come outside of fantasy to achieving imaginary plenitude, we will have a system in which the exchange value of ugly and uncomfortable shoes far exceeds the value of a human life, and in which there can be plenty of work to be done but no jobs, hungry people but fertile land unfarmed to keep supply low and profits up. Instead of wondering which charity to donate money to, why don't we begin to question, as Blake and Godwin did two centuries ago, why we *need* charities in the first place?

These are just some suggestions for a kind of practice which might lead to a real awakening, if awakening can be understood as seeing things as they really are instead of as achieving a blissful escape from the world. The most important first step in any effort to change the world is to change its ideology, because any practice can only take place in ideology. And note that this is not a matter of changing *yourself* first and allowing the world to change on its own, because you *cannot change yourself* apart from making a change in the world, in the kinds of social practices in which people engage. Changing our ideologies is always a matter of changing our practices, or consciously cultivating practices that might feel uncomfortable, dull, or difficult at first, or even for quite some time. We must realize that we can motivate our actions with our reasons, with help from other individuals, and break out of our reified and naturalized ideological obfuscation. Not out of ideology completely, of course, but into an awareness, that "Aristotelian mean" as Sachs describes it, awareness of the conventional nature of conventional truth.

The greatest impediment to this kind of change seems to me to be an incomplete understanding of what in Buddhist thought is called *anatman*. I will conclude, by considering what I take to be the most important concept in all of Buddhist thought, perhaps the most important insight in all of human thought, but also the most persistently difficult concept to think our way through.

Conclusion: *Anatman*, Mind, and Conventional Truth

I am going to argue for both the possibility and the value of an extreme version of the concept of *anatman* or no-self, one which refuses to hold onto even the most subtle kinds of essential, abiding, unconstructed being. In Western psychology, we typically think of individuals as having a "true self," a core that is unchanging, that is somehow separate from their bodies, and from all the social roles they play and activities they take part in. In the 1970s, it was common for therapists to ask a patient to write down a list of labels that describe them, then ask them to consider removing them one by one: you are not your job, your marriage, your friendships, your nationality, your political affiliation, these are not you—what is your "true" self? In Western Buddhism, this has often been taken to be the meaning of no-self: I am not my body, or my thoughts, I am the deep core of nebulous feeling that can transcend this *samsaric* world. In his book *No Self No Problem*, for instance, the Tibetan Buddhist Anam Thubten assures us that "no self" means that we are not our bodily self, but a "pure consciousness" which is our "true identity." What I want to suggest is that this gets it exactly wrong. The Buddhist teaching of no-self instructs us that all those roles we play in the world are exactly what we are, are the only "self" we have, we are nothing *but* them. What we *don't* have, according to the Pali canon, is this pure consciousness that somehow plays these roles, inhabits this body, and has these experiences. Instead, we just *are* these roles, this body, these experiences, *and nothing else*.

The importance of this cannot be understated. Because if we are only the sum of our roles and experiences, the very last thing likely to lead to any kind of liberation is attempting to become indifferent to the very phenomena which combine to make up the only self we have: a conventional self. In a text from the Pali canon, *Udayi Sutta*, the Buddha is asked about the nature of no-self and responds with the famous simile of the plantain tree:

"Doesn't intellect-consciousness arise in dependence on the intellect & ideas?"

"Yes, friend."

"And if the cause & reason for the arising of intellect-consciousness were to cease totally everywhere, totally in every way without remainder, would intellect-consciousness be discerned?"

"No, friend."

"It's in this way, friend, that consciousness has been pointed out, revealed, and announced by the Blessed One [with these words]: 'For this reason consciousness is not-self.'

"It's just as if a man going around wanting heartwood, seeking heartwood, searching for heartwood, would take a sharp ax and enter a forest. There he would see a large banana tree trunk: straight, young, without shoots. He would cut off the roof, cut off the crown, and unfurl the coil of the stem. There he wouldn't even find softwood, much less heartwood.

"In the same way, a monk assumes neither a self nor anything pertaining to a self in the six spheres of sensory contact. Assuming in this way, he doesn't cling to anything in the world. Not clinging, he is not agitated. Unagitated, he is totally unbound right within. He discerns that 'Birth is ended, the holy life fulfilled, the task done. There is nothing further for this world.'"

(Translated by Thanissaro Bhikkhu)

The implication of nihilism here is one reason, perhaps, that Westerners shy away from this radical understanding of no-self. If the goal is that there be "nothing further for this world," well, is that what we want to work toward? How is that different from the Jainist practice of simply sitting unmoving until one starves to death and escapes the cycle of life and death? We must begin with a correct understanding of the meaning of "birth" and of "this world": what we have escaped when we realize no-self is the reification of our ideology, our World, in Badiou's sense, our *loka* in Buddhist terminology. We are no longer interpellated into an ideology without awareness that it *is* an ideology, and the goal of the holy life is fulfilled. What we are seeking is a recognition that we are always and only the effect of the practices in which we are produced, and we need to be very careful to decide consciously, in rigorous philosophical thought, what kinds of practices we want to be made up out of, to avoid causing suffering for our (conventional) selves and for others.

Once we can dismiss this fear of suicidal nihilism, though, there is still another powerful difficulty that makes the concept of no-self so terribly hard for us to think within. All the major philosophical dilemmas of Western thought have turned on the assumption of the atomistic mind. The problem of free will and determinism, of consciousness, of the relationship of the mind to the body, the entire question of ethics—to all of these problems, Western philosophy has sought a solution which assumes the atomistic conception of minds. Both idealists, who see the solution in a consciousness or soul that inhabits the body, and materialists, who consider the mind as rising up out of the brain's interactions with the external world via the senses, can find no solution to these age old dilemmas. Even those Western philosophers who engage with Buddhism in a comparative philosophy that seeks to overcome our conceptual limitations tend to stop short of accepting the full implications of Buddhist thought. For instance, Teed Rockwell turns to Nagarjuna to avoid the endless problem of our inability to reduce the mind to the brain, but can only construe Nagarjuna as suggesting that the mind occurs in the interaction between individual brains and external stimuli. The "cause and reason for the arising of intellect-consciousness" mentioned in the *Udayi Sutta* above, then, is understood to be only physical objects of perception.

The important shift we must make, though, is to understanding those causes and reasons which give rise to consciousness as social practice, centrally including the capacity for symbolic language, which enable interactions *not* between the brain and a tree, but between two or more individual human animals. The mind is not in the brain, but in language, culture; in Lacanian terms it exists in the symbolic/imaginary system in which we live.

William James, in his seminal textbook *The Principles of Psychology*, saw the problem of free will as simply unsolvable within the atomistic paradigm of the discipline of psychology, but for James this was not a problem with atomism; instead, he saw this as evidence that there must in fact be a god and a soul, that empiricism was true only of the material, not the spiritual world. Many other thinkers insist this is "merely" a problem of language, of the inevitable tendency of our language to insist on an active subject. They will say, as Thomas Metzinger does in his book *The Ego Tunnel: The Science of the Mind and the Myth of the Self*, that "we mentally represent ourselves *as* representational systems" (5), and think this has solved the problem. When we ask who is the "we" who is doing the perceiving of this representation, the question is either dismissed as a problem of language, or we are offered the ultimate fallback answer: "certain aspects of consciousness are ineffable" (9). Hume, as we have seen, at least had the courage to confess that he was, in fact, relying on a subtle and implicit "self" in his system, and could see absolutely no solution to the problem.

Western Buddhist teachers have fared no better with this, tending to slip back into the insistence on a subtle *atman* just as they are trying to explain that there is not one. B. Alan Wallace, despite years of training as a Buddhist, cannot conceive of escaping the purely atomistic mind, and consistently resorts to the concept of a "substrate consciousness" which can transcend our material world, but which somehow is not, Wallace insists, an *atman* or soul. Wallace presents us with a version of Buddhism that seeks to uncover, through spiritual practice, a "brightly shining mind" that is unborn, eternal, and exists "in every being," although "veiled by adventitious defilements" (115). The "conceptual mind," which is conventional and impermanent, cannot access this "realm of consciousness," but the "brightly shining mind" can "influence the minds of ordinary sentient beings" (115) in ways that are "beyond the realm of philosophy" (116). Our greater freedom, it seems, is achieved by removing the defilements, conventional accretions inhibiting the ability of the pure consciousness to subtly and imperceptibly influence the conventional mind. He presents us, then, with the very definition of an *atman*: an abiding deep self, uncreated by causes and conditions, permanently existing, unchangeable, and alone capable of true and complete bliss. Similarly, Rodney Smith, the guiding teacher of the Seattle Insight Meditation Society, in a book specifically proposing to explain "the Buddha's liberating teaching of no-self," simply insists that the false "self" is the mind, and once we abandon our thinking and allow our deep self to simply feel emotions, we have achieved enlightenment, and the illusory phenomenal world is at our command: at one point, he suggests we would be able to walk up walls (*Stepping Out of Self-Deception*, 197-198).

There have been a handful of Western thinkers who have come closer to an understanding of consciousness as existing in social practices. Eighty years ago, V. N. Volosinov proposed this approach. "Consciousness," he suggested, "becomes consciousness only once it has been filled with ideological (semiotic) content, consequently, only in the process of social interaction" (11). Psychoanalysis, beginning with Freud and most thoroughly with Lacan, presented a radically empty subject, arising not from deep within but from without, in a socially produced symbolic network. Alain Badiou has suggested a theory of the subject that accepts all of the most radical implications of Lacan's thought: as individual organisms, we are nothing but automata; it is only as socially engaged subjects *to* a truth that we gain any agency—the subject is not an individual, but a social phenomenon. As such, it may very well transcend the limits of an individual organism's life, and experience the future effects of our present day actions. We will never find consciousness in the firing of neurons, because it exists only in the symbolic social interaction of multiple individuals.

If these approaches to understanding the collective nature of the mind have been persistently misread or simply suppressed, it is perhaps largely because of the troubling implications of this truth. Freud can serve as one powerful example:

> When I promised my patients help and relief through the cathartic method, I was often obliged to hear the following objections, "You say, yourself, that my suffering has probably much to do with my own relation and destinies. You cannot change any of that. In what manner, then, can you help me?" To this I could always answer: "I do not doubt at all that it would be easier for fate than for me to remove your sufferings, but you will be convinced that much will be gained if we succeed in transforming your hysterical misery into everyday unhappiness, against which you will be better able to defend yourself with a restored nervous system." (*Studies in Hysteria*, 232)

This is the source of the most common quip about psychoanalysis: that it can only convert misery into ordinary unhappiness. The point Freud is making, however, is much different. For Freud, it is imperative to accept that much of our human unhappiness is because of our social environment, and *that* is beyond the reach of psychoanalytic treatment; the really useful benefit of uncovering what is unconscious, what is invisible within our construal of the world, is that it might leave us "better able to defend" ourselves—to make real changes in those "relations and destinies" causing our "everyday unhappiness." The problem with psychoanalysis, the threat it posed, was not fear of the sexuality buried in our unconscious, but fear that examining the mind in this way would point to social, not personal, causes of unhappiness. In fact, Wallace quotes Kurt Danziger in support of his claim that abandonment of the introspective method occurred for "ideological rather than pragmatic" reasons (173). This is Danziger's point, but the ideological reason is not what Wallace implies; instead, the reason for the abandonment of introspection was that it "demonstrated that the nature of the object of psychological investigation was linked to the social structure of the investigative situation" (Danziger, 48). The problem wasn't materialist ideology, but the possibility that the contents of the psyche were produced by social structures; and so it would require social change to improve or cure the mind. Interdependence, it seems, was more troubling than incurable neurosis.

Spinoza, as well, whose work was banned throughout the West for centuries, saw this possibility. Balibar refers to "the most profound of all Spinoza's ideas" (*Spinoza,* 95): "knowledge is a process by which communication is continuously being improved. It can multiply the power of every individual, even if some individuals inevitably know more than others" (Balibar, *Spinoza,* 97). This improvement of knowledge in the collective Mind is, for Spinoza, the ultimate source of joy. But it must, it can only, be done collectively, because, as Balibar puts it, "if no man ever thinks alone, then we might say that to know really is to think ever less by oneself" (*Spinoza,* 98). Spinoza's ultimate aim was, in his own words, "to try to find out whether there was anything which would be the true good, capable of communicating itself, and which alone would affect the mind, all others being rejected—whether there was something which, once found, and acquired, would continuously give me the greatest joy, to eternity" (Spinoza, 3). But this could not be done alone: "it is part of my happiness to take pains that many others may understand as I understand" (Spinoza, 5).

Perhaps today we can grasp, with the help of the Buddhist concepts of no-self, dependent arising, and conventional truth, that we must practice together to make our reality, to invent practices capable of producing a better mind, and to do so in rigorous thought with constant conscious intention. This is no small matter, because the majority of individuals in our World are interpellated into one form or another of reactionary or obscurantist subjectivity, resisting at all costs the introduction of truth into our present knowledge of the world. They are insisting, that is, on a reification of the ideology of global capitalism, on refusing to see our ideology *as* ideology, and see our social World as a humanly created thing which is open to change by human agents.

If we can produce enough subjects structured by the aesthetics of the sublime, awake to the incongruity or lack or non-correlation between knowledge and truth, between concrete material practice and abstract thought, then we might produce enough sublime subjects to force a change in the World. To put it another way, if we could produce a collective subject faithful to the Buddha Event, to the recognition that our World is humanly created and impermanent yet inescapable and causally powerful, we could perhaps begin to live as fully conscious human beings.

Works Cited

Alter, Robert. Introduction. *Pleasure and Change: The Aesthetics of Canon.* By Frank Kermode, with Geoffrey Hartman, John Guillory and Carey Perloff. Ed. Robert Alter. Oxford: Oxford University Press, 2004. Print.

Althusser, Louis. "Ideology and Ideological State Apparatusses (Notes towards an Investigation." *Lenin and Philosophy.* Trans. Ben Brewster. New York: Monthly Review Press, 1971. Print.

Arnold, Daniel. *Brains, Buddhas, And Believing : The Problem Of Intentionality In Classical Buddhist And Cognitive-Scientific Philosophy Of Mind.* New York: Columbia University Press, 2012. Print.

Badiou, Alain. *Ethics: and Essay on the Understanding of Evil.* Trans. Peter Halward. New York: Verso, 2001. Print.

—. *Logics of Worlds: Being and Event 2.* Trans. Alberto Toscano. New York: Continuum International Publishing Group, 2009. Print.

—. *Second Manifesto For Philosophy.* Trans. Louise Burchill. Malden, MA: Polity Press, 2011. Print.

Badiou, Alain and Francois Balmes. *De L'Ideologie.* Paris: Maspero, 1976. Print.

Balibar, Étienne. *The Philosophy of Marx.* Trans. Chris Turner. New York: Verso, 1995. Print

—. *Spinoza and Politics.* Trans. Peter Snowdon. New York: Verso, 1998. Print.

Batchelor, Stephen. *Alone With Others: An Existential Approach to Buddhism.* New York: Grove Press, Inc., 1983. Print.

—. *Confession of a Buddhist Atheist.* New York: Spiegel & Grau, 2010. Print.

Bhaskar, Roy. *The Possibility of Naturalism: A Philosophical Critique of the Contemporary Human Sciences.* New York: Routledge, 1998. Print.

—. *From East to West: Odyssey of a Soul.* New York: Routledge, 2000. Print.

Cowherds, The. *Moonshadows: Conventional Truth in Buddhist Philosophy.* Oxford: Oxford University Press, 2010. Print.

Danziger, Kurt. *Constructing the Subject: Historical Origins of Psychological Research.* Cambridge: Cambridge University Press, 1990. Print.

de Man, Paul. *Aesthetic Ideology*. Ed. Andrzej Warminkski. Minneapolis: University of Minnesota Press, 1996. Print.

Eagleton, Terry. *Ideology: An Introduction*. New York: Verso, 1991. Print.

Freud, Sigmund, and Joseph Breur. *Studies in Hysteria*. Trans. A.A. Brill. Boston: Beacon Press, 1937.

Garfield, Jay, Translation and Commentary. *The Fundamental Wisdom of the Middle Way: Nagarjuna's* Mulamadhyamakakarika. Oxford: Oxford University Press, 1995. Print.

Garfield, Jay and Graham Priest. (2003) "Nagarjuna and the Limits of Thought." *Philosophy East and West*, 53(1) (2003): 1-21.

Gethin, Rupert. *The Foundations of Buddhism*. Oxford: Oxford University Press, 1998. Print.

Hamilton, Sue. *Early Buddhism: A New Approach*. New York: Routledge, 2000. Print.

Hayes, Richard P. "Nagarjuna's Appeal." *Journal Of Indian Philosophy* 22.4 (1994): 299-378.

Hegel, G. W. F. *Aesthetics: Lectures on Fine Art*. Vol. I. Trans. T. M. Knox. Oxford: Oxford University Press, 1998. Print.

Hume, David. *A Treatise of Human Nature*. Ed. David Fate Norton and Mary J. Norton. Oxford: Oxford University Press, 2001. Print.

Lamarque, Peter. *The Philosophy of Literature*. Malden, MA: Blackwell Publishing, 2009. Print.

Lusthaus, Dan. *Buddhist Phenomenology: A Philosophical Investigation of Yogacara Buddhism and the Ch'eng Wei-shih lun*. New York: RoutlegeCurzon, 2002. Print.

Metzinger, Thomas. *The Ego Tunnel: The Science of the Mind and the Myth of the Self*. New York: Basic Books, 2009. Print.

Ñanamoli Thera, Trans. "Cula-kammavibhanga Sutta: The Shorter Exposition of Kamma" (MN 135), translated from the Pali. *Access to Insight*, 14 June 2010, http://www.accesstoinsight.org/tipitaka/mn/mn.135.nymo.html. Retrieved on 27 September 2012.

Nhât Hanh, T. *Understanding Our Mind*. Berkeley: Parallax Press, 2006. Print.

Norris, Christopher. *Badiou's Being and Event: A Reader's Guide*. London: Continuum Press, 2010. Print.

Rockwell, Teed. "Minds, Intrinsic Properties, and Madhyamaka Buddhism." *Zygon* 44.3 (2009): 659-674.

Sachs, Joe. Introduction. *Nicomachean Ethics*. By Aristotle. Trans. Joe Sachs. Newburyport, MA: Focus Publishing/R. Pullins Company, 2002. Print.

Smith, Rodney. *Stepping Out of Self-Deception: The Buddha's Liberating Teaching of No-Self*. Boston: Shambhala, 2010. Print.

Spinoza, Benedict de. *Treatise on the Emmendation of the Intellect*. In *A Spinoza Reader: The Ethics and Other Works*, Ed. and Trans. by Edwin Curley. Princeton: Princeton University Press, 1994. Print.

Suzuki, D.T. *An Introduction to Zen Buddhism*. New York: Grove Press, Inc. 1964. Print.

Thanissaro Bhikkhu. "Samsara." *Access to Insight*, 5 June 2010, http://www.accesstoinsight.org/lib/authors/thanissaro/samsara.html. Retrieved on 26 September 2012.

Thanissaro Bhikkhu, Translator. "Kamma Sutta: Action" (SN 35.145), translated from the Pali. *Access to Insight*, 8 June 2010, http://www.accesstoinsight.org/tipitaka/sn/sn35/sn35.145.than.html . Retrieved on 27 September 2012.

—. "Udayi Sutta: About Udayin" (AN 5.159). *Access to Insight*, 3 July 2010, http://www.accesstoinsight.org/tipitaka/an/an05/an05.159.than.html. Retrieved on 29 September 2012.

Thubten, Anam. *No Self, No Problem*. Ithaca, New York: Snow Lion Publications, 2009. Print.

Volosinov, V. N. *Marxism and the Philosophy of Language*. Trans. Ladislav Matejka and I. R. Titunik. Cambridge, MA: Harvard University Press, 1973. Print.

Wallace, B. Alan. *Meditations of a Buddhist Skeptic: A Manifesto for the Mind Sciences and Contemplative Practice*. New York: Columbia University Press, 2012. Print.

Wordsworth, William and Samuel Taylor Coleridge. *Lyrical Ballads: 1798 and 1800*. Ed. Michael Gamer and Dahlia Porter. Peterborough, Onatario: Broadview Press, 2008. Print.

Zizek, Slavoj. "Love Beyond Law." *Lacanian Ink*. http://www.lacan.com/zizlola. Retrieved on 27 September, 2012. Web.

PART TWO

Speculative Non-Buddhism:
X-buddhist Hallucination and its Decimation

GLENN WALLIS

There are no arguments. Can anyone who has reached the limit bother with arguments?
—E.M. Cioran, *On the Heights of Despair*

The representation of the working class radically opposes itself to the working class.
—Guy Debord, *"Thesis 100," Society of the Spectacle*

[The] goal consists in wresting the vital potentialities of humans from the artificial forms and static norms that subjugate them.
—Marjorie Gracieuse, *"Laruelle Facing Deleuze: Immanence, Resistance and Desire"*

As long as man lives under the Decision or the Principle of Sufficient Philosophy, he lives also within an impotence of thought and within an infinite culpability.
— François Laruelle, *"Theorem oooooooooooo: On the Advent of Impotence"*

Preface

1   *Non-buddhism.* My overall goal in this section of *Cruel Theory|Sublime Practice* is to articulate a theory and practice that I call "speculative non-bud-dhism." The original impetus to my specific formulation of "non-buddhism" was my reading of François Laruelle's "A Summary of Non-Philosophy" together with his *Dictionary of Non-Philosophy* and *Philosophies of Difference*. As anyone who has read him can attest, Laruelle is simultaneously exhilarating and frus-trating. I have found the mere struggle to follow his thought exhilarating. In-deed, what is most stimulating about Laruelle is not that he creates new content for philosophy or makes spectacular breakthroughs concerning philosophy's ob-sessions with truth or being, for he makes no contribution to philosophy whatso-ever. Rather, what is stimulating about Laruelle is his very performance as think-er and writer. In attempting to follow his thought and to make out the significance of his work, I was catalyzed to consider new possibilities for thinking and writing about *Buddhism*. Laruelle is, however, at the very same time almost agonizingly frustrating. He thinks and writes at a level of, in my experience, unprecedented abstraction. As Ray Brassier says of this aspect of Laruelle's work:

> Those who believe formal invention should be subordinated to substantive innovation will undoubtedly find Laruelle's work rebarbative. Those who believe that untethering formal invention from the constraints of substantive innovation—and thereby transforming the latter—remains a philosophically worthy challenge, may well find Laruelle's work invigorat-ing. Regardless of the response—whether it be one of repulsion or fascination—Laruelle remains indifferent. Abstraction is a price he is more than willing to pay in exchange for a methodological innovation which promises to enlarge the possibilities of conceptual inven-tion far beyond the resources of philosophical novelty. ("Axiomatic Heresy" 24)

I should mention here that Ray Brassier's explication of Laruelle in his article "Axiomatic Heresy: The non-philosophy of François Laruelle" and in *Nihil Un-bound*, and Anthony Paul Smith's 2012 private online seminar "A Stranger Thought" were vital sources for my encounter with Laruelle's thought.

I want to emphasize, however, that non-buddhism is not a transposition of Laruelle's non-philosophical procedures for understanding the identity of phi-losophy over to a study of Buddhism. Rather, my conception of non-buddhism began on its own, received a defining jolt from Laruelle's non-philosophy, and then proceeded again on its own way. Certain Laruellen concepts in particular proved valuable in helping me articulate my own suspicions about Buddhism's identity, in particular, his concepts of radical immanence (synonyms are: the real; the Real; One-in-One; uni-versal vision-in-One; identity-in-person; determination-in-the-last-instance), philosophical decision, auto-position (also called specularity), and the stranger subject. Beginning at ¶10, I will briefly treat each of these terms. After citing Laruelle's definitions, I will appropriate and adjust Laruelle's concepts to show how they might serve the organon of non-buddhism. But first, some preliminary remarks.

[Note: Wherever I place some form of "buddhism" (x-buddhist, buddhistically, etc.) in brackets within a quote, it represents some form of "philosophy" (philosopher, philosophically, etc.) in the original.]

2   *Critique and performance.* This section of *Cruel Theory|Sublime Practice* offers two frameworks: "Critique" and "Performance." The goal of "Critique" is to outline a theoretical-critical framework for viewing and giving thought to the identity of Buddhism. It is intended ultimately to stimulate new perspectives concerning this identity—its structure, character, rhetoric, ramifications, potentialities. The theory is thus intended to frame the question: what is Buddhism's *identity*? The goal of "Performance" is to create tools and suggest ways of *doing things with* Buddhist material. The question driving this exercise is: what kinds of things happen to Buddhist materials when we perform non-buddhist critical operations on them? This question is ultimately driving at another: of what value might "decommissioned" or "de-dharmacized" Buddhist materials be for us?

To paraphrase Ray Brassier on non-philosophy, speculative non-buddhism is a theoretical practice proceeding by way of Buddhist axioms yet producing theorems that are buddhistically uninterpretable ("Axiomatic Heresy" 25). The reader should therefore not expect to encounter in this section yet another *interpretation* of "Buddhism." That is to say, the purpose of the theory that I am calling speculative non-buddhism is emphatically *not* to move cumbersomely through the morass of the Buddhist canons making proclamations *apropos* of this or that doctrine, ancient or modern. Neither is the purpose of this exercise to perform intricate philological surgery on the textual tradition or, indeed, even to explicate the "original meaning" of some doctrine or term. In the view of the theory itself, such a move would merely constitute more Buddhism. My aim is, rather, to create the conditions (critique) for pursuing (performance) an untraced and unconscious trajectory of primary Buddhist concepts and postulates, and hence, of the whole of Buddhism itself.

My overall ambition for this section is both more limited and farther-reaching than explicating some hidden facet of Buddhism. My theory is, first of all, concerned with western cultural criticism in the present. As such, it is being designed with three primary functions in mind: (i) to uncover Buddhism's syntactical structure (unacknowledged even by—especially by—contemporary Buddhists themselves); (ii) to serve as a means of inquiry into the viability of Buddhist propositions; and (iii) to operate as a check on the tendency of *all* contemporary formulations of Buddhism—whether of the traditional, religious, progressive or secular variety—toward blind ideological excess.

As I mentioned, my idea for the interpretive strategy that will permit this analysis—speculative non-buddhism—was initially inspired by François Laruelle's recent work in non-philosophy. I will not, however, attempt to summarize Laruelle's project. That refusal stems partly from the fact that Laruelle's severe abstraction defies such summation. More importantly, though, I do not see speculative non-buddhism as a mere transposition of Laruelle's non-philosophical procedures for understanding the nature of philosophy over to a study of Buddhism. Given the specific Buddhist discourse-related issues that interest me, a unique approach is required. Still, the insights of Laruelle and other thinkers do figure in this section; and I discuss these explicitly when necessary.

Critique

First Terms

3 *X-buddhism.* The term "x-buddhism" indexes the recursion of an abstract whole: Buddhism. A study of the whole would show it to be of the type of cultural-doctrinal systems that proffer specular authority concerning crucial human knowledge, such as religion, philosophy, and mythology. A study of the *x* would be historical and comparative. Such a study could conceivably produce a descriptive catalogue of Buddhist schools from *a* (Atheist) through *m* (Mahayana) to *z* (Zen), graphing their relations and tracing their divergences concerning, for instance, the means and end of the whole's specular authority. From such a study we would begin to see that the whole, Buddhism, breeds infinite interpretation not only of the world, but of itself. Hence, Buddhism splinters into unending modifiers, *x*. Yet, this same study of protean variation would suggest clues as to the function producing such difference-of-the-same. (After all, each modifier indicates membership in a single set: Buddhism.) In the present text, my interest stems from the function of the same—from the identifying mark of the set as a whole. "X-buddhism" thus intends to capture the fact that the whole is indeed a unity, but a splintered unity, a pluralized singular. Abstract and inert "Buddhism" devolves to the concrete and spirited interpretive communities of limitless "x-buddhisms."

Devolvement ensures replication. And, indeed, what we find in each and every *x* is the sign of the whole. Following François Laruelle, I name this sign *decision*. My contention is that we can trace the authority of each *x* back to a simple yet powerful syntactic operation, an operation that is embedded in, indeed, constitutes, the whole. Decision, I will show, functions as an algorithm of infinite iterations (*x*) of the whole (Buddhism, The Dharma). That is the general sense of the term "x-buddhism."

4 *Hallucination.* Isolation of this recursive function-of-the-same in buddhistic discourse is in itself an important advance toward a critique of x-buddhism. My concept of hallucination allows the critique to advance yet further in that it reveals x-buddhism to be something other than the specular authority that is conjured by its rhetorics of self-display. Namely, it reveals x-buddhism to be, at most, quasi-knowledge or a type of pseudo-science, and, at the least, a *genus* of desire. An extensive exposé of this facet, however, is not my concern here. I am interested in both more and less. More, because my critique of x-buddhism is situated within a broader cultural criticism. Less, because the final aim of the critique is, in Wallace Stevens's words, "nothing that is not there and the nothing that is" ("The Snow Man")—that is, in resetting the function of one's specific linguistic-cultural situation devoid of x-buddhistic representations.

The animating idea of this text is thus as follows: The practitioner's faith in the authority of x-buddhism implicates him or her in a particular form of commitment, called decision. Given the complexion of decision, detailed in ¶12, this commitment ensures that the practitioner views the world through a transcendental prism. Thus, the commitment, both affective and cognitive in nature, creates a rending (de-cision) from reality. (What I mean by this unnecessarily problematic word "reality" is discussed in ¶12.) However, within the very rhetorics of self-display that initiate the rending (in short, the x-buddhist inventory of doctrine, social relations, and forms of practice) is to be found the cure to that rending. X-buddhism's rhetorics of self-display are thus the means whereby a specific representation of reality (namely, x-buddhism's) is simultaneously ruptured and repaired. A crucial point here is that the sacrifice and its sacrament are confined entirely to a circle of x-buddhism's own creation. Reality itself remains untouched. X-buddhism, *as x-buddhism*, does not offer up *knowledge* of anything whatsoever other than of itself. This is why I say that Buddhism is an instance of a specular authority: like Narcissus's pool, reality remains forever Buddhism's mirror. X-buddhism names a matrix of hallucinatory *desire*—the manufactured desire of the x-buddhist for realization of x-buddhism's self-created world-reparation. This is the general sense of the term "hallucination." The purpose of the present text is to create a critical theory and apparatus that enables the investigator to uncover this hallucinatory quality of x-buddhistic rhetorics. In the act of investigation, it may indeed become evident that divested x-buddhist materials offer crucial human knowledge after all. But they can never do so *as* x-buddhist materials.

5 *Decimation*. This term is intended both metaphorically and literally. Decimation refers to a procedure in digital sound processing whereby the sampling rate of a signal is reduced via filtering. In practice, this reduction often requires discarding, or "downsampling" extraneous data. Technically, sampling refers to the digital measurement of an analog audio signal. In its more colloquial musical connotation it involves taking discrete-time sound units from an original contin-uous-time whole, and inserting them into a new whole—as beat, vocal phrase, chord progression, chorus, loop, etc. Both of these senses are in play here. Deci-mation of the audio signal becomes necessary when the output system operates at a higher sampling rate than the desired input system can accommodate. An additional benefit of decimation is that it reduces noise and distortion in a signal while maintaining consistent signal power, a combination that improves signal-to-noise ratio. Because it requires fewer operations to implement (e.g., fewer data, smaller band-width requirement, less filtering, reduced memory), decima-tion is more economical than higher-rate sampling. Indeed, the prime motiva-tion for decimation is its *lower cost*. Applied metaphorically, x-buddhism can be seen as a high-frequency, broad-band, complex data signal-system.

It is also possible to view the various iterations of x-buddhism as samples in the other sense, as *mixes*. They vary, that is, not in their continuous-time wholes, since they consist of identical data, but rather in their combinations or composi-tions *of* that data. Non-buddhism, by contrast, can be understood as the inter-ruption of the continuous-time whole of x-buddhism through discrete-time analyses. Via the non-buddhist heuristic (¶20ff.), x-buddhism's signal is filtered and reduced. Samples may be extracted, but never reintroduced into a new whole. Some original high-frequency x-buddhistic signal data are discarded al-together. Decimation, moreover, levels the data, eliminating specularity.

As the metaphor suggests, I also intend a literal sense of the term "decima-tion;" namely, *destruction of a great portion*. Via heuristic filtering, speculative non-buddhism reduces the x-buddhist postulates (tones them down) to such an extent that the original *vibrato* becomes indiscernible. The excess data can be said to be thus destroyed. (Heidegger's notion of *Destruktion* captures the sense of destruction I have in mind. I say more about this term in ¶9). This is the gen-eral sense of decimation: filtering, reduction, leveling, lower cost, elimination, destruction.

6   *Non.* Speculative non-buddhism is a way of thinking and seeing that takes as its raw material *Buddhism*. The prefix *non* thus does not signal a negation. *Buddhism*, as a positive value, must remain intact for non-buddhism to proceed. Non-buddhism is a thought-experiment concerning precisely *Buddhism*, but one that assumes the need to think the subject matter unbeholden to its complex

system of values, premises, claims, beliefs, and so on. The *non* signals, then, a multifaceted function.

The first task of *non* is to disable Buddhism's, or more precisely, x-buddhism's, network of postulation. It puts pause to the unquestioned dynamism inherent in all *isms*, in all, that is, self-proclaimed comprehensive knowledge systems, of which x-buddhism is the instance that concerns us. A question implicit in this particular task of *non* is: shorn of its transcendental representations, what might x-buddhism offer us? This question points to the second task of *non*. Laruelle holds that philosophy thrives on difference. Specific philosophies posit, of course, specific differences (e.g., Heidegger's horizontal ekstasis as differential to being/beings, Kant's pure synthesis as differential to the transcendent and the empirical, etc; see Brassier, "Axiomatic Heresy 26); but, more crucially for this point, philosophy as a discipline depends on difference *per se*—difference between, namely, itself and everything else: politics, aesthetics, ethics, science, and so on. Difference ensures that all things become philosophizable. Philosophizing *Y* delivers *Y* over to philosophy's sovereignty: it is philosophy, and not *Y*—not science, art or linguistics—that then controls the terms of understanding.

X-buddhism operates in a similar fashion. It "dualizes" the world: on one side of the knowledge divide is x-buddhism (or its magistrate, The Dharma); on the other side is everything else. From this vantage point, x-buddhism charts the contours of the discourse—on, for instance, mind, consciousness, the person, ethics, cosmology, psychology, even art, philosophy, and science. The *non* subtracts this difference by equalizing—or, in Laruelle's term, "unilateralizing"—the duality of x-buddhism's making, and thereby establishes parity among discussants.

It is toward precisely that end that *non* indicates a critical practice. But at the same time it serves to modify the nature of the critique. The aim of this text is to create a critical theory for evaluating x-buddhist raw materials. Conceivably, a critical-constructive methodology could emerge from the interface of the non-buddhist apparatus and x-buddhist materials. *Non*, however, would radically reshape the contours of any such constructive project. For, speculative non-buddhism—its way of proceeding, its critical practice, its ideas—renders x-buddhism unrecognizable to itself. While *non* indicates an approach to analyzing and critiquing precisely x-buddhist teachings, it necessarily results in buddhistically untenable, indeed, buddhistically uninterpretable, theorems. While this process results in a re-description of x-buddhism, *non* indicates that speculative non-buddhism is not an attempt to reformulate or reform,in any sense of the term, x-buddhism. Neither is it concerned with ameliorating x-buddhism's (or indeed the abstract whole's) relationship with contemporary western secular values.

Non means: this is not a negation of x-buddhism; but neither is it a re-inscribed, "purified" x-buddhism. *Non* says: we are concerned with para-zero reality—with, that is to say, radical representational deflation; and, to that end alone, with the dialectics of knowledge.

7   Organon. In the sense just indicated, speculative non-buddhism is an *organon*. It is an instrument for doing a certain kind of thinking. As an instrument, it enables a practical operation on a body of purported knowledge, namely "x-buddhism." The kind of thinking it enables, though, is not such that can be either agreed to or disputed. The critique does not offer a doctrine or world-view. What it offers is speculation on usage. The uses of this speculative non-buddhist approach can only be determined once it has been employed. As such—as practical criticism—the best approach to explaining what speculative non-buddhism does is to name the methodological moves of which it consists as well as some of the assumptions underlying those moves. The heuristic beginning at §20 serves this end. It will, finally, be helpful to the reader to explain what I mean by the terms "speculative" and "non-buddhism."

8   *Speculative*. It may appear ironic that the substantive that names the critical practice I have in mind is modified by a mental operation universally eschewed by x-buddhism itself. For it is precisely when views and perspectives (Pali *diṭṭhi*, Sanskrit *dṛṣṭhi*) become "speculative" that trouble begins. The paradigmatic example of this attitude is found in the *Cūḷamālukya Sutta* (*Majjhimanikāya* 63), where the Buddha figure warns against the futility of speculating on indeterminate questions and on concerns that he, in his wisdom, left "undeclared." My use of the term "speculative" thus gives notice that as a critical practice, as a way of looking and thinking, speculative non-buddhism is of necessity disinterested in "what the Buddha said" and unbeholden to Buddhist values. Most importantly, it reaches this neutral position precisely via speculation. For speculation, as its cognate *perspicuity* reveals, names a clear, plain, and intelligent *seeing through* of a matter. Such seeing through presupposes a unique relationship to the matter at hand. In our case, the matter at hand is "Buddhist teachings," "Buddhism," "The Dharma," and any and all *x* varieties thereof. A

speculative position toward x-buddhism neither embraces nor rejects x-buddhism's postulates, *in the first instance*. On the contrary, its operation *requires* full acceptance of the x-buddhist status quo *as is*—nothing changes. If this were not the case, speculation would immediately devolve into a series of indicative statements that compete with those under consideration.

Speculation begins with interrogation. Therein lies its importance to a critical method. In fact, given the importance of criticism to the speculative non-buddhism project, a brief excursus might be useful here. The term *critical* is derived from the Greek word meaning "to separate," *krinein*. Separation creates *crisis* in the professed whole that is under examination. A person—and only such a person—who enables separation and instigates crisis is qualified to be a *krites*, a judge. The guarantor of this qualification, moreover, is the judge's newfound skill as *kritikos*—a person who is able *to discern*, a person who is thus precisely *able* to judge. The term *kritikos*, in addition, carries an important nuance: the person does his or her separating, discerning, and judging *with care*. An animating contention of speculative non-buddhism is that throughout its history, right down to the present-day x-buddhism's dichotomies—traditional-progressive, eastern-western, ancient-modern, conservative-liberal, religious-secular, overt (Zen, Vipassana)-covert (MBSR, mindfulness), etc.—x-buddhism has persistently failed or refused, indeed is perhaps wholly *unable*, to perform the kind of self-critical evaluation of itself that is required for maturation beyond visionary or dogmatic forms of knowledge. Speculative non-buddhism sees as a result of x-buddhism's critical opacity a continuous circling in on itself to the point of incessant redundancy.

9 *Speculation as precursor to rupture and disruption*. Speculation thus serves the critical project in that the question-asking of the sort I have in mind is a precursor to rupture; and from rupture ensues disruption. Speculation breaks open the closed system, the abstract one, the whole, of Buddhism. A term from the heuristic will be useful here. That term is "destruction." The organon of speculative non-buddhism fixes on x-buddhism *in the afterglow* of its destruction. The destruction that ensues from this analysis, though, is closer to Heidegger's notion of *Destruktion* in *Being and Time*, than it is to an "end of Buddhism/end of religion" rhetoric. It will be instructive to quote Heidegger at length here. (Interestingly, regarding ¶5, Heidegger employs a signal-processing metaphor in this passage.)

When tradition thus becomes master, it does so in such a way that what it "transmits" is made so inaccessible, proximally and for the most part, that it rather becomes concealed. Tradition takes what has come down to us and delivers it over to self-evidence; it blocks our access to those primordial "sources" from which the categories and concepts handed down to us have been in part quite genuinely drawn. Indeed it makes us forget that they have had such an origin, and makes us suppose that the necessity of going back to these sources is something which we need not even understand. (43)

Speculative non-buddhist methodology makes proximate to the practitioner x-buddhism's specular oracularity, thereby "unblocking" the "primordial 'sources'" (concepts and practices indexing phenomenality, such as *sunyatā, anattā, anicca*, etc.) from which those utterances are, ostensibly, drawn. While this unblocking of tradition's occlusion constitutes a destruction of canonically sanctioned infrastructure, it may also provide a speculative opportunity for a vivification of the "sources." Speculative non-buddhism aims to "go back to the sources"—*conceptually and creatively*, not philologically and "responsibly," and to do so unburdened by tradition's concealing and coercive tessellation.

It is not difficult to see, then, how the rupture of x-buddhism also creates its disruption: the normative claims underlying x-buddhism's ostensible continuity and unity (as, for instance, The Dharma, Zen Buddhism, or indeed as Buddhism pure and simple), is, in the interrogation of speculation, interrupted. What ensues from such an interruption? Perhaps discontinuity or even disassembly. Perhaps radical transmutation or even destruction. Certainly disruption of some form and extent. But we cannot know until we speculate. And we cannot speculate until we have created an organon or critical heuristics for doing so.

Laruellen Terms

10 *Radical immanence* (also called: the real; the Real; One-in-One; universal vision-in-One; identity-in-person; determination-in-the-last-instance). My claim that x-buddhism is a form of hallucination invites a question: hallucination of what? My immediate answer would be "of reality." And I would add that if our concern were not with "reality" then we'd be wasting our time here. For, what, other than "the real" could ultimately justify our effort at thought? But that answer would only serve to throw this text into the fraught sphere of x-buddhism's sovereignty. For, "reality" is x-buddhism's very theme and problematic. X-buddhism exists for no other reason than to conceptualize "reality," elucidate "reality," prescribe strategies for the practitioner to operate skillfully on, with, in, and through "reality." So, how can non-buddhism avoid speaking of "reality" without becoming either just another version of or foil to x-buddhism? Laruelle's concept of "radical immanence" will assist toward that end.

In the disciplines of religious studies and philosophy, "immanence" describes a doctrine that either permits the intermixture of some transcendent force or agent and this world, or refuses the transcendent variable altogether, so that there is only "this world." X-buddhism prides itself on being a system of knowledge wholly immersed in "the real." (The canonical term that I would select as an equivalent to "real" is Pali *sacca*/Sanskrit *satya*. This term, however, is invariably translated as "truth." That translation ignores the fact that the verb at the root of sacca/satya is √*as*, "to be;"hence, *sacca/satya* as "real.") So, doctrinally, x-buddhism would seem to be in agreement with the general notion of radical immanence. In its traditional and religious x-buddhist expressions, however, knowledge of the real posits a purely visionary epistemological basis for itself in, for instance, some variation of the myth of the three watches of the night (including contemporary versions revolving around the enlightened teacher, the force of clear insight, the perspicuity of naked awareness, the power of meditative absorption, and so on). In more secular and scientistic forms of x-buddhism, such as "mindfulness," knowledge of the real is grounded in various versions of an ostensible phenomenology, one that typically fetishizes "the present moment." In either case, though, "the real" as immanence is, for x-buddhism, impossible. X-buddhism qua x-buddhism is incapable of knowledge of the real. The operative reason for this failure is "decision," a conceptual splitting off of the real into some transcendent enabler, such as "The Dharma," even in ostensibly "naturalized" phenomenological versions of x-buddhism. (I will discuss decision later.) The actual reason for this failure, however, is the real itself.

X-buddhism is nothing if not an extensive directory of the real (i.e., of reality-as-it-as, things-as-they-are—*yathābhūtaṃ, tathatā, saṃsāra*, etc.). Laruelle insists, however, that the real is not a subject that can be given over to or extracted from a system of thought for proclamation and description. The real is by definition wholly "foreclosed" (*Dictionary* 61) to such systems of thought. One reason for this inaccessibility is that such thought is comprised of "mixtures" of the world and the systems' own particular representations of the real (Laruelle designates the product of this mixture "the World" or the "thought-world;" *Dictionary* 87). Ironically, the mixture ensues from a "desire" of the practitio-

ner-formulator (of philosophy, of x-buddhism) to possess the real. Yet, the practitioner-formulator *qua* practitioner-formulator of x-buddhism invariably inter-
prets the real in the representational terms given by x-buddhism itself. Hence, as
Laruelle says, "[The real] becomes the object of desire rather than of knowledge" ("What Can Non-Philosophy Do?" 174). Bar desire for the real along with
desire's construction of the real, and what is left is:

> the One [i.e., the real; radical immanence, etc.] in flesh and blood, which does not tolerate
> either internal transcendence or external, operational transcendence. It is not the object of
> a construction or of an [x-buddhistic] desire deployed within the realm of what is operation-
> ally intuitable. ("What Can Non-Philosophy Do?" 174)

The real, radical immanence, is thus "non-intuitive phenomenality" (Laruelle, "Summary" ¶3.1.4.). It is "'in the flesh;' that which is no longer attribute or
even subject" ("Summary" ¶3.1.3.). Being neither attribute nor subject, radical
immanence cannot even be said to "be" or to "exist," for such locutions force on
it cognition together with its inevitable, and inevitably transcendental, representations ("Summary" ¶3.1.5.). Radical immanence is thus "given-without-
givenness" and "separated-without-separation" (Laruelle, *Dictionary* 61). X-buddhism may *posit* radical immanence, but radical immanence is by definition
wholly extricated from and eminently indifferent to any such postulation. Reality is not x-buddhism's to posit *as priority*, to give *as term*, or to separate from
some transcendent, differential second term. A designation such as "real" or
"radical immanence," is, says Laruelle, a "non-conceptual first term" (*Dictionary*
62) or a "first name" (*Dictionary* 18). With it, non-buddhism "interrupts for itself
the [x-buddhistic] path of the real" (*Dictionary* 62), which path originates in and
flows from x-buddhism's insatiable desire to project itself into all things, beginning, as it always does, with "reality."

Unlike x-buddhism, non-buddhism does not begin by postulating "reality" as
a term prior to some subsequent cataloging *of* reality. Rather, non-buddhism:

> conserves [reality's] primacy without priority, thus a non-metaphysical primacy over
> thought...[Non-buddhism] is only a primary thought because it lacks effect over...radical
> immanence or identity through and through. No ontic or ontological content, not even feel-
> ing, affectivity, or life, can serve to define the essence of [radical immanence], lest it intro-
> duce a hidden transcendence into it. (*Dictionary* 62)

The real's primacy is conserved because it is the very condition that permits thought in the first place. And it is for that same reason that thought is foreclosed to the real. Contrary to non-buddhism, x-buddhism cannot fulfill this charge of conservation because it presumes to arrive at its thought of "the real" (*satya, śūnyatā, saṃsāra, yathtābhūtaṃ*, etc.) via the transcendental splitting of immanence, called "decision," along with the employment of decision's specular paradigm. This latter point will be discussed in §12.

So, how can we guarantee conservation of the real? According to Laruelle, there is only one way to do so: axiomatic formulation.

> Even "immanence" only serves to name the Real, which tolerates nothing but axiomatic descriptions or formulations. Its function does not exceed that of [a] first term having primacy over others. It cannot be a question of a simple formal symbol, precisely because axiomatic is, if not the Real, at least in-Real or according–to-the-Real. (*Dictionary* 62; see also "What Can Non-Philosophy Do?" 186)

Radical immanence (reality, the real, etc.) is thus "axiomatically determined rather than presupposed through vague theses or statements" ("What Can Non-Philosophy Do?" 175). Radical immanence is, moreover, presupposed "as utterly empty and transparent, void of any and every form of predicative content, whether it be empirical or ideal" in order to establish "the minimally necessary precondition for thought" (Brassier, "Behold the Non-Rabbit" 69). Perhaps like zero in mathematics, it functions for thought as an "empty condition, rather than a positive, ontologically sufficient or substantive state of affairs," in order to make possible otherwise disabled operations.

Following this principle of axiomatic formulation, we can claim for non-buddhist thought that it is anchored in radical immanence; that is to say, at a minimum it *thinks alongside of the real*. No ontic or ontological claims *vis à vis* the real need be made. No special access need be posited. Contrary to x-buddhism, non-buddhism, for this very reason, has no interest in clarifying or even attempting to describe the real. *Non-buddhism's interest is in clarifying "x-buddhism."* The real, for non-buddhism, is an axiomatic function that serves our clarification of x-buddhism. As such, it functions *to suspend* x-buddhism's claim on the real. To that end, the non-buddhist heuristic contains the postulate of *empty reality*. Like Laruelle's "the real, radical immanence," etc., "empty reality" is an axiomatic function. It will be helpful to say more about the axiomatic nature of this particular function.

The non-buddhist postulate of "empty reality" presents an example of what I call a "recommissioned" x-buddhist postulate; namely, *emptiness; zero; sūnyatā/ śūnyatā*. As such, the practice of postulate recommissioning is similar to Laruelle's idea of a "first name." A first name is a "Symbolic element...formed on the basis of a philosophical concept and entering into the constitution of axioms that describe the One [the real; radical immanence, etc.]" (*Dictionary*, 18). In Heidegger's terms, from the earlier quote, postulate recommissioning, or taking "emptiness" as a first name, is the very move that permits resistance to tradition's "[taking] what has come down to us and [delivering] it over to self-evidence." It is the move that unblocks "our access to those primordial 'sources' from which the categories and concepts handed down to us have been in part quite genuinely drawn." Laruelle likens this move to a result from "cloning." In our case, it is a cloning *of* an x-buddhist term, *by* reality, *for* non-buddhism. Like Laruelle, I find in this operation "the hope of breaking the circularity" (*Dictionary* 18) of the term that is triggered by its function as an element in the network of x-buddhistic postulation. Deprived of its x-buddhistic representational (abstract) sense, "emptiness" or "empty reality" can be placed alongside of "the concrete real," re-stated as an axiom, and reactivated as a postulate. It is, however, no longer x-buddhism's postulate—of emptiness, *sūnyatā,* or anything else. In other words, non-buddhism is not concerned with what *sūnyatā* "really is," but with how the concept functions within x-buddhism's symbolic system. (This is the sense in which non-buddhism renders x-buddhism uninterpretable to itself.)

11 *Decision.* In the first instance, and in the last, radical immanence itself constitutes the reason for x-buddhism-*qua*-x-buddhism's inability to possess knowledge of the real. In nonetheless insisting to claim for itself exigent knowledge of the real, x-buddhism reveals an *operative* reason for this inability as well. That reason is "decision," a concept I am adapting from Laruelle's usage.

Laruelle refers to the "abyss of philosophical decision" (*Philosophies of Difference* 203). As it relates to a critique of x-buddhism, Laruelle's comment can be glossed as follows. "X-buddhism" names a hub of a specific type of interpretation (of what is real, of the person, of mind, of the world, of existence, etc.). X-buddhistic interpretation is infinite because it originates not in what is real or even in some axiomatically given real, but in a (hallucinatory) transcendence of x-buddhism's own making. Lacking, therefore, any regulatory constraint, the whirl of x-buddhistic interpretation never ceases. On the contrary, the whirl breeds an "abyss of an absolute contingency." Recourse to the "logic" of such interpretation is precisely what constitutes a person as "x-buddhist." Such recourse ensues from decision, a "veritable *principle of real choice*." Although the specifics of interpretation vary from one x-buddhism to another, decision itself accounts for "the strange rapport maintained among its diverse systems." Speculative non-buddhist critique can be understood as an attempt to "[modify] the possibility and the limits" of x-buddhistic decision. (See *Philosophies of Difference* 203-204.)

We can now be more specific. Decision, contends Laruelle, "corresponds to a certain invariant, explicit, or repressed distribution of transcendental and empirical functions" (*Dictionary* 56). As such, decision is "an operation of transcendence which believes (in a naïve and hallucinatory way) in the possibility of a unitary discourse on Reality...To philosophize is to decide Reality and the thoughts that result from this" (*Dictionary* 56).

Laruelle gives his concept of decision in the following definitions of, first, non-philosophy *per se* and, second, non-philosophy's subject material, philosophy.

Non-philosophy typically operates in the following way: everything is processed through a duality (of problems) which does not constitute a Two or a pair, and through an identity (of problems, and hence of solution) which does not constitute a Unity or synthesis. ("Summary" ¶2.1.2)

[Philosophy] is a faith, with the sufficiency of faith, intended by necessity to remain empty but which necessarily evades this void by its repopulation with objects and foreign goals provided by experience, culture, history, language, etc. Through its style of communication and "knowing" it is a rumor—the occidental rumor—which is transmitted by hearsay, imitation, specularity and repetition. Through its internal structure, or philosophical 'Decision,' it is the articulation of a Dyad of contrasted terms and a divided Unity, immanent and transcendent to the Dyad; or the articulation of a universal market where the concepts are exchanged according to rules specific to each system, and from an authority with two sides: one of the philosophical division of work, the other of the appropriation of part of what the market of the concepts produces. The philosopher is thus the capital or a quasi-capital in the order of the thought. Or the shape of the World understood in its more inclusive sense. (*Dictionary* 57-58)

Every authoritarian utterance, every word written with certitude, every convinced claim of the type "x-buddhism holds" or "the Buddha taught" or "according to the *Heart Sutra*/Pali canon/*Shobogenzo*/this or that teacher," every attempt to formulate *from conviction* an "x-buddhist" (including crypto-Buddhist "mindfulness") response/solution to Y invariably instantiates buddhistic decision. This decisional operation constitutes the structural syntax of buddhistic discourse, and, in so doing, governs all such discourse—the most scientistically covert and the most secularly liberal no less than the most religiously overt and most conservatively orthodox. Without it, there would be no Buddhist discourse, no Buddhist utterances, no Buddhism, no Buddhists. Such is the scope of x-buddhistic decision.

X-buddhists *qua x-buddhists* are incapable of discerning the decisional structure that informs their affiliation. One reason for this failure is that admittance to affiliation ensues from a blinding condition: reflexivity. Indeed, reflexivity is *commensurate* with affiliation. The more instinctive the former, moreover, the more assured the latter. Optimally, x-buddhism, like all covertly ideological programs, aims for hyper-reflexivity. The degree to which this goal is accomplished, however, is also the degree to which decisional structure, the very internal structure of all of x-buddhist discourse, becomes unavailable to the x-buddhist. Non-buddhist theory is needed, in part, in order to discern the decisional machinery, and thus the overt identity, of x-buddhism. Non-buddhism, as neither Buddhism nor a negation of Buddhism, aims to stimulate the cognitive and affective conditions that render decision intelligible.

12   *X-buddhistic decision.* What, then, is the decisional structure that regulates all things "Buddhist"? First of all, unlike Laruelle, and as my comment about "reflexivity" indicates, I would like to speak of decision having an affective as well as cognitive dimension. (Like its cognitive counterpart, the affective quality of decision is occluded commensurate with the degree of the practitioner's reflexivity.) The word "x-buddhist" names a person who has performed a psychologically charged determination that Buddhism, The Dharma, in some form or another (i.e., some *x*), provides thaumaturgical refuge. In this sense, affective decision is an emotional reliance on or hopefulness for the veracity of x-buddhist teachings. As such, affective decision violates the methodological spirit of all legitimate knowledge systems, whether in the sciences or in the humanities. Because x-buddhism cloaks itself as a purveyor—indeed, as *the* purveyor *par excellence*—of the most exigent knowledge available to human beings, this violation cancels the very warrant that x-buddhism grants itself as supreme organon of wisdom. In so far as affective decision operates on personal identity and world-view, this particular machination of decision, moreover, provides coercive ideology with an inroad into x-buddhism.

In its cognitive dimension, x-buddhistic decision consists in the positing of a dyad (and countless ensuing sub-dichotomies) that serves to split reality in an attempt to comprehend reality, together with a unifying structure that grounds the dyad transcendentally *and*, simultaneously, by virtue of the necessary inter-mixture, partakes of immanence. "Decision" is thus meant literally. It involves a cutting off, a scission, of reality in the positing of particular terms of representation. The purpose of scission is to come to an understanding of the actual, immanent world (though axiomatically posited, and conceived non-ontically, as "the real, radical immanence, One," etc.). In the very process of understanding, though, decision divides the world between immanence and a transcendence that ostensibly grounds that immanence. The decisional division is between (1) a major dyad, consisting of a conditioned *given* and that which conditions it, a *fact,* and (2) a prior *synthesis* necessary for grounding (transcendentally) and guaranteeing the (immanent) unity of the dyad. In being both intrinsic to the dyad and constituting an extrinsic, transcendent warrant, *synthesis* is thus a "divided unity."

Decision is, given its specifically x-buddhist terms and the representations that ensue from those terms, *always, already, and only* an x-buddhistic understanding of the world. It is in embodying this understanding that the x-buddhist person becomes "the shape of the World understood in its more inclusive sense." X-buddhistic decision is, moreover, precisely constitutive of that understanding, that World. Although phenomenality is implied in the terms *given (datum), fact (faktum)* and *synthesis,* no components of the x-buddhist decisional structure need necessarily be arrived at empirically or rationally. Like all ideological systems, x-buddhism, of course, holds that its postulates are inextricably implicated in phenomenal reality and given to the most perspicuous thought. This, even though reality is, as a major x-buddhist axiom has it, "empty of inherent existence." Indeed, x-buddhism's estimation of itself as paladin of empty reality coupled with its fertile representations *of* reality is what constitutes it as "a faith, with the sufficiency of faith, intended by necessity to remain empty but which necessarily evades this void by its repopulation with objects and foreign goals provided by experience, culture, history, language, etc."

Specifically, x-buddhist cognitive decision consists in positing *spatiotemporal vicissitude (samsara)* as a conditioned *given* and *contingency (paticcasamuppada)* as its conditioning *fact.* (The machinery of x-buddhist decision is particularly relentless, furthermore, in that it produces a seemingly inexhaustible reserve of sub-dichotomies that obtain from the dyad: suffering/ease, form/emptiness, delusion/awakening, boundedness/liberation, grasping/release, desire/renunciation, detrimental/beneficial, cause/effect, proliferation/concentration, and so on.) Finally, the structure that synthesizes, and thereby articulates the algorithmic syntax of x-buddhist decision is *The Norm (dharma;* in contemporary x-buddhist writing, this word is almost invariably topped, like the point of a Prussian *Pickelhaube,* with a Germanic capital *D*: The Dharma). *Dharma* is a multivalent term; but its salient sense for non-buddhism's purposes can be summed up in the statement *The Dharma is The Dharma because it mirrors The Dharma::X-buddhist teaching (dharma) is the norm of existence (dharma) because it mirrors cosmic structure (dharma).* Hence, *The Dharma* as *The Norm* (the following capitalized words are synonymous with "norm"): the cosmic Ought machine establishing the Scale of the All, the physical and perceptual-conceptual cosmos, in relation to humans; revealing the Patterns governing humans in the face of the All; setting the Standards of behavior of humans toward one another and toward all sentient beings; proclaiming the Archetypal Equation of the All and x-buddhist teachings; Founding the teachings in the worldly sphere of human being; and providing the Touchstone for human beings to the teachings. (I will, for reasons that should become clear, leave the term largely untranslated as The Dharma.) The Dharma is the x-buddhistic algorithm in that it constitutes a recursive procedure out of which a virtually infinite sequence of x-buddhisms can be generated.

In x-buddhistic decision, The Dharma is the function that synthesizes the dyad of spatiotemporal vicissitude and contingency. Crucially, the dyad obtains nowhere, bears no sense, outside of this idealized representation. In order to serve as the dyad's synthesizing (and necessary) guarantor within the world that the spatiotemporal-vicissitude-contingency dyad aims to lend intelligibility, however, The Dharma must simultaneously be extrinsic to the world given by the dyad. The function of The Dharma, and nothing else whatsoever, articulates the syntactical relationship of contingency and spatiotemporal vicissitude.

The Dharma—the tripartite buddhistic *dispensation, truth, and cosmic structure*—functions, then, as a gathering together of reality's splintered whole. In performing its function, The Dharma must necessarily operate as both an intrinsic or immanent and extrinsic or transcendent feature of reality: intrinsic precisely because spatiotemporal vicissitude-contingency immanently instantiates it; extrinsic because it transcendentally (ideally—*in thought*) grounds that instantiation. This operation constitutes an inescapable circularity. The premise (*The Dharma is the case*), is contained in the conclusion (*thus spatiotemporal vicissitude-contingency*), and the conclusion, in the premise. In other words, the entire decisional structure of Buddhism amounts to an *explanans* (The Norm: The Dharma), that is always and already present in every instance of the very *explanandum* (phenomenal manifestation: *spatiotemporal vicissitude-contingency*), and an *explanandum*, every instance of which always and already attests to the truth of the *explanans*. In x-buddhistic terms: The *samsara-paticcasamuppada* dyad (including the countless posited dichotomous realities that flow from its fecund font), is visible through the pristine speculum of The Dharma. And The Dharma is visible in the contingent and dichotomous unfurling of the samsaric swirl that it, The Dharma, minutely indexes. Indeed, it is true: *The Dharma is The Dharma because it mirrors The Dharma.*

13   *The force of decision.* X-buddhistic decisional circularity renders x-buddhism a world-conquering juggernaut from which nothing can escape. As passengers, x-buddhists of all varieties—as those who possess reflexive commitment to buddhistic decision—are granted perspicuous knowing of all exigent matters related to human existence. "Buddhist" thus names a person who, as Brassier says of the philosopher, "views everything (terms and relations) from above" ("Axiomatic Heresy" 26). Thus, to cite Brassier further:

> [D]ecisional specularity ensures the world remains [x-buddhism's] mirror. [X-buddhistically theorizing] the world becomes a pretext for [x-buddhism's] own interminable self-interpretation. And since interpretation is a function of talent rather than rigor, the plurality of mutually incompatible yet unfalsifiable interpretations merely perpetuates the uncircumscribable ubiquity of [x-buddhism's] auto-encompassing specularity. Absolute specularity breeds infinite interpretation—such is the norm for the [x-buddhist] practice of thought. (26-27)

The interminable debates ("infinite interpretation"), past and present, concerning the nature of Buddhism—its proper expression, its time-place-appropriate formulation, and so on—are merely instances of what Laruelle calls, in our earlier quote, "the articulation of a universal market where the concepts are exchanged according to rules specific to each system, and from an authority with two sides: one of the [buddhistic] division of work, the other of the appropriation of part of what the market of the concepts produces [Secular Buddhism, MBSR, Zen, etc.]. The [x-buddhist affiliate or practitioner] is thus the capital or a quasi-capital in the order of the thought. Or the shape of the World understood in its more inclusive [i.e., x-buddhistic] sense" (*Dictionary* 57-58).

"The World," for an x-buddhist, is the "thought-world" shaped by buddhistic decision. An "x-buddhist" is by the same measure the representative of that thought-world "in the order of the thought" that is precisely the x-buddhist dispensation. And herein lies a crucial task for speculative non-buddhism. It concerns empty reality, or what, as we saw above, Laruelle calls "radical immanence"—reality shorn of that "hallucinatory" representation that x-buddhist rhetorics of self-display, born of desire, drapes over it. The human world is empty of x-buddhism's dharmic inventory. "X-buddhism," contrary to its narcissistic estimation of itself as custodian of "things as they are," indexes nothing in the world. Indeed, in hyper-fulfillment of itself as principal *representer* of exigent human knowledge, the term "x-buddhism" indexes an *occlusion* of the world. X-buddhistic specularity is impossible without the splitting of The Dharma into both immanent and transcendent functions. Such splitting, however, irrevocably corrodes x-buddhism's integrity as arbiter of empty reality, of radical immanence. Stripped of specularity, x-buddhism is, in virtually every instance of its dispensation, quickly overrun by science and the humanities. X-buddhistic decision therefore constitutes an unbending resistance to the very world that it aims to index, reflexively projecting its dharmic dream onto every instance of empty reality's unfolding. Indeed, without this resistance, there is no x-buddhism. But in the same vein, without this resistance there is no non-buddhism either. For, as Brassier says of non-philosophy:

> The decisional resistance to radical immanence provides [non-buddhism] with the occasional cause which it needs in order to begin working. It is what initiates [non-buddhistic] thinking in the first place...[Non-buddhism] is the conversion of [Buddhism's] specular resistance to immanence into a form of non-specular thinking determined according to that immanence. ("Axiomatic Heresy" 29-30)

The current debates concerning all manner of x-buddhisms amount to endless permutations of the same: buddhistic decision conjoined with resistance to radical—i.e., representationally minimal—immanence. Given x-buddhism's numerous tropes touching on empty reality—*śūnyatā, yathtābhūtaṃ, anattā, anicca, tathatā, nirvāṇa*, a finger pointing to the moon, discarding the raft, dismounting the donkey, killing the Buddha, and so on—this resistance is darkly ironic. It suggests that the twin impulses of flinching before empty reality and of evading x-buddhism's own intimation of itself as an ultimately occluding representation *of* reality are native to the very reflexivity that is required for an embrace of x-buddhism. From the perspective of non-buddhism, the result is the extravaganza of x-buddhisms that currently swirl in our midst.

14 *Auto-position.* Blindness to its decisional syntax ensures that x-buddhism remains trapped in an incessant looping in on itself. We see this internal looping in the virtually endless exemplification of The Dharma produced by both intrabuddhistic discourse and x-buddhist-interreligious discourse. Again and again, x-buddhism serves to explicate one matter and one matter only: x-buddhism. This narcissistic self-positing is what Laruelle refers to as "auto-position." It is "the highest formal act" of x-buddhistic decision because it is the move that permits x-buddhistic "faith in the real...in an illusory way" (*Dictionary* 3); namely, the way posited by, indeed *given* in, x-buddhist rhetorics of self-display. X-buddhistic auto-position is thus the x-buddhistic hallucination of reality. Auto-position is tantamount to a form of opaque drapery thrown over the world. As such "the world" becomes, for the x-buddhist, a dharma-induced vision. As the person who fills its prescriptions and embodies its vision, the x-buddhist becomes "the shape of the World." Auto-position is the result of decisional circularity. It is what accounts for x-buddhism's "specularity," its narcissistic beholding of itself in all things, its inherent sense of self-sufficiency. Non-buddhism shares non-philosophy's contention that "Auto-position (its sufficiency, its desire for mastery, its violence), is annulled while non-philosophical thought renounces every idealism so as to be allowed-to-be determined-in-the-last-instance by the Real" (*Dictionary* 3).

15 *Counter-premise to x-buddhistic auto-position.* Karl Marx begins *The German Ideology* with a premise that, in its simplicity and obviousness, seems hardly worth stating. "The first premise of all human history," he writes, "is, of course, the existence of living human individuals" (163). Why is it necessary to state this premise? The reason, Marx suggests in the *Preface*, is the requirement to "discredit the philosophic struggle with the shadows of reality" that so heavily influenced the "dreamy and muddled German nation" of his day. He is referring, of course, to the Young or Left Hegelians' "innocent and childlike" belief in the primacy of consciousness as the force of human history (162-163). Even if, as some Left Hegelians believed, Hegel ultimately sought to improve the concrete world, he still believed that the primary task was to provide humanity with the proper *ideas, concepts,* and *thoughts,* namely, those which necessarily "correspond to the essence of man" and to the world (162). Marx, by contrast, held that "Consciousness can never be anything other than conscious existence, and the existence of men in their actual life-process" (169). Precisely because the contents of consciousness—concepts, thoughts, etc.—are "formed in the human brain," they are, "necessarily, sublimates of [humans'] material life-process" (169). He thought, in other words, that the Hegelians (i) had it exactly the wrong way around, and (ii) were therefore committing a fundamental error:

> In direct contrast to German philosophy, which descends from heaven to earth, here we ascend from earth to heaven. That is to say, we do not set out from what men say, imagine, conceive, nor from men as narrated, thought of, imagined, conceived, in order to arrive at men in the flesh. We set out from real, active men, and on the basis of their real life-process we demonstrate the development of the ideological reflexes and echoes of this life-process...Morality, religion, metaphysics, all the rest of ideology and their corresponding forms of consciousness, thus no longer retain the semblance of independence. They have no history, no development; but men, developing their material production and their material intercourse, alter, along with this their real existence, their thinking and the products of their thinking. Life is not determined by consciousness, but consciousness by life. In the first method of approach the starting-point is consciousness taken as the living individual; in the second method, which conforms to real life, it is the real living individuals themselves, and consciousness is considered solely as *their* consciousness. (169-170)

In failing to recognize that "men are the producers of their conceptions, ideas, etc.—real, active men," the Left Hegelian project insured that they, the Left Hegelians, would alone stand at guard like wolves before the arsenal of thought. It is to accomplish "the aim of uncloaking these sheep, who take themselves and are taken for wolves; of showing how their bleating merely imitates in a philosophic form the conceptions of the German middle class" (162), that Marx "starts out from the real premises [namely: "men"] and does not abandon them for a moment" (170).

In a similar vein—to stem the force of x-buddhist auto-position—I offer the following self-evident premise. Premise: A crucial fact, *easily forgotten,* devoid of which non-buddhism would be just one more of the infinite iterations of an idealistic x-buddhism: non-buddhism aims to reclaim from x-buddhism the person of flesh and blood, who lives in the world of timber, shit, and stone, emptied, that is to say, of the dharmic dream. X-buddhism is a sacrificial rending from reality. Its rhetorics of self-display—whether secular, traditional, or scientistic—constitute an act of high pageantry, whereby empty reality is both ruptured and repaired. But the sacrifice and its sacrament are confined entirely to a circle of x-buddhism's own creation. Reality remains untouched. X-buddhism does not offer up *knowledge* of real processes. It is, rather, a matrix of hallucinatory *desire*—the manufactured desire of the x-buddhist for realization of x-buddhism's self-created world-reparation.

Subjectivity

16 *The subject: interpellation, disidentification, strangeness.* What is the purpose of one's recognizing the x-buddhistic decisional act and the force of its auto-positioning? What is gained? What is lost? Does "recognizing the decisional act" amount to yet another promise of enlightenment—a non-buddhist enlightenment? Does it merely constitute a new specular vantage point from which to craft our newly-won wise pronouncements *vis-à-vis* the world? Most importantly, how might we characterize the *person* for whom x-buddhistic representation is rendered transparent? Three lines of thought will be helpful here: Louis Althusser's idea of "interpellation;" Michel Pêcheux's concept of "disidentification;" and Laruelle's formulation of the "stranger subject."

First, though, a brief comment about the word "subject." I use the term "subject" to stand for the processes through which a particular type of person is formed. So, while in the end, I want to describe a concrete being, a subject is, in the first instance, an abstraction. As I am conceiving it, the subject/person relationship can also be considered in the terms of reader-response theory's model-reader/empirical-reader distinction. The model reader is not a real person. It is an inchoate complex of signals given in the text. Umberto Eco says, for instance, that the model reader "is a sort of ideal type whom the text not only foresees as a collaborator but tries to create" (*Six Walks* 9). He says, furthermore, that a text is a "lazy machine" that requires a real reader to activate its signals. This suggests that, for Eco at least, empirical readers can at least *approximate* ideal or model ones. Similarly, Althusser's interpellation as a "calling into being" suggests an actual shift from the abstract to the real. I understand the subject thus to be mainly the *conceptual model* for a person in thought and action.

16.1 *Althusser and interpellation.* The concept of subjectivity allows us to speak of the "person" in a way that avoids recourse to overly determinate conceptions of agency, such as psychology's "the personality," neuroscience's "the brain," biology's "the incentive system," etc. In so doing, it permits us to reflect on specific ways in which we *become* the persons we are—why, that is, we come to hold the beliefs that we do; to act, speak, and think as we do; to understand the world and interpret everyday events as we do; to hold, in short, the particular values that give shape to our lives. In Louis Althusser's famous formulation, we can go a long way in explaining our subjectivity by considering the "ideological state apparatuses" that continually "interpellate" or "hail" us into being (171). We are formed via our participation in and response to institutions such as family, religion, school, political organizations, mass media, legal systems, and so on. It is through our participation in our society's institutions that we acquire not only the particular values and ideas that we do, but, also the linguistic-symbolic means of grasping and then reproducing those values. To the extent that we share institutions-*cum*-values, Althusser speaks of "ideology in general" (159). (Think of how much you would have in common with a countryman you encounter in a remote Mongolian village. That shared identity would be a result of ideology in general.) Within these shared social frameworks, of course, we also find significant differences. In all but the most totalitarian societies, institutions offer an array of specific values and ideas. Most Catholic schools, for instance, emphasize conformity to God and country. Quaker schools, by contrast, emphasize critical thought and individuality. Althusser terms such variation "particular ideology" (159). (Think of how that American you meet in Mongolia—say, a conservative, wealthy southerner—comes across to you—say, a liberal, middle-class northerner—after a few moments of conversation.)

Althusser's thinking on ideology and subjectivity is useful here for several reasons. First, it recognizes the impossibility of *not* being formed into some sort of subject. We cannot avoid the subject-forming nexus of biological, social, and symbolic systems. In this way, he advances on earlier (yet still prevalent) thinking in which ideology was equated with the distortion of reality by (false) consciousness. For Althusser, ideology is not a distortion; it is, rather, the particular view, the particular understanding of the world that a person acquires in heeding the call of his society's particular institutions. Given, of course, the multitude of possible hailings and varying understandings of the world, we have to add that ideology is "the *imaginary* relationship of individuals to their real conditions of existence" (162; emphasis added). This fact, though, suggests another way that Althusser's notion of ideology and subjectivity is useful here. For, once we reject the possibility of an objective account of the world—and that *our* ideology necessarily contains that account—we are free to *reject the hail*. Doing so would require, in Althusser's terms, that we subject ourselves to different subject-forming institutions. And this possibility suggests a third: we can imagine things differently. Rejecting the hail and imagining things differently assume a degree of critical recognition that we do, in fact, possess an ideology. It is the realization that we have been viewing the world in *quite certain* terms, and not in certain *other* terms. Althusser holds that such a realization is possible only through a critical practice or "science" of ideology.

16.2 *Michel Pêcheux and disidentification.* Pêcheux, a student of Althusser's, was not alone in finding that his teacher did not offer a clear enough account of how the conditions for such a critical practice arose for the (always, thus already, subjugated) individual. For many, it seemed that Althusser's emphasis on the institutional nature of subject formation via ideological state apparatuses allowed too little room for vigorous rejection of the subject-forming hail.

> As many commentators have pointed out, one of the most perplexing aspects of Althusser's formulations on ideology is the absence of an elaborated stance regarding the possibilities for the realization of a resistant or counter-hegemonic politic at the level of the text-subject encounter. How to succeed in making "common sense" uncommon? (Montgomery and Allen n.pag.)

Given the determining force of Althusser's ideological state apparatuses, how can the subject gain insight into the manner in which his ideology goes about "naturalizing" or making self-evident (*cf.* the x-buddhist claim on *things as they are*) its portrayal of the world? Another way of asking the same question is: how is a change of subjective view possible? Pêcheux offers three means for answering this question. His first step is to de-reify the process of subject formation by recognizing the possibility of contradiction and resistance inherent *within* that process. Our ideological apparatuses, in other words, are the site of both formation and de-formation. Second, drawing on Lacan, he emphasizes the role that language and other symbolic systems play in the formation (and de-formation) of subjectivity. Third, he articulates the three decisive ways of *positioning* oneself within those structures. We can look at these points a little closer by concentrating of the final one. I will discuss it in terms of x-buddhist subject formation.

As I mentioned earlier, non-buddhism is concerned with cultural criticism in the present. So, when I speak of "the x-buddhist subject," I mean a specific re-fashioning of a contemporary westerner. Such a person comes to x-buddhism as an already-formed subject of some other kind. Encountering the x-buddhist symbolic system (words, expressions, theses, beliefs, propositions, prescriptions, axioms, mythos, narratives, etc.), the person is convinced, to some degree, of the naturalness and inevitability of the x-buddhist doctrines. For Pêcheux, this moment of consent characterizes "the effectivity of hegemonic ideology" or "the '*winning out*' of the reproduction of social divisions over their transformation" (Montgomery and Allen n.pag.). The person now *identifies* with x-buddhism. He sees the world through its categories and narratives; and, in participating in the community, he is implicated in reproducing its forms. He learns the rituals and protocols, and ascribes to them the values claimed by the community leaders. He accepts the social hierarchies of the community, and knows and takes his place therein. *Identification* is thus the first manner in which an individual can position himself in relation to x-buddhist ideology. The individual who identifies with x-buddhism is, moreover, the "good" subject.

> It would appear that this relation [i.e., identification] provides "already available" subject positions for the *good* subject who, realizing his or her subjection in the form of the "freely consented to," "*spontaneously*" assumes the position offered by the universal Subject "in all liberty" (Pêcheux 114, 156). This subject accepts the image of self [that is] projected by the dominant discourse. (Montgomery and Allen n.pag.)

Such spontaneous identification, however, may be threatened by the individual's recognition of contradiction. He begins to question the supposed naturalness or self-evidence of the community's interpretive categories. We now have, then, the potential of a subject who rejects the self that is prescribed—and indeed *naturalized*—in x-buddhist discourse. Pêcheux names this position within the ideology *counter-identification*. From the perspective of the community, the subject who thus opposes its claims is the "bad" subject. He is the "trouble-making" subject, who calls into question the very foundation of the community's ideology *as natural and self-evident*. Insight into contradiction may be more specific, too. In terms of x-buddhism, this may mean to challenge the historical grounds on which the Buddha's authority is assumed; the reliability of the canonical literature; the efficacy of the rituals; the relevance of the teacher's "wisdom" for contemporary life; the coherency of the central x-buddhist narrative, and so on. Because he takes a purely oppositional stance within the x-buddhist community, the "bad" subject, in an important if paradoxical sense, nonetheless perpetuates the power of the dominating x-buddhist ideology. That is to say, he *lets stand* the dominant ideology that informs the community. He does not attempt to construct an alternative to it, and certainly not *from* it.

The discourse of what then becomes a *bad* subject "turns against" the dominant identification, primarily by *taking up a position* that consists in initiating a separation, challenge or revolt against "what the 'universal Subject' gives him to think: a struggle against ideological evidentness on the terrain of that evidentness, an evidentness with a negative sign, reversed in its own terrain" (Pêcheux 157). That is, Pêcheux argues, the "trouble-making" subject does not recognize those meanings lived by the good subjects as being "obvious" or "natural," but rather as achieved contradictorily; and therefore the identity on offer is refused.

> The philosophical and political forms of a counter-discourse will then produce in the "bad" subject a *counter-identification* with the discursive formation imposed on him or her by interdiscourse, yet one where the evidentness of meaning remains complicit with it, in this case to be rejected. (Montgomery and Allen 1992 n.pag.)

The prefix "non" in non-buddhism does not signify brute opposition for precisely the reasons articulated above. An oppositional account of x-buddhism preserves the terms of x-buddhism's symbolic system. It remains complicit in the "evidentness" of the x-buddhist symbolic system, though "with a negative sign, reversed in its own terrain." So, counter-identification is incapable of creating a subject who is free from the shaping power of the x-buddhist apparatus. How, then, is such a "free" subject possible? Pêcheux's answer is: through *disidentification*. The disidentified subject alone is able to enact the crucial distinction between subjugation by an ideology and what Althusser calls the critique or "science" of one's ideology.

In his "Letter on Art in Reply to André Daspré," in *Lenin and Philosophy*, Althusser draws a distinction between art and science that will be useful here. Art offers us perceptions that *allude* to the world. Science offers perceptions that *know* the world.

> Art...does not give us a *knowledge* in the *strict sense*, it therefore does not replace knowl-
> edge (in the modern sense: scientific knowledge), but what it gives us does nevertheless
> maintain a certain *specific relationship* with knowledge. This relationship is not one of iden-
> tity but one of difference. Let me explain. I believe that the peculiarity of art is to "make us
> see," "make us perceive," "make us feel" something which *alludes* to reality. If we take the
> case of the novel, Balzac or Solzhenitsyn, as you refer to them, they make us *see, perceive*
> (but not *know*) something which *alludes* to reality. They make us "perceive" (but not know)
> in some sense *from the inside*, by an *internal distance*, the very ideology in which they are
> held. (222-223)

Specifically, what art offers us in the form of "seeing," etc., is "the ideology
from which it is born, in which it bathes, from which it detaches itself as art, and
to which it alludes" (222). Science has a different task; namely, to provide a "theoretical practice" for distinguishing between *seeing as* and *knowledge of*. Pêcheux
casts this distinction in terms of the *representations* of ideological hailing and the
concepts of scientific process. The former furnish *meaning*, while the latter perform a *function*. Significantly, both thinkers hold, when we employ a "theoretical
practice" such as science (or non-buddhism), when we, that is, operate within a
"discourse which claims to be scientific" or critical-theoretical, we are, in an important sense, subject-less. For, in Althusser's terms, "there is no 'Subject of science' except in an ideology of science" (171).

> In opposition to the empiricist model of knowledge production, Althusser proposes that
> true or scientific knowledge is distinguished from ideology or opinion not by dint of an his-
> torical subject having abstracted the essence of an object from its appearances. Instead,
> this knowledge is understood to be produced by a process internal to scientific knowledge
> itself. Though this transformation takes place entirely in thought, Althusser does not main-
> tain that scientific knowledge makes no use of facts. However, these facts or materials are
> never brute. Rather, specific sciences start with pre-existing concepts or genera such as "hu-
> mors," "unemployment," "quasars," or "irrational numbers." These genera may be ideo-
> logical in part or in whole. Science's job is to render these concepts scientific. This labor is
> what Althusser terms "theoretical practice." The result of this practice is scientific knowl-
> edge. Scientific knowledge is produced by means of applying to these genera the body of
> concepts or "theory" that the science possesses for understanding them...The result of this
> application of theory to genera is the transformation of the "ideological generality into a
> scientific generality." (Lewis n.pag.)

It should be clear that the Althusserian axiom "man is an ideological animal by nature" dispels the notion that scientific discourse is performed by pure, non-ideological, subjects (171). Indeed, it is worth recalling that the "two conjoint theses" that form the foundation of Althusser's theory of interpellation are: (i) there is no practice except by and in an ideology; and (ii) there is no ideology except by the subject and for subjects (170). The crucial point for our purposes is that a conceptually-oriented, or "scientific," critical theory such as non-buddhism keeps in its sights the *very topic* of subject formation.

> In the conceptual process of knowledge, the determination of the real and its necessity...is materialized in the form of an articulated body of concepts which at once *exhibits* and *suspends* the "blind" action of this same determination as subject effect (centering-origin-meaning)." (Pêcheux 137)

It is in this moment of suspension of the ideological representations that *disidentification* becomes possible. It constitutes a "transformation-displacement" of the identifying and counter-identifying subject.

> The ideological mechanism of interpellation does not disappear, of course—there is no "end of ideology" as a result of science—but it does begin to operate in reverse, on and against itself, through the "overthrow-rearrangement" of the complex of ideological formations and the discursive formations that are imbricated with them. In short, Pêcheux maintains that the appropriation of scientific concepts by the subject-form tends to undermine ideological identification in a way that other ideological discourses, for example, literature, cannot since they are trapped within a field of representation-meaning constituted by and for the subject-form. (Resch 147)

Although the distinction is somewhat crude—and indeed Althusser's failure to elaborate has elicited criticism—we can usefully apply it to our subject matter, x-buddhism. Althusser's basic distinction captures a feature of x-buddhism that is obscured—indeed, one that x-buddhism itself both conceals and eludes—when we let stand its self-presentation as knowledge system akin to science or even to art history as opposed to an ideological system that has more in common with literature and art. A final passage from "Letter on Art in Reply to André Daspré" should make this clear:

> Ideology is also an object of science, the "lived experience" is also an object of science, the "individual" is also an object of science. The real difference between art and science lies in

the *specific form* in which they give us the same object in quite different ways: art in the form of "seeing" and "perceiving" or "feeling," science in the form of *knowledge* (in the strict sense, by concepts). (223)

How can this distinction between forms be made transparent from within the x-buddhist ideological system? How, in other words, can x-buddhism's *allusion* to reality be *perceived* as such and hence become a form of *knowledge*? Pêcheux, recall, wants to insist on the role of both the "material character of meaning" in subject formation and the subject's position in relation to that meaning: "All my work," he says, "links the constitution of meaning to that of the constitution of the subject which is located in the figure of interpellation" (Pêcheux 101). Similar to Heidegger's claim that tradition becomes our "master"—that it successfully hails us to the extent that we identify with it—by delivering itself "over to self-evidence" (Heidegger 43), Pêcheux holds that ideology functions in large part by delivering over to the subject the self-evidence (or, in translations of Pêcheux, "self-evidentness") of its supplied meanings. Again echoing Heidegger, Pêcheux believes that subject-forming institutions accomplish this by causing us to "forget" the relationship between ideological interpellation and its very supply of meaning. For both thinkers, two key elements in both the masking and unmasking of interpellation is the transparency of language and one's position relative to that language.

> [W]ords, expressions, propositions, etc., change their meaning according to the positions held by those who use them, which signifies that they find their meaning by reference to those positions, i.e., by reference to the ideological formations...in which those positions are inscribed. (Pêcheux 111-113)

We can now look more closely at the position of the non-buddhist subject in relation to the x-buddhist social-symbolic system.

16.3 *The stranger subject.* An apt motto for the stranger subject might be: *sabotage all representation!* (paraphrase, The Invisible Committee, *The Coming Insurrection*). For, as Laruelle writes, "The Strangers are radical subjectivities" (Kolozova 61). As Katerina Kolozova points out, for Laruelle a given Y is "radical" if it correlates precisely not with some system of representation or reflection, but with "the real" (59). The stranger subject's identity is concomitant with that of the real. Echoing Marx (and Althusser), for whom the economic was *in the last* *instance* determinate of social formations, Laruelle, holds that the stranger subject is "determined-in-the-last-instance by the real, or radically immanent Ego" (*Dictionary* 71). It is what one becomes when one thinks and acts alongside of radical immanence. Another way of saying the same thing is that the stranger subject is the subject of the self that has evaded alienation from the real by resisting the seduction of arbitrary ideological representations. By virtue of this resistance, moreover, the subject effectuates immanence.

How is that so? Representation is as unavoidable as it is transcendental. Language, cognition, and culture implicate us all, in some form and to some degree, in representation, reflection, and ideology. Real *correlates* are also, of course, transcendental—they are *conceptual reflections about* the real, i.e., held in mind and articulated in speech. But we can speak of them as being at least minimally so. For our purposes, we can say that a real correlate is a representation, reflection or ideological component that is *maximally* denuded of x-buddhist concepts. Whereas *representational Y* (for example, "*anicca*") "follows the syntax of," in our terms, the x-buddhist network of postulation, *real Y* ("impermanence")— as *concept,* in the first instance, keep in mind, not as a material entity or essential quality—is transcendentally minimalistic, hence, follows "the syntax of the Real" (Kolozova 2011, 60). "The Real," recall, is neither the object of science nor the empirically verifiable environment. It is, in Laruelle's unique usage, "axiomatic." It is "the minimally necessary precondition for thought" (Brassier 2001, 69). The real is posited without position, given without givenness, and so on—for how could it possibly be granted position or given *to* thought? To attempt to do so is to once again pile up the detritus of transcendental representation; and the real must *necessarily* be indifferent to our claims on its nature, modes, and meanings. Stranger subjects are similarly radicalized subjects in this peculiar Laruellean sense, and not "persons, individuals or subjects in the technical transcendental sense of the word" (Kolozova 2011, 61). "Subject" as aspect of philosophical decision (and as philosopheme) creates yet another split between person and world in their immanent aspects. Laruelle wants to avoid this "estrangement," and instead affirm *unilaterally* (from the side of the real only; for to add another side is to rev up transcendence once again) the irreconcilable difference between the "mute real" (Kolozova 64) and the (linguistic) subject, which affirmation also affirms, in Kolozova's words, "the lived reality of the radical estrangement as taking place in the Real. The lived is what takes place on—or makes—the plane of the Real" (Kolozova 60). In short, Laruelle says that the stranger subject is made of "the sheer lived." But note, too, that one of the "first names" of the real is also "lived." So, the subject that is "molded from and into" it, the "mute real"—that is to say, the stranger subject—is capable of thought and action that is precisely "affected by immanence" (Kolozova 64). The stranger thinks and acts, namely, "in fidelity to the Real" (Kolozova 64).

17 *The non-buddhist subject.* In the terms given in §16.3, the aim of the non-buddhist critique is the articulation of a subject who, though initially *hailed* by the x-buddhist material, eventually comes to *disidentify* with its decisional representations, and thereby reinvigorates thought alongside of the real, as *stranger*. X-buddhistic thought is thought that is laden with maximal representation. Reinvigorated thought is thought devoid of those representations, so that it is again minimally representational. Such a subject has transformed the *symptom* that manifests as reflexive belief in the self-sufficiency of dharmic minutiae back into the *capacity* for speculative human knowledge. The non-buddhist subject thus knows *what to do with* the de-dharmacized x-buddhist material. (The reader should remember that it is not claimed here that the subject knows *how to be done with* x-buddhism. Non-buddhism may have overtones of anti-buddhism, but it is not quite that.) Unlike the thought of the x-buddhist-subject, which, given the extravagant dharmic inventory, is infinitely expandable, the thought of the non-buddhist subject is unremarkably collapsible—it collapses always back into the identity of mere man/woman. Therefore, in terms of subjectivity, the aim of non-buddhism is the mirror-image of that of x-buddhism. Consider Laruelle's "Theorem oooooo: On the Suicide Disguised as Murder," reworded to suit our needs. [X-buddhism] has but one goal: to make man believe that he must identify himself with [x-buddhism]; to make man assume this suicide, a suicide disguised as murder charged against man. ("Theorems")

Although this language of suicide and murder may sound unnecessarily menacing, anyone who has spent time within the thaumaturgical refuge of x-buddhism, and observed the formation of ventriloquized subjects there, will, I think, appreciate the violence of those words. Acquiescence to the point of reflexivity—a product of decision—requires evasion of oneself. This self-killing/evasion is the reason for the person's "infinite culpability." Non-buddhism is a radical laying bare of the brutal refusal of x-buddhism to honor its most basic pledge: abetment of liberation. If, as in classical-buddhism, liberation entails unbinding from the constraints of delusion, the liberated subject will not—indeed, by definition, *cannot*—subscribe to the x-buddhist program of subject-forma-tion. Paths of liberation necessarily bend toward disintegration of prescribed forms and discontinuity of static cohesive programs, and so are unbearable to systems such as x-buddhism. Hence, the interminable postulation that consti-tutes the inventory of dharmic self-sufficiency— the *binding* of the person within the dharmic fortress, fastened down by the "natural" and "self-evident" connec-tives that constitute the interminable items of the dharmic inventory.

One way of conceiving of the subject of non-buddhism is in terms of the trope of "incidental exile" from the dharmic fortress refuge, given in the heuris-tic below. Exile involves a sloughing off of the hallucinated x-buddhist identity, acquired via participation in the refuge. Another way of understanding the same thing is Laruelle's "Theorem o, or the Transcendental Theorem: On Nontransfer-able Identity," which states:

> Nothing can, except through illusion, substitute itself for man and for his identity. And man
> cannot, except through illusion, substitute himself for [x-buddhism], for the [Dharma], etc.
> Man is an inalienable reality. There is no reversibility between man and [x-buddhism]. ("The-
> orems")

To repeat, recalibrated identity is the aim of non-buddhism. X-buddhism, as self-described dispeller of delusions, must ostensibly desire the same. Yet it does not. It desires rather *to connect everything* via the decisional tension, and to do so in order to maintain and preserve its *dharma-samsara-paticcasamuppada axis mundi.* What x-buddhism *desires* is to see its own narcissistic visage perpetually reflected, from on high, in the mirror of the world. And for that, x-buddhism de-sires, because it *requires*, an unthinking ventriloquized subject. For, in the words of the Generic Zen Master: "Only without thinking can we return to our True Self" (Empty Gate Zen Center).

"Non-buddhist" is a term that names a subject *of theoretical practice.* The non-buddhist stranger subject is patterned on radical immanence or the real. As we have seen, the real is wholly indifferent to the proclamations of x-buddhism, non-buddhism, or anything else. It posits nothing, not even itself. It indulges no dualities because it is deaf and dumb. It cannot even be said to exist (because that would require the dualizing concept of non-existence). But what sentient human can deny that it—the real—*is*? (And this supposition is the reason that, in order to avoid further discussion—and to get on with our work—we, like Laruelle state "the real/radical immanence" *axiomatically*, or performatively, as is the case in mathematics.) The stranger subject, then, in being patterned on radical immanence, stands in contrast to the x-buddhist subject, which is modeled on the transcendental material constituted by the x-buddhist decision. The non-buddhist subject continues to utilize—to think with and perhaps act on—x-buddhist material. It does so, however, *not* to fulfill the (circular, dharmic) demands of decision, but precisely to break free of those demands in order to effectuate, to whatever degree possible, radical immanence. When the decisional cyclone becomes still, all of x-buddhism's postulates thrash against, and then lie alongside of, radical immanence. (They never tumble *into* immanence because the real is foreclosed to them—*they* are synthetic reflections and representations *of* the real, which is always, as Laruelle puts it, One, a simple identity.) Whereas acceptance of dharmic decision creates a subject that stands in an unequal, subordinate, vertical relationship to x-buddhistic postulates, the non-buddhist subject stands in an equal, horizontal one. How? By taking its place alongside of the real, in so far as it eschews superfluous representations. The non-buddhist subject, in performing this decisional suspension, creates a newly ordered relationship to the original x-buddhist material. The non-buddhist subject, then, is one who is determined not by decision but by the real lived, whose immanence the subject effectuates via the theoretical practice. We now turn to this practice.

Performance

> To really place [x-buddhism] in question, even if we are obliged to make use of [x-buddhistic] procedures, we must invalidate it in one blow and without remainder. We must presuppose every conceptual term to be already divested of all power.
> —François Laruelle

18   *Decimated performance.* The way to "invalidate x-buddhism in one blow" is *not* to consign its materials to the trash heap of fantastic irrelevancies. As "Performance" aims to show, the way to do so is to place that material under the demands of thought that has broken with the principle of sufficient Buddhism. This is not an easy task, for, borrowing Laruelle's rhetoric of violence, x-buddhism has a vast arsenal at its disposal. To disarm it, we have to call into question for the practitioner his or her very desire for x-buddhism's assault on reality. What is left at the end of this struggle? As Laruelle says, such a struggle entails "more than a break or than a new primary decision, it is the subordination of the non-philosophical decision to its immanent cause, the vision-in-One" (see Smith 6). What is left, in other words, is what stood there prior to the invasion: radical immanence. The task of non-buddhist performance is likewise to enable the subordination of x-buddhist decision to that which presupposes it: the real lived.

The goal of this section is to offer non-buddhist tools for practice. As stated earlier, the question driving this exercise is: what kinds of things happen to x-buddhist postulates and practices when we bring the non-buddhist critique to bear on them? This question is ultimately driving at another one: what might be the human uses of a disempowered (de-dharmacized) x-buddhist apparatus?

I am using "performance" in two, related, senses here. First, application of the theoretical-heuristic framework is an *ideal* performance realized by an *ideal* subject. In that sense, performance is akin to a thought-experiment. In our case, such a practice, I suggest, reveals a decimated figure, one that has been reduced, cleared out, and abated. That figure is, of course, x-buddhism divested of its transcendental warrant, its specularity, its sufficiency, and so on. Speculative non-buddhism is practice-oriented or performative in the sense that it is an exploration *in thought* into the means and conditions of the x-buddhist network of postulation as human awakening apparatus. It is, that is to say, a manner of thinking about the force of de-dharmacized x-buddhist postulates and practices for assisting the practitioner in negotiating the division between decision-driven ideology and self-reflective critique, or a science of ideology. As such, a decimated x-buddhism would, if not constitute the means for establishing such "para-zero" subjectivity, at least provide material for such a constitution. Subject, however, to the vertical vacillation of decision, the line of dharmic postulation must be reestablished horizontally, parallel to the lived, human gaze. The first requirement of non-buddhism is thus to *forcibly open a new line of vision*—to *divest* the primary classical-buddhist conceptual terms of their dharmic account. In practice, that means we must radically re-read, and only then recommission, x-buddhist postulates and practices.

19 *Heuristic.* Speculative non-buddhism aims to stall the swirl of x-buddhist decision so that, dust settled, we may gain a fresh perspective on x-buddhist thought and practice. In light of the machinations of buddhistic decision, this perspective must necessarily be neither from within nor from outside of x-buddhism itself. The investigator must remain unbeholden to x-buddhism's structural schemes, rhetorical tropes, and decisional strategies. To these ends, speculative non-buddhism offers specific methodological operations, or a heuristic. The terms of the heuristic may be viewed as exploratory postulates. As such, the investigator may choose to perform a critical-constructive dialogue with a given form of Buddhism on the basis of discoveries made via the heuristic—articulating, for instance, what a "Secular Buddhism" or an "Ordinary Mind Zen Buddhism" might look like given the operation of speculative non-buddhism heuristics. As stated at the outset, however, speculative non-buddhism itself is wholly disinterested in any reformulation of Buddhism. Indeed, from a speculative non-buddhist perspective, reformulation is an empty exercise because Buddhists of each and every variety play with "loaded dice" (Laruelle's term): Buddhism, and by extension its acolyte, always and already *knows*. (This is what is meant by "specularity.") "Being Buddhist" means: refusing to silence the Siren-like *vibrato* of buddhistic decision. Thus, another function of performance is to enable the investigator to navigate away from Buddhism's representational Scylla.

This is not to suggest that speculative non-buddhism is merely a destructive project. To view its constructive, or really vivifying, contribution, we can briefly review the function of the *non* in "non-buddhism." Laruelle says that the *non* in "non-philosophy" is akin to that in "non-Euclidean geometry." The difference between Euclidean and non-Euclidean geometry lies, of course, in the behavior of a line. Euclid's fifth postulate assumes parallelism. In upholding this postulate, along with the other four, Euclideans radically limit the field of possible forms. Rejecting this postulate (though preserving the other four), non-Euclidean geometry envisions, so to speak, radical new possibilities; namely, it permits elliptical and hyperbolic curvature.

This image is instructive. "Non-buddhism" makes no decision about (1) what structures or postulates *properly* constitute "Buddhism," or (2) the value, truth, or relevance of any of the claims made in the name of "Buddhism." Such non-decision enables a speculative, and perhaps even applied, curving toward or away from, as the case may be, that which is indexed by "the teachings of Buddhism." Crucially, though, the criteria for any given move lie wholly outside of "Buddhism's" value system. From within the fold, such a move is unpalatable, even heretical; for, the integrity of the system—its premises, authorities, and institutions—must, axiomatically, remain inviolate, for they are precisely what constitute "Buddhism." Non-buddhism stands outside of the fold, but not as a violent revolutionary storming the gates of venerable tradition. Enabling the x-buddhist postulate of requisite "disenchantment" (a term in the heuristic) non-buddhism is too disinterested in "Buddhism" for such a destructive stand. This disinterest, however, does not manifest in rejection. Non-buddhism is acutely interested in the potentialities of x-buddhist teachings, but in a way that, again, remains unbeholden to—and hence, unbound by and unaccountable to–the (dharmic) norms that govern those teachings. As Laruelle claims for non-philosophy, I claim for non-buddhism: only once we have suspended the structures that constitute x-buddhism, only once we have muted x-buddhism's cosmic *vibrato*, are we free to hear fresh, lived, *terrestrial*, resonances.

We can now turn to the heuristic that enables speculative non-buddhism to do its work.

20   *Heuristic index.*
Ancoric loss
Aporetic dissonance
Aporetic inquiry
Buddhemes
Buddhism
Buddhist
Cancellation of warrant
Curvature
Decision
Desire
Destruction
Detail fetish
Devitalization of *charism*
Dharma, The
Disinterest
Disruption
Empty reality
Exemplificative braggadocio
Fitting proximity
Gotamic calculus
Great Feast of Knowledge, The
Humophobia

Ideological opacity
Incidental exile
Material
Postulate deflation
Principle of sufficient Buddhism
Protagonist, The
Recommission of postulates
Rhetorics of self-display
Saliency of requisite disenchantment
Spiritual narcissism
Thaumaturgical refuge
Ventriloquism
Vibrato
Voltaic network of postulation
World

21 *Ancoric loss*. An affective condition. The irreversible termination of hope that some permutations of x-buddhism, including crypto-buddhist formulations such as "mindfulness," index the thaumaturgical refuge adduced in its rhetorics of self-display. Speculative non-buddhist investigation presupposes an attitude of *having no hope* in the ultimate efficacy of the x-buddhist dispensation. Interestingly, ancoric loss resembles x-buddhism's own perquisite dispensation of "disenchantment" and echoes its trope of "leaving home."

22 *Aporetic dissonance.* An affective condition. The believer's *discovery* within himself or herself of a dissonant ring of perplexity, puzzlement, confusion, and loss concerning the *integrity* of x-buddhism's self-presentation. It involves an apprehension that x-buddhistic rhetorics of self-display are but instances of acataleptic impassability. This ring is the signal for aporetic inquiry.

23 *Aporetic inquiry.* A cognitive, investigatory feature of speculative non-buddhism ensuing from an affective condition, namely aporetic dissonance. The act of vitiation augured by such dissonance effectively suspends x-buddhism's network of postulation, thereby devitalizing x-buddhism's *charism*. Such vitiation alerts the practitioner to (i) fissures, gaps, *aporia*, in the x-buddhist dispensation and (ii) the possibility that x-buddhist rhetorics of self-display constitute precisely an attempt to stock *aporia* with x-buddhistic phantasmagoria or evade the *aporia* altogether.

24 *Buddhemes.* The iterative vocabulary, phrases, and sentences that comprise virtually one hundred percent of x-buddhistic discourse. Buddhemes are abundantly displayed in all x-buddhist journals, blogs, magazines, dharma talks, canonical literature, commentaries, secondary books, dialogue, and Facebook pages. In reflexively speaking and writing in buddhemes, x-buddhists effectively reduce reality to the descriptive terms provided by x-buddhist discourse. Significantly though, buddhemic usage evades its own ostensible indexing of empty reality by simultaneously repopulating reality with, and on, its own terms. In light of the speculative non-buddhism heuristic, such reflexive usage appears as symptomatic not only of decision, but of blind ideological subscription. Buddhemic speech usurps and over-determines the practitioner's potential expression of his or her own lived experience. Speculative non-buddhism suspects that buddhemic utterance, like the employment of all borrowed language, is a sign of evasion, of taking comfort in the warm embrace of the thaumaturgic *sangha*. But, again, such utterance functions at the expense of the very purpose that that community is (ostensibly) meant to serve, namely, the combustion of representational delusion *vis-à-vis* empty reality.

25 *Buddhism.* An explicit representation or thought-world founded on a universally accepted syntax, or decisional structure. As the history of Buddhism exemplifies, this structure permits perpetual mutation, wherein decision is re-inscribed in ever-developing expressions of "x-buddhism." Doctrinally, "Buddhism" names a specular, covertly ideological system founded on teachings given canonically to a literary protagonist named "the Buddha." Aesthetically, "Buddhism" names a consistently recognizable rhetoric of self-display (texts, costumes, naming customs, statuary and iconography, hair styles, painting, ritual artifacts, architecture, etc.). Institutionally, "Buddhism" names the manufacturer and conservatory of a particular variety of spiritualized *charism*. In the terms of its own rhetorics of self-display, "Buddhism" names the principal and superior representer of exigent human knowledge. Yet, as mentioned earlier, given the inexhaustible inventory of reality engendered by buddhistic decision—indeed, given the very syntax of decision itself—"Buddhism" can be formulated and arranged in innumerable guises. The word "Buddhism" thus indexes a consistent multiplicity: consistent, given its omnipresent decisional syntax; multiple, given its protean adaptability. The history of Buddhism shows it to be, to cite Laruelle again in this context, "the articulation of a universal market where the concepts are exchanged according to rules specific to each system, and from an authority with two sides: one of the [buddhistic] division of work, the other of the appropriation of part of what the market of the concepts produces" (*Dictionary* 57-58)—for instance, morphological innovations, such as Dzogchen, Soto Zen, Mindfulness Based Stress Reduction, Secular Buddhism or even Post-traditional Buddhism.

26 *Buddhist*. A person who is reflexively beholden to the structural syntax of buddhistic decision. The embodiment of ("the shape of"), hence the central agent in, the buddhistic thought-world. A person whose speech concerning exigent matters is constructed from buddhemes. Given the radically protean nature of decisional adaptation, the possible modifications (*x*-) of the abstract noun "Buddhist" are illimitable, hence "x-buddhist."

27 *Cancellation of warrant*. A major consequence of applying speculative non-buddhist heuristics: the comprehensive withdrawal of buddhistic verity. Indeed, given the coercive function of decision, the work of speculative non-buddhism cannot proceed until cancellation of warrant occurs. Cancellation is not an intentional act. It is the sudden dissipation—affective and cognitive—of a *fata morgana* (warrant).

28 *Curvature*. Analogous to non-Euclidean geometry, whereby decommissioning of a single postulate—thus severing Euclidean geometry's integrity—permits elliptical and hyperbolic curvature. Speculative non-buddhist heuristics yield a distorted image of Buddhism. Lines of connection, juxtaposition, and intersection intended by Buddhist rhetorics of self-display appear as in a hall of mirrors. Yet, in distortion and contortion, new patterns may become visible.

29 Decision. An affective and cognitive operation. Affectively, "decision" is used in its colloquial sense. It involves a psychological and emotional (and, in many cases, economic) determination to accept a particular condition or state of affairs over and against other options. In this case, the *decision* involves (i) adherence to x-buddhism's claims to verity and (ii) dependency on its charism.

Cognitive decision is a technical usage. Derived from Laruelle, it involves a fissure between an immanently and axiomatically given (empty reality of the world) and a transcendentally idealized (dharmic representations of the world). This splitting permits x-buddhism the specularity that constitutes it as the totalizing dispensation given in it rhetorics of self-display. Simultaneously, however, decisional splitting excludes x-buddhism from the community of knowledge. Speculative non-buddhism unmasks this decisional syntax, which operates without exception in every instance of x-buddhism.

30 *Desire.* In the x-buddhist dispensation, desire is the preeminent cause of pain and suffering. It is a kind of insatiable craving that exacerbates the inherent unease of the human condition. X-buddhism claims knowledge regarding the uprooting of this desire, this craving. But in the very voicing of its claim, x-buddhism ensures that, as Lacan says, desire does not give up on desire. (For Lacan, of course, such persistence is favorable. For x-buddhism, it is detrimental.) The voicing of this claim stimulates in the hearer affective decision. Decision, in turn, requires the birth of a specific variety of desire: the desire for reparation of x-buddhism's self-imagined world-fracture. Ironically, x-buddhism is an instance of what Ordinary Mind Zen teacher Barry Magid calls a "curative fantasy":

> A curative fantasy is a personal myth that we use to explain what we think is wrong with us and our lives and what we imagine is going to make it all better. Sometimes these fantasies are quite explicit: we're sure we know what's wrong and we're sure we know what we're after. (*Ending* 6)

To see the irony of this statement, we have to read it against Magid's intention. X-buddhism continually reveals itself as just such a saving "personal myth." X-buddhism is a "curative fantasy" writ large. It is sure it knows what's wrong with you, and it is sure it knows what you should be after. X-buddhism, therefore, aims, for your sake, to foster in you the proper genus and force of its unique desire.

31 *Destruction.* What is not being destroyed is *buddhistic decision*. For, in order for speculative non-buddhism to do its work, that structure must, in the first instance, remain intact. For, obviously, only if intact can it be exposed. Once exposed, however, a re-description occurs that has destructive consequences. Speculative non-buddhism, it can be said, is eminently interested in viewing x-buddhism in the afterglow of its destruction. But, as I mentioned, the destruction that ensues from its analysis is closer to Heidegger's notion of *Destruktion* in *Being and Time*, than it is to an "end of Buddhism/end of religion" rhetoric. It will be instructive to quote Heidegger at length again in this context:

> When tradition thus becomes master, it does so in such a way that what it "transmits" is made so inaccessible, proximally and for the most part, that it rather becomes concealed. Tradition takes what has come down to us and delivers it over to self-evidence; it blocks our access to those primordial "sources" from which the categories and concepts handed down to us have been in part quite genuinely drawn. Indeed it makes us forget that they have had such an origin, and makes us suppose that the necessity of going back to these sources is something which we need not even understand. (43)

32 Detail fetish. See Exemplificative braggadocio.

33 *Devitalization of charism.* The x-buddhist vallation is sealed by *charism*. X-buddhistic *charismata* are the incalculable averred "gifts" of wisdom, knowledge, community, teacher-student relationship, healing, and so forth, that cascade out of the dharmic dispensation. Such gifts exert a binding influence on the x-buddhist. One result of charismatic influence is the blinding of the x-buddhist to decisional structure and decisional commitment. Enactment of speculative non-buddhist heuristics enables the x-buddhist to unbind and unblind from the coercive yet largely unconscious effects of the *charism*. Imaginative curvature—speculatively applied reconfiguration—is impossible until this *charism* is quelled.

34 *Dharma, The.* The specular *omen pontificator* of samsaric contingency. Like God, Justice, Logos, Rta, The Dao, and so on, The Dharma (English: The Norm as buddhistic trinity of dispensation, truth, and cosmic structure) is the architect of the cosmic vault and the keeper of its inventory. As such, The Dharma engenders the buddhistic hallucination of reality. In its decisional function, The Dharma is the transcendent-immanent operator that synthesizes the purely immanent dyad of spatiotemporal vicissitude (*samsara*) and contingency (*paticcasamuppada*). The hallucinatory quality results from the fact that The Dharma is a function of a purely idealized (transcendent) grammar that produces oracular statements *infinitum* concerning the finite world (immanence). The Dharma is the axis on which turns around and around and around the x-buddhist world-conquering juggernaut. It is the buddhistic gathering together (under the authority of The Dharma) of reality's posited (by The Dharma) splintered whole, which splintering is exhibited by the (dharmically indexed) world condition articulated (by The Dharma) as spatiotemporal vicissitude-contingency.

35 *Disinterest*. An affective quality. The speculative non-buddhism investigator forfeits his commission if he serves as either the shape of the buddhistic thought-world or as a revolutionary storming the gates of the x-buddhist vallation. Disinterest's physical corollary, when confronted with charismatic x-buddhist omens, is a shrug of the shoulders, followed by a concerned glance toward the harbinger. For, to someone disinterested, interest appears symptomatic of a dissociating yearning for the thaumaturgic *sangha*.

36 *Disruption*. X-buddhism's network of postulation is a power grid pumping buddhistic *charism* through the lines of venerable transmission. Steadied by its rhetorics of self-display, the network extends to *sangha* sub-stations and into the affective-cognitive-decisional apparatus of the individual x-buddhist person. Speculative non-buddhist heuristics enable an interruption of the power surge in order to inspect its machinery and analyze its juice.

37 *Empty reality*. Another name for radical immanence. In other words, the most banal, disappointing, uninteresting, unremarkable, indeed, vacuous, fact of life imaginable. In one register it is: nothing that is not in the world, and the nothing that is. In another register it is: everything that is not yet in the world, and the everything that already is. Ontically, science charts empty reality. Ancestral statements about the earth's accretion and cell formation as well as descendent statements concerning cell dissolution and the earth's incineration point toward empty reality. Culture adds its representations. The primary purpose of enacting speculative non-buddhist postulates is to encourage us 200,000-year-old *homo sapiens* apes *to settle alongside of* empty reality with, *initially* at least, whatever culturally minimal representation is required to get along. Dispelling occlusion of empty reality—which occlusion ensues from incognizant, e.g., x-buddhistic, representation—constitutes speculative non-buddhism's very reason for being. Against the narcissistic impulses of the *homo sapiens* ape to reify and aggrandize his evanescent cultural fictions, empty reality must not be re-inscribed as x-buddhistic *śūnyatā*, no-self, "things as they are," dependent origination, or anything else. Empty reality is given in the "just so" of everyday life. The term "empty reality" is used because it names the intimately real, the radically immanent, while refusing to pluck the heartstrings of the soul's *vibrato*. X-buddhicized terms, like "*śūnyatā*," do the latter. *Śūnyatā*, for instance, is "Joe Ji-kyo Jones Roshi" to *empty reality's* "Joe Jones;" it is, namely a rhetorical flamboyance that serves to occlude what it purports to name precisely because it *overwrites* what it names (with its grandiosity, cultural-historical complexity, etc.). X-buddhists, as the shape of Buddhism, may attempt to comment on empty reality; but, in doing so *qua x-buddhists* via buddhemic utterance, this would amount to yet another inscription of buddhistic decision—yet another turn on the circularity of the dharmic axis. Empty reality is not an issue for x-buddhism. It is none of x-buddhism's business. Empty reality is nothing at all. Could the term express that point with any more directness and clarity? To a great extent, the term "Buddhism" names a particular manner of *representationally stylizing* empty reality. As terms such as *śūnyatā* intimate, finally, a dark irony is at hand here: x-buddhism encodes its own undoing. But no x-buddhist is able to undo it. That would be impossible. Hence: non-buddhism.

38 *Exemplificative braggadocio.* Also known as the x-buddhistic "detail fetish." It refers to a form of behavior. It is a manner of argumentation in which minute details about *x-buddhism* are made load-bearing structures in arguments about various facets of *reality*. X-buddhist exemplificative braggadocio is a primary manifestation of x-buddhist faith in the principle of sufficient Buddhism. It is the way of x-buddhist commentators to cite as evidence for their position *an example*: sutta/sutra/tantra-a-b-c maintains x, y, z; buddhistic-school/teacher-a-b-c maintains x, y, z, etc. I could add, without exaggeration, that they cite their examples *ad infinitum*. For, exemplification is an essential feature of dharmic discourse. Given the long history and vast cultural-geographic range of the dispensation, there is virtually no end to the x-buddhists' salvo of dharmic exemplification. That is why I say that x-buddhism is a world-conquering juggernaut from which nothing can escape: there is nothing under the sun for which x-buddhism cannot provide an example. The examples it proffers, moreover, derived as they are from buddhistic decision, ensure that "x-buddhist" names a person who, as Ray Brassier says of philosophers, "views everything (terms and relations) from above." Like Wittgenstein his slabs and Heidegger his hammer, the x-buddhist is entranced by his *examples*.

Contrary to x-buddhism, non-buddhism sees the perpetual crowing of dharmic exemplification not as the specular instantiations of reality that those examples are meant to demonstrate (concerning mind, matter, consciousness, perception, sensation, etc.) but rather as symptomatic displays *in need of analysis*. It is, in fact, via an analysis of buddhistic exemplification that I arrived at my specific adaptation of Laruelle's axiom of decision in relation to x-buddhism. Endless dharmic exemplification presents the most rigorous basis for the operation of decisional circularity, or what Laruelle calls "auto-position" (specularity), in all of x-buddhism. It is worth repeating Brassier again in this regard:

> [d]ecisional specularity ensures the world remains [x-buddhism's] mirror. [Buddhistically theorizing] the world becomes a pretext for [x-buddhism's] own interminable self-interpretation. And since interpretation is a function of talent rather than rigor, the plurality of mutually incompatible yet unfalsifiable interpretations merely perpetuates the uncircumscribable ubiquity of [x-buddhism's] auto-encompassing specularity. Absolute specularity breeds infinite interpretation—such is the norm for the [x-buddhist] practice of thought. (26-27)

The illuminating irony of x-buddhists' citing diverse examples to other x-buddhists is that, from a non-buddhist perspective, they are only exhibiting—meta-exemplifying!—the unity of buddhistic syntax. Doing so is all the more illuminating because their examples are not, as they purport to be, examples from and of reality, but from and of x-buddhism itself, and only itself.

39 *Fitting proximity*. A relation of the investigator to x-buddhism's vallation. Too close, and the effulgence of x-buddhism's *charism* blinds; too far away, and the embers turn cold.

40 *Gotamic calculus*. The first names or primary raw terms— derived from the canonical protagonist, Siddhattha Gotama, the Buddha—that a given x-buddhism employs to chart its model of being and becoming. In general terms, a calculus is concerned both with the tangent or trajectory of continuous instantaneous change and the area or space that ensues, even if only momentarily, from that change. As such, a calculus is concerned with the quantification of real-world limits. Newton's use of the calculus allowed a mathematical description of physical phenomena. Mathematical equations were, then, the terms of Newton's calculus. By contrast, Gotama is concerned with *qualitative* real-world limits. His major terms are the concepts that make up the dharmic inventory. Different x-buddhisms employ various major terms. An example of a classical-buddhist gotamic calculus might be: disenchantment, ancestral anamnesis, vanishing, symbolic identity, nihility, conceptual proliferation, contingency, world, surface, perspicuity, unbinding-extinction (*nibbida, sati, anicca, anattā, suññatā, papañca, paticcasamuppāda, loka, sabba, paññā, nibbāna*). These foundational concepts are viable candidates for a gotamic calculus because they are arguably the *sine qua non* of classical-buddhism (hence, they are first names, or primary raw terms). Devoid of them, the earliest dispensation is hardly anything more than a platitudinous ethical system conjoined to superstitious devotional practices situated within a pedestrian philosophical framework. It is precisely because of its robust existential postulates, such as "vanishing" and "radical contingency," that classical-buddhism has consistently attracted the interest of the world's thinkers, including philosophers, physicists, and artists. The great irony here is that the classically-oriented x-buddhisms themselves (e.g., the Secular, Atheist, Agnostic, Thai Forest, traditional Theravadin, Insight, Vipassana, MBSR, and a few others) evade the ultimate and invigorating conclusion—the, or *a*, seemingly inevitable outcome—of their own terms. The result of this evasion is that these terms haunt x-buddhist discourse. The calculus seems to permit, if not outright dictate, an alternative trajectory. Even as nodes in the network of x-buddhist postulation, a series of fair, yet unexplored, questions presents themselves: don't concepts such as nullity and radical contingency cast a shadow on x-buddhism's modern-day Epicurean path to *eudaemonia*? Don't ideas such as vanishing and extinction hang like a cloud over that path's destination, *nirvana*, when construed as a healing garden that "slakes the thirst with a natural cure"? The heuristic tool "gotamic calculus" asks the investigator to perform such recalculations of x-buddhist first names, and to give relentless thought to what unexpected sums might be derived, no matter where such thought might lead.

41   *Great Feast of Knowledge, The.* X-buddhistic decision is a specular court of justice that rules from above. Its representatives include, for instance, Enlightenment, Compassion, Suffering, Delusion, Mindfulness. Consideration of any of these representatives devoid of the royal warrant provided by decision reveals these representatives to be, as buddhistically presented, unfit, unusable, unreliable, and even suspect, characters. For, deflation acts to make manifest the representatives' display of self-importance, necessity, obviousness, assumed desirability, pretense to natural truthfulness, etc. Speculative non-buddhism escorts x-buddhism's representatives to the Great Feast of Knowledge. Seated at the table there, the representatives must hold their own alongside of local knowledges such as art, philosophy, literature, biology, psychology, physics, and so on. From a speculative non-buddhist estimation, the x-buddhist representatives, devoid of their dharmic body guards (the network of postulation), lose all status in such an exchange. That status, founded on the specularity given in decision, is thereby deflated. Sitting at the Great Feast of Knowledge radically alters the contribution of x-buddhism's representatives. (I hear art and evolutionary biology, for instance, holding forth passionately on the absolute necessity and glorious fruits of one of x-buddhism's foremost undesirables, "delusion," to take but a single instance).

42 *Humophobia.* "Above all, we should cease postponing the act of becoming what in fact and essence we are," says Henry Miller (*Plexus* 64). What we, in fact and essence are, of course, is human. The force of x-buddhist subjugation can be understood as an effort to repress this fact and reverse or even obliterate this "essence." It does so by offering a pantheon of realized types—from the traditional arahant and bodhisattva to the contemporary mindful practitioner—skilled in the enlightened arts of wisdom, compassion, kindness, non-judgmental clarity, and a host of other salvific dispositions. X-buddhist typology cynically belies fear of the human *of flesh and blood*, and thus fashions in its place fantastic constructions of enlightened mutants. The only way the x-buddhist typology can function is both to subsume and to overcome the human. That is, x-buddhism first determines what the "the uninstructed worldling" is (lustful, deluded, hostile, unskilled, etc.), and then instructs him on how to surpass himself.

43 *Ideological opacity.* X-buddhism is nothing if not a vortex of participation and identity. It aims both explicitly and implicitly to form particular types of subjects, and to do so in its own image. The basis of its transformational program is, furthermore, its own prescribed practices (social, linguistic, devotional, contemplative, etc.). All of this is, finally, accompanied by robust institutional commitment, or hyper-reflexivity. Such features describe not a contestable program of knowledge or skill acquisition, but rather an ideological system of indoctrination. It describes, that is, a systematic program of personal transformation and social reproduction whose ideas—beliefs, goals, actions—derive not from individual agents, but from a pre-established putative norm, in this case: The Dharma. Speculative non-buddhism is constantly alert to any signs in buddhistic decree that indicate a comprehensive view of self, society, and cosmos. Indeed, the very fact that, unmolested by the kinds of methodological moves that speculative non-buddhism makes, The Dharma operates unseen (it is just "how things are," it is natural and self-evident, etc.), is evidence of the ideological machination of x-buddhism. The question is whether the non-buddhist intervention may enable transparent insight into such opaque machination of x-buddhist ideology.

44 *Incidental exile.* An exile is someone who finds himself or herself in fitting proximity to Buddhism's vallation. I say "finds" because exile, in this case, is not forced: it occurs *incidentally and unexpectedly*. Aporetic dissonance initiates it; aporetic inquiry further drives it. The process goes something like this. Contentedly ensconced within x-buddhism's thaumaturgical refuge, you find yourself soothed by tradition's self-proclaimed "compassionate" *charism*. (A sufficient apprenticeship within x-buddhism's workshop—locking oneself onto the grooves of borrowed x-buddhistic thought—may be a necessary precondition for exile even to be an option.) But, for whatever reasons, at some point you discover within yourself a sense of ancoric loss and aporetic dissonance. On examination, you hear this ring as the resonance of a complex of disturbing emotions and thoughts: perplexity, puzzlement, confusion, disappointment, and loss. You discover, to your surprise, that x-buddhism leaves much to be desired. You become suspicious of the way it postures as the giver of solutions, as the harbinger of peace. It may answer many questions, but, you are beginning to realize, it all too often does so in a facile and hasty manner. It even encourages superstitious belief and new forms of neurotic attachment. And in the meantime, it is creating for you many questions which it seems impotent to answer. Suddenly, you find yourself incidentally and unexpectedly exiled from the thaumaturgical refuge, from the innocent embrace of the pure dispensation. What will you do? You may, of course, abandon the project altogether and wander on your way, seeking refuge in another self-described specular dispensation or in a desert of confusion or in nothing at all. Another possibility: you engage the bewildering aporias that have opened before your unsuspecting mind. Hence, you set up camp in fitting proximity—fitting, that is, for an exile.

45 *Material.* Speculative non-buddhism is a critique of x-buddhist *material*. The material that it takes into its purview includes the numerous forms that make up x-buddhist thought and practice: *sanghas* and practice groups, retreats and retreat centers, rituals and ritualization, protocols, concepts, language usage, rhetoric, websites, blogs, forums, popular and academic books and magazines, canonical literature, paraphernalia, altars, artifacts, iconography, hair styles, naming practices, clothing, and beyond. As the term *material* suggests, specifically x-buddhist configurations of these forms occur always in the second instance only. Decimation of the material thus constitutes a reclamation of the human by the human and for the human.

46 *Postulate deflation*. Deprecating the charismatic braggadocio of x-buddhism's conceptual magistrates so that they are forced to join the table of common-law discourse. *See* Great Feast of Knowledge.

47 *Principle of sufficient Buddhism*. Parallel to Laruelle's "Principle of Sufficient Philosophy," which states that everything is philosophizable. X-buddhistic decision is similarly a pretension of that mechanism's creators (i.e., x-buddhists) that all things under the sun are matters for x-buddhism's oracular pronouncements, and that the totality of pronouncements (the network of postulation) constitutes an adequate account—a unitary vision—of reality. "Buddhism" thus names, for "Buddhists," a sufficiency. As postulate deflation reveals, however, this view of sufficiency is maintained only insofar as x-buddhism successfully avoids conversing with the sciences and humanities at The Great Feast of Knowledge. This avoidance amounts to a myopia whereby Buddhism only *appears* sufficient. This appearance, given the blighted field of reality that it entails, amounts to buddhistic hallucination, whereby "the x-buddhist view of Y" is confused with—seen in place of—"Y."

48 *Protagonist, The*. Also called "the Buddha-figure." The progenitor of the Buddhist dispensation. He is referred to by various names, such as "The Buddha," "Gotama," and "The Blessed One." Speculative non-buddhism's designation "the protagonist" is intended to indicate the irrefutable fact that "the Buddha" is a historical figure entirely overwritten by a literary one. Not the slightest wisp of evidence has survived that sheds light on the historical progenitor. Any reliable historical evidence that once existed has been reduced to caricature by the machinations of internecine x-buddhist institutional shenanigans and the stratagems of ideological dupery. The figure of the Buddha in the classical Pali texts is a concoction of the collective imaginations of the numerous communities that, over several centuries, had a hand in the formation of the canon. Add to this imaginative mélange the imaginings—cultural, political, fantastic, ignorant—of all the iterations of all forms of x-buddhism, and the result is the Buddha as Cosmic Magic Mirror, reflecting all things to all people. A viable composite human figure "the Buddha" can be salvaged from this protean symbol of buddhistic vanity only with force of the darkest, most atavistic yearning of puerile nostalgia for The Great Father.

49   *Recommission of postulates.* Once deflated, muted, decimated, subjected to the inquiries of the participants at The Great Feast of Knowledge, and otherwise divested of charismatic potency, x-buddhism's postulates may be released back into the world. The result, however, is, in every instance, a buddhistically uninterpretable result. For instance, the postulate of the second preeminent reality (*idaṃ dukkhasamudayaṃ ariyasaccam: taṇhā*) claims exigent and superior knowledge of the cause of human unease or "suffering" (*dukkha*), namely "craving" (*taṇhā*). Stripped of specularity, derived as it is from the transcendental dharmic inventory, the postulate may be brought into dialogue with, for example, bio-science's biological incentive system (BIS). BIS identifies the reward-punishment mechanism that explains human craving *vis-à-vis* evolutionary adaptation. In short, the notion of "uprooting," "extinguishing," or otherwise extirpating craving (all additional classical-buddhist postulates) in light of BIS looks not only unfeasible but outright hackneyed. Or perhaps not. We won't know how well the recommissioned postulate holds up at The Great Feast of Knowledge until we observe it in vigorous dialogue.

50   *Rhetorics of self-display.* The entrancing nimbus enfolding the palace of The Dharma. The aesthetic affectation of thaumaturgy—clothing, naming, hair styles, painting, sculpture, architecture. To wit: The cult of the book; the exaltation of the dharma talk; the apotheosis of the teacher. To wit: Buddhas and bodhisattvas arrayed in magnificent robes, sitting majestically in their heavenly abodes—their buddha fields—exuding auras of healing light. Magical flesh and bone, fresh as the breath of the Blessed One, efficacious as *amritya*, nectar of the gods. Magnetic mantras—*nembutsu, daimoku, dharani*—sound tsunamis surging throughout the universe. Ritual paraphernalia—statues, bells, a twirling wheel clutched like a crucifix in the dark. Those living exemplars, as charismatic and clairvoyant as the Buddha walking unscathed on an open road: Roaring roshis, shamanic lamas, wizardly tulkus, and wonder-working arahants. (= A rhetorically-charged display of x-buddhist rhetorics of self-display.)

51 *Saliency of requisite disenchantment.* "Disenchantment" is, of course, an eminently buddhistic notion. The protagonist posits it as the catalyst *par excellence*, indeed, the requisite affective condition, of "home-leaving," of embarking on the "holy life." In good speculative non-buddhism fashion, however, we can divest it of the limit circumscribed by x-buddhism. Doing so, we claim it as a value of flesh and blood, and turn it back on "home-leaving," back on "the holy life," back on x-buddhism. Indeed, disenchantment—with the buddhistic specular oracularity—is the catalyst to speculative non-buddhist enquiry.

52 *Spiritual narcissism.* The x-buddhist subject is doubly narcissistic. First, it is so in a manner consistent with the general, wide-spread condition found among all religious adherents; namely, exalted self-importance. The x-buddhist subject is the holder of the key to the cosmic vault of wisdom (i.e., The Dharma). It is the progeny of the Enlightened One. The elixir-like *mana* of mindfulness courses through its consciousness. As such each and every x-buddhist has the potential—and the *right*—to outflank interlocutors from every manner of local knowledge, whether of the sciences or of the humanities, and, lead, like Delacroix's *Liberty*, the embattled masses from the front. This form of x-buddhist narcissism is on open display. The second type is more subtle, and so less visible. This insidious type of spiritual narcissism has the potential for what Laruelle's "Theorem oooooo" names "the suicide disguised as murder" (see §17). It is as Ovid says in *Metamorphoses*: Narcissus died "because he could not lay hold of himself, and yet perceived himself as other." Like Narcissus, the Buddha's progeny becomes (like the progenitor himself) "tired of hunting and the heated noon"—of stress and unease born of the slow samsaric burn. She or he, too, sits down, "attracted by the peaceful solitudes and by the glassy spring"—the promise that infuses the rhetoric of x-buddhist "refuge-taking." And yet, as the x-buddhist stoops to quench his thirst "another thirst increases," for:

> While he is drinking he beholds himself reflected in the mirrored pool—and loves; loves an imagined body which contains no substance, for he deems the mirrored shade a thing of life to love. He cannot move, for so he marvels at himself.

A Narcissus, the x-buddhist becomes entranced with the watery image of a transfigured self—the realized subject shimmering in the dharmic dispensation. Yet he fails to recognize that before him is—*always and only*—himself alone. Or, put the other way around, he has fallen for the illusion that the x-buddhist subject can replace his identity. The heuristic thus implores the x-buddhist, as Ovid's narrator does Narcissus,

> Avert your gaze and you will lose your love, for this that holds your eyes is nothing save the image of yourself reflected back to you. It comes and waits with you; it has no life; it will depart if you will only go.

We implore, of course, to no avail—the lustful fantasy for the realized subject now has a real, if liquid and ungraspable, form. And so the x-buddhist Narcissus must eventually admit:

> This fatal image wins my love, as I behold it. But I cannot press my arms around the form I see, the form that gives me joy.

53   *Thaumaturgical refuge.* The affectation of x-buddhist teachers to wonderworking community (*sangha*). Telling signs of thaumaturgical display among x-buddhist teachers include: masking identity with special naming, clothing, and hair styles; exalted utterance, verbal demiurgy; narratological seizure; assumption of privileged status as ritual officiate; wielding unique power objects; functioning as high pageantry eminence; serving as guardians of the sanghic *axis mundi*. Such displays communicate to the practitioner what the anthropologist Pascal Boyer calls "hidden causal essence." Given the role that thaumaturgical refuge plays in ideological allurement, it will be instructive to quote Boyer at length:

> Notions of ritual specialists are based on non-religious notions of causal essence. People think of such ritual specialists as having some internal, vaguely defined quality that sets them apart from the common folk. Learning to perform the rites [is secondary]; what matters most is possession of that internal capacity, conceived in quasi-biological terms. This is where, once again, what may have seemed a specifically religious phenomenon is derived from common cognition. The notion of a hidden causal essence that cannot be observed yet explains outward form and behavior, is a crucial feature of our spontaneous, intuitive way of

thinking about living species. Here, it is transferred upon a pseudo-natural kind, as it were: a sub-kind of human agents with different essential characteristics. (Boyer 2004: 33)

The notion of "enlightenment," is a prime example of "hidden causal essence." Why does the Dalai Lama present himself in the way he does? Because he is, of course, an "enlightened" being. His actions are impelled by this "essence," hence it is "causal." The essence, moreover, is invisible to us; hence, it is "hidden." Being hidden, how are we affected by it? An all-too-common result of this imputation of hidden causal essence is that we easily—indeed, spontaneously and "naturally"—elevate certain humans to an exclusive status. Cognitive science aims to show that such a move results from the habits of everyday cognition. We assume that entities, whether human, animal, or even imagined (such as "God"), possess qualities that are intrinsic and, indeed, essential to that kind of entity. Buddhist teachers, in North America as in Asia, excite and encourage assumptions of their, and by extension their "sangha's," special, hidden, causal—in a word, thaumaturgical—essence.

54   *Ventriloquism.* The x-buddhist person manifesting buddhistic representation via speech and writing. Ventriloquism is an instance of the x-buddhist as "the shape of the [dharmic] World" (see "World"). Evidence of ventriloquism is the predictable iteration of buddhemes in everything from canonical literature to dharma talks and blog posts. At its most extreme, ventriloquism manifests as follows. In dialogue: the x-buddhist's mouth is moving, but it is tradition that speaks. In writing: it is a form of spiritualized automatization—a mediunic experience akin to cryptomnesia. At its most extreme, it is a species of stupidity.

55   *Vibrato.* Any statement that assumes–whether tacitly or explicitly–that x-buddhism reigns over the court of knowledge resounds with a *vibrato* that originates within x-buddhism's own orchestration. That *vibrato* results from the strike of multiple postulation. Non-buddhism mutes this *vibrato*, and thereby enervates the postulates' potency. It does so, in part, by abstaining from enabling buddhistic decision about the value of the postulates lying there, now diminished or outright decimated. Speculative non-buddhism views this deflation as salutary. Whereas the inflated (x-buddhist) postulates cast shadows on the ground of thought, non-buddhism's deflation clears a bright space for speculation. Whereas x-buddhist inflation attempts to determine the course of thinking (always back to itself), the course of thought and application ensuing from non-buddhist deflation is undetermined.

56   *Voltaic network of postulation.* A self-generating totality that constitutes the Buddhist dispensation. It is the totality of premises, claims, propositions, presuppositions, beliefs, axioms, and so on, coupled with the totality of utterances, talks, interpretations, commentaries, sub-commentaries, secondary literature, and so on. Because of the colossal and intricate accrual of this twenty-five hundred year old dispensation, infinite x-buddhisms, each complete in itself, may be generated from this network.

57   *World.* The result of a *mixture*; namely, of x-buddhism and the immanent sensorium. Together with "the person" and "the mind," "the world" forms a primary reference point for x-buddhist doctrinal assertions (*loka, kṣetra, cakravāla*). The horizon of the x-buddhist "world" includes, but potentially reaches far beyond, the terrestrial sphere, encompassing numerous heavenly and hellish realms in a multi-tiered cosmos and even multiple universes or a multiverse. For the reflexive x-buddhist practitioner, assertions about "the world" become the interpretive basis for the specifically x-buddhist thought-world or the world fashioned from the x-buddhist conceptual materials. It is in this sense that the x-buddhist is, as Laruelle says of the philosopher, "the capital or a quasi-capital in the order of the thought. Or the shape of the World" (*Dictionary* 58). Another way of conceiving of an x-buddhist is thus as the embodied product of the dispensation's hallucinated thought-world.

Final Words

58   The alphabet of x-buddhisms runs virtually from A (as in Atheist) to Z (as in Zen). Fragmentation and splintering is endemic to all cultural forms, so that is not surprising. Neither is it surprising that along with the twenty-first century and the proliferation of the Internet many new forms have emerged. The result is that a robust debate is taking place in the West concerning the status and relevance of traditional forms of Buddhism. A "whither Buddhism" mood hangs over countless books, blogs and journals. Some argue that the details of how these new forms will distinguish themselves from more traditional forms are still being worked out. The heuristic reveals: it does not matter. For, in light of specu-

lative non-buddhist heuristics, all forms of x-buddhism—from the most scientistically covert, such as MBSR and "mindfulness," to the most progressively,
agnostically, atheistically, secularly, liberal, to the most religiously overt and
conservatively orthodox—are identical. "Buddhism," I have argued, names a
particular variety of sameness. What makes all x-buddhisms the same is that
each is governed by buddhistic decision: the mixing of the immanently given
world, empty reality as spatiotemporal vicissitude (*samsara*)/contingency (*pat-
ticcasamuppada*), with its transcendently given warrant, The Dharma (as norm).
X-buddhism claims to offer exigent, superior knowledge concerning human being (i.e., of the immanently given). To do so in the terms that it advocates (exi-
gency, superiority, etc.), however, x-buddhism must intermix its "identity" (The
Dharma) into its own description of "difference" (spatiotemporal vicissitude/
contingency).

The result of this representational circularity is precisely what we have seen
throughout the history of Buddhism down to the present: a fecund supposition
of uncircumventable validity that manifests as infinite iterations of x-buddhism.
The progeny of Buddhism, namely, all x-buddhisms, replicate the decisional syntax, however they may modify and adjust the terms of the primary supposition.
Speculative non-buddhism is unconcerned with operating on this supposition
precisely because doing so would constitute yet another iteration of x-buddhism. The "non" is, for that reason, subtractive. What it subtracts from Buddhism—its subject—is decision. The act of subtraction is like tilting Buddhism's
vertical line (the world-Dharma axis) to a horizontal position (world-world-world
all the way through). In the tilting, the ground of thought is littered with the
transcendental flotsam and jetsam of The Dharma.

Speculative non-buddhism sifts through this debris and decimates the excess. Operating from an open space, x-buddhism, as system of postulation, is
escorted over to The Great Feast of Knowledge for interrogation and robust discussion. But here x-buddhism must stand face to face with, and subject itself to,
the same rules of engagement as all of the sciences and the humanities, as all
local knowledges. X-buddhism is thus stripped of its aristocratic regency. And in
the process, it becomes democratized. How well does it do? Can x-buddhism,
devoid of its dharmic caduceus, make the adjustment to democratic citizen of
knowledge? Devoid of their precious transcendental warrant, how do, say, the
claims of *vipassana* or *shikantaza* as special, indeed superior, *eudaemon*, hold up
in conversation with local spheres of knowledge such as cognitive psychology or

rhetorical criticism? Given the unbounded catalog of The Dharma, there is virtually no end to such questions. As one concrete example of a possible way for-
ward, I will end this section of *Cruel Theory|Sublime Practice* with a thought ex-
periment.

Coda

A Thought Experiment: Recalculating X-Buddhist Terms as Non-Buddhist
First Names

The Stranger or the identity of the real is non-reflected, lived, experienced, consumed while
remaining in itself without the need to alienate itself through representation.
—François Laruelle

"First name" or "first term" is a Laruellen concept. Laruelle defines first terms as:

Fundamental terms which symbolize the Real and its modes according to its radical immanence or its identity. They are deprived of their philosophical sense and become, via axi-
omatized abstraction, the terms—axioms and theorems —of non-philosophy. (*Future Christ*
xxvi)

What might foundational x-buddhist terms offer us once they are divested of
their specifically x-buddhist ideological force and shorn of their decisional transcendence? Might they contribute collectively to a non-buddhist organon of
what Laruelle refers to above as "the identity of the real"?

We can begin our thought experiment with the following non-buddhist determinations:

Our need, *in the first instance*, is to fully inhabit the situation we are in.
X-buddhist terms, *as x-buddhist terms*, are deceptive nodes in a vast, subjugating network of representational postulation.
A consequence of opaque x-buddhistic ideological subscription is living alienated through representation.

To these determinations, we can add the following hypothesis: Foundational x-buddhist terms, viewed as a decimated calculus, offer valuable materials for the non-buddhist stranger subject of the practice of theory. The value of the materials lies precisely in their identification of human truths. (It is for this reason, too, that the x-buddhist Pali and Sanskrit terms are translatable.)

Experiment design. We can employ the gotamic calculus as our experiment design (see ¶40). As mentioned, the terms of the calculus are derived from the teachings of the classical protagonist, Siddhattha Gotama, as presented in the Pali canon. The x-buddhist terms (with common translations) and their non-buddhist first names are now given as a thought experiment.

The Thought Experiment

Nibbida **(revulsion, aversion, disgust)** → **Disenchantment**. *The truth of requisite disappointment.* The x-buddhist term functions to hoist an ancient ascetic religious value onto our contemporary secular lay situation. *Nibbida* says: through insight born of extensive contemplation, the mature practitioner comes to see the unsatisfactory nature of the "aggregates," the self-structure that conditions individual subjective experience. So seeing, he becomes disgusted, turns away from the contents of sensory data, and achieves peace. The non-buddhist first name decimates the x-buddhist term, arriving at simple *disenchantment* or *the truth of requisite disappointment*. Disenchantment is the disposition that prepares the cognitive and affective apparatuses for the unflinching acceptance of all human truths. It is born of an irrefutable discovery; namely, the fact that no system of thought and no single person, not even the protagonist-as-thaumaturge, can identify an ultimate refuge, "absolute lucidity being incompatible with the reality of the organs" (Cioran, 91). In its most mature form, disenchantment enables ancestral anamnesis.

Sati **(present-moment awareness; mindfulness)** → **Ancestral anamnesis**. *The truth of the non-correlational memorial sacrifice.* The x-buddhist term valorizes a quality of mind that remains perpetually "present," uncontaminated by "past" and "future." As the parable of the beauty queen and the pot of oil suggests (*Sedaka Sutta, Saṃyuttanikāya* 42.20), it is a condition of undistracted

myopia whereby attention is "immersed in the body." In its modern-day incarnation, it is celebrated as a condition of ostensibly non-judgmental and non-reac-
tive "mindfulness" directed toward "just this moment." Divested of its network
of postulation, this condition of mind is obviously neither feasible nor desirable.
Yet, its resonance remains: *remember! remember!* As "ancestral anamnesis," it
thus names *the truth of the non-correlational memorial sacrifice.* It is the lived
corollary to the liturgical reminiscence of the Christian believers, who make sacrificial memory of God's salvific deeds. As such, it is recognition, in thought, of
the horizon that precedes and enables all thought. This horizon appears as consciousness of our irreversible concurrence with the natural world. Natural science employs ancestral statements to illuminate this horizon, thereby catalyz-
ing our recognition. For instance, it reminds us that: The universe is 13.7 billion
years old. Our earth accreted nearly 5 billion years ago. Life, as simple cells, began to rustle on Earth 3.5 billion years ago. Our ancestors, *homo habilis,* appeared on the scene only 2 million years ago. Behaviorally modern humans appeared only 50 thousand years ago. And because ancestors produce offspring,
science further reminds us, we may include descendant statements to complete
the line of horizon. The philosopher Ray Brassier offers us this compelling vision:

> Roughly one trillion, trillion, trillion (10^{1728}) years from now, the accelerating expansion of
> the universe will have disintegrated the fabric of matter itself, terminating the possibility of
> embodiment. Every star in the universe will have burnt out, plunging the cosmos into a
> state of absolute darkness and leaving behind nothing but spent husks of collapsed matter.
> All free matter, whether on planetary surfaces or in interstellar space, will have decayed,
> eradicating any remnants of life based on protons and chemistry, and erasing every vestige
> of sentience—irrespective of its physical basis. Finally, in a state cosmologists call "asymp-
> topia," the stellar corpses littering the empty universe will evaporate into a brief hailstorm
> of alimentary particles. Atoms themselves will cease to exist. Only the implacable gravita-
> tional expansion will continue, driven by the currently inexplicable force called "dark ener-
> gy," which will keep pushing the extinguished universe deeper and deeper into an eternal
> and unfathomable darkness. (*Nihil Unbound* 228)

This horizon—this consciousness—catalyzes a searing, living memory of our
ancestral-descendent scope. It establishes a line of horizon that sacrifices all
consoling notions of the inevitability, much less primacy, of the human race and
of the earth and cosmos as "home." How much more so does it obliterate fantasies of an unscathed exit, such as heaven or rebirth? The non-buddhist evacua-
tion of spiritualized x-buddhist values from *sati* renders the fetishized "present"

hollow. More seriously, it renders infinitesimally puny the ostensible cognitive fizzle known as "enlightenment." Ancestral anamnesis, like decimated *sati*, indeed means: *remember, remember!*

Anicca (impermanence) → **Vanishing**. *The truth of dissolution.* Dissolution is self-evident. It obtains immediately in every instance of perception, conception, and sensation. Over greater spans of time, such as a lifetime, it is made evident through memory and comparison. Science traces it over eons, before the advent of human beings. Dissolution is instantaneous and continuous. It is to extinction what a molecule is to mass, argon to vapor. Extinction describes more than the absolute cessation of objects and entities: it describes the condition that negates even the possibility of their being further extinguished. Extinction is patient: it waits for the final instant. Its purview is immense, vast. It sees its object after millions of years. Dissolution occurs in the midst of things—in the salience of their rising, persisting, and fading away. Its view is minute and narrow. It sees its object in an instant of intimate, if destructive, embrace. Yet, being instantaneous and continuous, dissolution is not extinguished. Although a concept itself, dissolution is one that hovers near the fact it names, rendering it intelligible. Dissolution as concept lends lucidity to what, without it, remains a dark, foreign, and harrowing domain. The concept dissolution makes possible the seeing of the truth of dissolution. Intelligibility and lucidity suggest thought wading into the surging sea of immanence.

Anattā (no-self, insubstantiability) → **social-symbolic identity**. *The truth of communal selfhood.* Like vanishing, social-symbolic selfhood is as readily discernible in thought and practice as it is resisted and denied. Social-symbolic identity derives from the unavoidable inter-subjective truths that "I" share a social world with "you;" and that "we" negotiate this world via ideological conventions of thought and practice formed, moreover, from shared conceptual-linguistic habits of communication. Negatively, x-buddhist *anattā* is the refutation of a substantial, fully and uniquely self-conscious agent that determines its destiny from its own center. Positively, it intimates a social-symbolic self that is, moreover, ever-altering in its dependent relation to its social-symbolic world.

Suññatā/śūnyatā (emptiness) → **nihility**. *The truth of void.* Realization of nihility is the antidote to the inexorable human drive toward transcendental illusion. As Alenka Zupančič explains, "transcendental illusion is the name for something that appears where there should be nothing. It is not the illusion of something, it is not a false or distorted representation of a real object. Behind this illusion there is no real object; there is only nothing, the lack of an object" [Zupančič, 69]. If the interpretations of various x-buddhist usages of *suññatā* are consonant with this truth, the x-buddhist project as a whole, abbreviated as "The Dharma," is transcendental illusion writ large. The irony of a system that simultaneously *names the truth of void* and stuffs the minds of its acolytes full of strategies for evading that truth is stupendous. For, the dharmic catalogue is nothing if not a compendium of evasion of what is for what isn't. As a non-buddhist first name unencumbered by the demands of *suññatā/śūnyatā*, we can think void afresh.

Papañca (conceptual proliferation, cognitive elaboration, diffuseness) → **thinking**. *The truth of thought's inevitability.* Contemporary western x-buddhism esteems the unthinking subject, one who is capable of "mindfully" (i.e., non-judgmentally, non-reactively, non-reflectively) mining the pre-linguistic, non-conceptual wisdom slumbering in the depths of the body or in "the moment." This possibility requires, of course, an additional one: cessation of thought. And that possibility belies a hidden value: the very *desirability* of such a state. "No-thought" can only speak, in other words, to those who would subscribe to the ascetic values and desires that drive worldly *escape*. Ironically, for them, the Buddha-figure—their ascetic *exemplar*—proclaims as a crucial feature of his calculus of awakening the unavoidable reality of *papañca*. The term says: "subjective life"—that which unfolds where the phenomenal world meets the individual sensorium—is manifold, diffuse, and prone to differentiation and expansion. X-buddhism concludes from this premise: therefore, stem the expansion—*think less!* Non-buddhism concludes from the same premise: therefore, thought is inevitable—*think better!*

Paticcasamuppāda (dependent origination, conditioned genesis) → **Absolute contingency**. *The truth of chance over law.* In the ascetic law of the Buddha-figure, *paticcasamuppāda* is invoked to navigate between the nihilistic cliffs of chaos and the mechanistic rocks of determinism. In other words, the x-buddhist *dharma*, like the Christian *logos*, establishes *order*. Unrestrained reality, furthermore, thus brought to order, enables the x-buddhist to ground his or her most salient beliefs, such as: causality and ethics (*karma*); metaphysics (*suññatā/śūnyatā*); psychology and ontology (*anātman*); eschatology (*punabbhava*); and cosmogony (the twelve *nidāna*). As the latter, *paticcasamuppāda* constitutes the source and foundation of the x-buddhist belief in the primal origin of human suffering: ignorance (*avijja*) of the nature of arising. It is thus not difficult to understand why x-buddhism denies the force of its own term, *paticcasamuppāda*. The series of inter-relational, interlocking, multiple factors that attend each and every arising has no grounds *in reason* to come to a stop *in reality*. X-buddhism constrains *paticcasamuppāda*, giving it license to recognize only that "multiple," "numerous," "compound" or "manifold" conditions attend a given arising. As a non-buddhist first name, absolute contingency forces on it no such unwarranted constraint (just as, indeed, *paticcasamuppāda* permits *itself* no such constraint). We can thus think *paticcasamuppāda* along the lines of Meillassoux's hyperchaos:

> Hyperchaos simply denotes that everything either *could* or *could not* change without reason; it could remain in perpetual flux or could remain in the same state for an indefinite duration (as it appears to be the case, for instance, with the "universal" laws of physics). In fact, it's entirely conceivable that hyperchaos might just as well result in a world wholly comprised of fixed objects, without any becoming whatsoever. Hyperchaos denotes a Time whereby everything could be abolished just as readily as everything could persist in an eternal becoming. From the vantage of hyperchaos, everything is contingent—even disorder and becoming themselves. This is why the fact of our present order itself –e.g. the perpetuation of universal laws–does not disqualify the hypothesis of hyperchaos. (Meillassoux 13)

Sabba (the all) → **The Universe**. *The truth of intransitivity.* The ascetic Buddha-figure proclaims "Without directly knowing and fully realizing *sabba* you will not be able to eliminate distress (*dukkha*)" (*Saṃyuttanikāya* 35.26). And yet, both the ancient protagonist and his contemporary acolytes restrict the *sabba,* the all, to a miniscule *part*. The part comprises one side of a presumed correlation: that between brute world on the one hand, and that same world filtered through ideology, culture, and the quirks of perception—in short, human consciousness—on the other.

> I will teach you the all (*sabba*). Listen to what I say. What is the all? The eye and forms, the ear and sounds, the nose and scents, the tongue and tastes, the body and tactile objects, the mind and thoughts. This is called the all. Someone might say, "I reject this all, I will declare another all." But because that is simply a groundless assertion, such a person, when asked about it, would not be able to explain, and would, moreover, meet with distress. What

is the reason for that distress? Because *that* all is not within his or her sensorium. (*Sabba Sutta; Saṃyuttanikāya* 4.25.2.)

Transformed into a non-buddhist first name, *sabba itself* "declares another all." Once the myopic ascetic vision of the all *as sensorium* is decimated, the all becomes unrestricted. As a non-buddhist first name, *the universe* indexes the intransitive reality of the *extra-sensorial*. But this is not to give license to grand mystical claims about "the ineffable." It is not, that is, to reconstitute yet another transcendental illusion. *The universe*, as non-buddhist first name, simply acknowledges that, contrary to the Buddha-figure, there *is*, in fact, a mind-independent world. Atoms, for example, functioned as atoms prior to human conceptions of atoms; and they will do so after the last human consciousness has flickered out. And all along, from Thales to CERN, humans will construct knowledge of atoms. Insofar as this knowledge is conditioned by the vagaries of culture and its conditioned consciousness, it is always provisional, that is to say, *transitive*. Yet, much is known about the intransitive, consciousness-independent, aspect of reality. Science is the organon of this knowledge. X-buddhism, of course, prides itself on being compatible with science. However, because of its refusal to think *sabba* to the end, it has disqualified itself as a viable "scientific" interlocutor yet again. Non-buddhism's decimation of *sabba* remedies this lapse.

Paññā (understanding, wisdom) → **Perspicuity.** *The truth of immanental transparency.* In the ancient dispensation, *paññā* is a cleansing void. It cools the afflicting cognitive-affective conditions that fuel ignorance (of *anicca, anattā, paticcasamuppāda*, etc.), thereby revealing the vista of *how things are*. This vision, in turn, constitutes the x-buddhist *terminus*, named by our devout contemporaries "enlightenment." As an x-buddhist term, *paññā* is the major nodule in the gargantuan voltaic network of postulation called "Buddhism." For *paññā* to whir and hum, the x-buddhist practitioner must activate this sprawling nexus of practices, values, conceptual claims, premises, ideology, belief, institutional commitment, and so forth and so on. The dharmic *vibrato* that rings through this network is transferred to the practitioner, becoming a subjugating siren. Stripped of such excess signal, the non-buddhist first name "perspicuity" indicates *free and open access* to the constituents of wisdom—to, that is to say, *vanishing, social-symbolic identity, absolute contingency, nihility*, and all the rest.

Nibbāna/nirvāṇa **(extinguishment, blowing out)** → **Extinction**. *The truth of annihilation.* X-buddhism cannot bear to think an *actual* end. Who would sign up for such a deal? So, instead, it offers the age-old spiritualist guarantee: *a way out.* Rather than follow its own premises (*anicca, anattā, etc., etc.*) to their most obvious and logical conclusion, x-buddhism opts "to stave off the 'threat' of nihilism by safeguarding the experience of meaning" (Brassier, *Nihil Unbound* jacket cover)—in this case, as is usual with the world's spiritualists, of *ultimate meaning*. *Nirvāṇa* is ultimate meaning proffered at the expense of doctrinal integrity and cohesion. Like every other spiritual chimera, *nirvāṇa* is not merely misleading: it is a term of violence. For x-buddhism, *nirvāṇa* is the prime subjugating magistrate in the service of The Dharma. And yet, for anyone willing to listen closely through the dharmic static, *nirvāṇa* sends a vital signal. Decimated, *nirvāṇa* blows open a clearing for the intelligibility of a devastating fact for human consciousness to accommodate: extinction.

Bodhi **(awakening, enlightenment)** → **Flesh and blood humanity**. *The truth of human sufficiency.* Everyone—no exclusions, no exceptions, no conditions—may legitimately proclaim along with the Buddha-figure: "Knowledge and insight arose in me. My freedom is certain. This is my last birth. Now there is no rebirth" (*Dhammacakkapavattana Sutta*).

The person of flesh and blood is an inalienable reality. Reversibility between the person of flesh and blood and the x-buddhist subject is impossible. Liberated from the perpetual force of the anti-human dharmic differential, termination of the statute of decision spontaneously exposes the raw, radical identity of the person of flesh and blood.

Works Cited

Althusser, Louis. *Lenin and Philosophy*. Trans. Ben Brewster. New York: Monthly Review, 1971.

Boyer, Pascal. "Out of Africa: Lessons from a By-Product of Evolution." *Religion as Human Capacity*. Lawson, E. Thomas, Timothy Light, Brian C. Wilson, Eds. Leiden, Brill, 2004: 27-44.

Brassier, Ray. "Behold the Non-Rabbit: Kant, Quine, Laruelle," *Pli* 12 (2001): 50-82.

—. "Axiomatic Heresy: The non-philosophy of François Laruelle." *Radical Philosophy*, September/October (2003): 24-35.

—. *Nihil Unbound: Enlightenment and Extinction*. Basingstoke: Palgrave Macmillan, 2007.

Cioran, E.M. *The Temptation to Exist*. Chicago: University of Chicago Press, 1998 [1956].

—. *On the Heights of Despair*. Trans. Ilinca Zarifopol-Johnston. Chicago: University of Chicago Press, 1992 [1934].

Debord, Guy. *Society of the Spectacle*. Trans. Black and Red [Fredy Perlman and Jon Supak]. 1977 [1967]. Retrieved on 8 June 2013 <http://www.marxists.org/reference/archive/debord/society.htm>

Eco, Umberto. *Six Walks in the Fictional Woods*. Cambridge: Harvard University Press, 1994.

Empty Gate Zen Center. "True Self, Authentic Self." Retrieved on 8 July 2012 <http://emptygatezen.com/empty-gate-zen-center/true-self-authentic-self>

Gracieuse, Marjorie. "Laruelle Facing Deleuze: Immanence, Resistance and Desire." *Laruelle and Non-Philosophy*. John Mullarkey and Anthony Paul Smith, eds. Edinburgh: Edinburgh University Press, 2012. 42-59.

Heidegger, Martin. *Being and Time*. Trans. John MacQuarrie and Edward Robinson. London: Blackwell Publishing, 1962. [1927].

Invisible Committee, The. *The Coming Insurrection.* Retrieved on 20 July 2012 <http://tarnac9.wordpress.com/texts/the-coming-insurrection>.

Kolozova, Katerina. "The Figure of the Stranger: A Possibility for Transcendental Minimalism or Radical Subjectivity." *Journal for Cultural and Religious Theory,* Vol. II, No. 3 (Fall 2011): 59-64.

Land, Nick. *The Thirst for Annihilation: Georges Bataille and Virulent Nihilism.* London: Routledge, 1991.

Laruelle, François. "Theorems on the Good News." Trans. Alexander R. Galloway. Unpublished. Originally published as: François Laruelle, "Théorèmes de la Bonne Nouvelle," *La Décision philosophique* 1 (May 1987): 83-85.

—. *Dictionary of Non-Philosophy.* Trans. Taylor Adkins. Paris: Editions Kime, 1998.

—. "A Summary of Non-Philosophy." Trans. Ray Brassier. *Pli* 8 (1999):138-148.

— "What Can Non-Philosophy Do?" Trans. Ray Brassier. *Angelaki: Journal of the Theoretical Humanities* Vol. 8, No. 2, August (2003): 169-189.

—. *Future Christ.* Trans. Anthony Paul Smith. New York: Continuum, 2010.

—. *Philosophies of Difference.* Trans. Rocco Gangle. New York: Continuum, 2010.

—. *Anti-Badiou: the Introduction of Maoism into Philosophy.* Trans. Robin Mackay. New York: Continuum, 2013.

Lewis, William. "Louis Althusser." *The Stanford Encyclopedia of Philosophy.* 1 Retrieved on 16 June 2012 <http://plato.stanford.edu/archives/ win2009/entries/althusser>.

Magid, Barry. *Ending the Pursuit of Happiness.* Somerville: Wisdom Publications, 2008.

Meillassoux, Quentin. "Contingency & the Absolutization of the One." MS of a lecture delivered at the Sorbonne for the symposium "Metaphysics, Ontology, Henology." Trans. Benjamin James Lozano. No Date. Retrieved on 1 December 2011 <http://speculativeheresy.files.wordpress.com/2011/03/contingency-and-absolutization-of-the-one.pdf>.

Miller, Henry. *Plexus: The Rosy Crucifixion.* New York: Grove Press, 1994 [1963].

Montgomery, Martin, and Stuart Allan. "Ideology, Discourse, and Cultural Studies: The Contribution of Michel Pêcheux." *Canadian Journal of Communication*

17.2 (1992): no page numbers. Retrieved on 10 August 2012 <http://cjc-on-line.ca/index.php/journal/article/view/661/567>.

Mullarkey, John, and Anthony Paul Smith, eds. *Laruelle and Non-Philosophy*. Edinburgh: Edinburgh University Press, 2012.

Ovid. *Metamorphoses*. Trans. Brookes More. Boston, Cornhill Publishing Co., 1922.

Pêcheux, Michel. *Language, Semantics and Ideology*. New York: St. Martin's Press, 1982.

Resch, Robert Paul. *Althusser and the Renewal of Marxist Social Theory*. Berkeley: University of California Press, 1992. Retrieved on 12 July 2012 < http://ark.cdlib.org/ark:/13030/ft3n39n8x3>

Smith, Anthony Paul. "Philosophy and Ecosystem: Towards a Transcendental Ecology. Unpublished paper.

Stevens, Wallace. "The Snow Man." *The Best Poems of the English Language*. Ed. Harold Bloom. New York: Harper Perennial, 1999. 831-832.

Zupančič, Alenka. "On Love as Comedy." Addendum. *The Shortest Shadow: Nietzsche's Philosophy of the Two*. Cambridge, Mass: The MIT Press, 2003.

PART THREE

Control

MATTHIAS STEINGASS

I was strolling through some boutiques, department stores and high end outlets on the golden side of the small but rich city. I was on the lookout for a present. This was on the street that runs from the main station to the lake in one of Europe's most expensive cities. An espresso costs more than four dollars. You can't get a good meal with a glass of wine below fifty. Gorgeous, high-heeled women everywhere. Very up to date, restrained—and expensive. Men in the unobtrusive costly custom made suits that quietly signal the top end of the social ladder. Every accessory a statement of superiority and wealthy understatement. The watch, the handkerchief in the breast pocket, the glasses, the tie, the tiepin, the light-color shirt, cuff links, and just the right gait: not too fast, one hand in a pocket, no need to hurry. Controlled, powerful, mighty. The women an adornment. Beautiful fragile creatures, woven from airy, dear substances. All silk and cashmere, fine leathers, evanescent perfumes in an air like a breeze. A laid back summer day in Sukhavati. Little birds twitter. People sit in cafes and even the waitresses look so beautiful serving their customers. Even the personnel in the boutiques all look blessed as they demonstrate how to wear all these luxurious alms.

I couldn't find what I was looking for. Not exactly knowing what I wanted I waited for the moment of recognition. Some little treasure would signal that it would be just right. It would be an intuition. A thing to express myself and my feeling to let her know that I recognized her in her uniqueness. An object that would be translated through the act of decision into a meaningful gift. But I couldn't find anything. In one of the side streets there was a little bookstore that specialized in photography. I knew it well. I went into the cool air-conditioned atmosphere and began scanning the volumes superficially. My eyes caught the back of a big volume. James Nachtwey, the war-photographer. I already knew his work. His eyes look into another world. Not from this planet. Not at this paradise here. Never would the darkly screeching sound of an incoming mortar suddenly fill the air of the street outside. No such sound here, nor the brutal punch of the detonation, the echoes from the surrounding mountains decaying into the lighter noises of falling debris hitting the ground, finally sealed off with the numbing silence of death. This, here, is the light side of the tree of life. I pulled

the heavy book from the shelf and put it on a table. A black cover with red let-
ters. I opened it somewhere in the middle. A bit tired, I began looking through it
absentmindedly. After some moments, I realized what I was looking at and began noticing. I turned a page and there was a bony little black human. Kneeling
in the sand. The head already a skull. Irrecoverable absolute vulnerability. A few
feet next to it a vulture. The big bird quietly awaiting the death of its prey. An
elderly woman within arm's length looked at the picture too and then suddenly
turned away. It felt like I was watching some obscene forbidden X-rated graphic
display. Pornographic imagery right in the middle of the decent and the righ-
teous. I closed the book and went outside. I walked a bit and sat down in one of
the cafes. I had to control my voice ordering something. The pictures I saw
caught me off guard. They were a shock. One we normally take great pains to
avoid. My phone rang. A customer wanted urgent advise. I put on my sunglasses.
I slowly managed to regain my composure. What didn't go away was a certain
feeling tone. Not that I was enraged about the sudden visibility of another unbe-
lievable reality. Somehow my perception had changed. The life of the city
seemed even quieter now, more subdued and slower. The colors a bit paler. A
woman dropped a little bag. When she picked it up again, she was forced to bow
down in an awkward move because of her high heels and her tight skirt. Her el-
egant, controlled movements collapsed into an insecure posture. Her beautiful
untouchable ease became unbalanced. She nearly fell. The thought crossed my
mind to jump up and help. The waitress brought an espresso. Some sugar, bitter-
sweet liquid, soothing atmosphere—and I was already forgetting. A couple
walked hand in hand. Lovers, immersed in their transpersonal realization.

Some weeks later, I was on a meditation retreat. A little remote village in a
valley at the southern slopes of the Alps. A romantic place. Old houses, narrow
little pathways, nice and friendly people from a sangha I had known for two or
three years. We sat around a table after dinner and talked. Somehow, we came
to the topic of unease, the first noble truth, and through the associative pattern
of our speech I began relating my experience. While talking I got a bit excited
about the bewildering moment I had gone through. I tried to describe the mood
I'd experienced. A grey aura. Something clear and quite. A dark temper, a bit
sombre. In trying to portray it I realized that it developed again. A shining melan-
cholia. A sad insight. When I ended, there was a short uneasy silence. Then a
woman asked, "Why would you even look at a book like that if it makes you de-
pressed?"

Bliss

Pure Consciousness is bliss. To realize no-self is to get rid of any confusion about being. The only prerequisite is to get rid of the self. The self is the problem. The ego. This manic, materialistic, constantly moaning beast inside our head. Endlessly, it is demanding input and entertainment. Endlessly, it is engaged in a constant unstoppable chatter about everything that comes into its reach. It is the cynical non-believer with a firm conviction that this life is the only life and that therefore nothing is of real value. There is no karma and no last judgment, therefore no basis for any ethics. And therefore, too, nothing is true and every-thing is allowed. This kind of thought and self is the problem. This materialistic platitude. "Your 'self' is always busy terrorizing you. You have a terrorist in your brain, coming out of your own instincts and culture, who is pestering you all the time" (Thurman, 2004, 50). "The ordinary mind is the ceaselessly shifting and shiftless prey of external influences, habitual tendencies, and conditioning. ... [F]lickering, unstable, grasping and endlessly minding other's business; its en-ergy consumed by projecting outward. ... [T]he ordinary mind has a false, dull stability, a smug and self-protective inertia, a stone-like calm of ingrained hab-its. [It] is as cunning as a crooked politician, skeptical, distrustful, expert at trick-ery and guile ... (Sogyal, 2002, 47).

Those are descriptions of two of the most important advocates of modern Buddhism—the form of Buddhism which has blossomed in the so-called devel-oped world in the period since World-War II, and which evolved especially into the gestalt known today since the 1970s when the influx of Tibetan Lamas trig-gered a new phase in the reception and assimilation of Buddhism. It is a develop-ment paralleling important achievements in society, such as freedom of expres-sion, the decay of rigid social structures and the growth of a huge material power to support new freedoms. Although the depiction of the thinking self as a crook and liar seems a bit exaggerated, put forward by two exotic proponents of pop-culture, this notion, with its particularly negative connotation of the ego as an expert at trickery and guile, is rather common in contemporary Buddhism. As modern Buddhist pop-culture has it, any advanced level of human conscious-ness and any way to the holy grail of everlasting compassion is hindered by the deceptive experience called "self"—an illusion. It is said that from earliest Bud-dhism onward the one major tenet concerns "no-self," the self that doesn't exist in reality. Proponents of the diverse Buddhisms today consequently follow this tenet. The self isn't really there. It is the grand illusion without which the world would be a truly peaceful place. It hinders the true self of open presence and compassion from unfolding its glory.

To underpin this notion of a true self, Robert Thurman portrays pre-1959 Tibet as the blueprint for a world of peace and happiness, one that attained the true, blissful self on a nationwide scale. He advocates a Tibetan Buddhism as the ultimate cure to get rid of the dark ego of modernity: "We can join the peaceful, cool, inner revolution. Why don't we have year-round blissful vacation? It could be summer all the time. Gradually, more disenchanted people would join us. That's what Tibet was like before the Chinese invaded. Since 1409, they were on a blissful vacation, many people wandering on pilgrimage or staying still on retreat. They were on vacation, the whole country—I mean it. ... With all its grime and low-tech infrastructure, it was the closest any human society so far ever came to experience the delightful quality that the Buddha tells us is our birthright, our destiny" (xxi). Thurman isn't joking here, and this is no caricature. What he declares here is his deep conviction: Tibetan society was the most developed society on earth. They were on a blissful vacation for hundreds of years, and they reveal to us the fact that a state of permanent bliss is achievable right here and now.[1] We are blessed with a simple and straightforward cure for all our modern illnesses, and we are told today that it is really simple to achieve such a blissful transcendence of everyday life. Once the evil self, the dark ego, is abandoned and substituted by pure consciousness, only then does eternal bliss unfold.

Thurman's terrorist in your brain seems to be a pretty good explanation for why we are not yet at peace with all our wealth. There is an evil entity *coming out of your own instincts and culture.* Luckily, parallel to a culture in which everything can be planned and achieved, in which consumer goods are available at once via credit card and computer download, bliss is available instantly, too. As Buddhist lore has it, suffering is a result of the conditioned. It originates in the compound. Nothing uncompounded could ever suffer or cause suffering, and so the self or individuality, which is a composition of social and biological structures, coming out of your own instincts and culture, has to be abolished. Modern pop-culture has brought this thought to its culmination: the end of the ego is the end of suf-

---

1   What Tibet does he mean? 1409 is the date the blissful vacation started. This is the founding year of the Gelugpa order, to which Thurman belongs—determined by the foundation of the Ganden monastery by Je Tsongkhapa (1357 - 1419). This would mean he equates the blissful vacation with the teachings of the Gelugpa. Do the Gelugpa, and thereby the Dalai Lama, hold the golden key to eternal bliss?

fering. That's it. And this end is accomplished through the end of thinking. The end of thinking is the end of the compound and thereby the end of the terrorist in our brains. Pure consciousness is the unconditioned, which isn't stained by thought. "We suffer because we identify ourselves with conditioned things, and act as if what happens to them happened to us. By persistent meditation and mortification, we must reject and renounce everything but the highest, which is the Unconditioned [sic!] alone" (Conze, 1951, 23).

Edward Conze, a Buddhist scholar writing in the 1950s and 1960s, here fore-shadows Buddhist thinking today. Identification with the conditioned is suffering. Dis-identification with the constructed no longer constricts us to a world in which every undertaking is always doomed and constantly exposed to a possible sudden de-centering that throws us into doubt, distrust and disbelief. The only real absolute center of certainty is the zero of nirvana—"the Absolute [sic!] [which] has no relation to anything" (111). To be non-relational is to be free of suffering—the third noble truth accomplished. Non-relation is being without thought. Thought is discourse and discourse is engagement. Non-relation is dis-engagement. And the center-point of critique is always the so-called self, which is nothing but a gangster occluding an entity which is somehow non-relational, unconditioned and unthinking. The annulment of the worldly ego is the prerequisite for a higher being that is total non-relation and therefore unstained and pure beyond any measurement. The ultimate solution for the problem of the ugly self, the evil persona terrorizing us like the Alien, is pure consciousness. The path of modern Buddhism is the path leading us from the delusive everyday self to knowledge of the true self. It's the terrorist vs. pure consciousness, the impure vs. the pure, the unlawful combatant vs. Uncle Sam. It must be killed by any means.

Welcome to the desert of the real

In treating the question of "misknowledge," Thurman quotes Dharmakirti: "All successful action is preceded by accurate knowledge" (56). He goes on to say that actually being wrong "*is the only way* for us to discover what is truly right and truly wrong" (his emphasis). In the discussion that then follows, Thurman makes it clear that "certain knowledge of a 'self' is actually 'misknowledge'—a fundamental misunderstanding, a delusion" (58). That is the fundamental tenet of Buddhism regarding no-self. But the emptiness of the self of any rigid structure stands for far-ranging flexibility. The absence of a substantial entity stands for the *openness* to every influence. And in fact only this openness makes creativity possible. This leads to a difficult and challenging consequence: the malleability of no-self means that we are, to a great extent, products of chance and circumstance. But it means, too, that those with enough knowledge can produce whatever self is necessary. Growing knowledge about the malleability of the self leads to the development of technologies to consciously influence the individual person. This is the simple truth that people are manipulable.

The Thurman brand of Buddhism, at first sight, seems well equipped against such danger of a manipulated human. Contemplation of a thoughtless, blissful true self is treated only as the crowning of the path after several lessons that demonstrate how to build up a moral structure. "[I]t is never advisable to merely launch into deep contemplation for its own sake, simply to attain mental stability: it often ends up reinforcing our egocentrism" (225). "The danger of deep contemplation, even for advanced practitioners, lies in the fact that the experience seems to be unquestionably absolute in its reality" (227). And he even mentions the worst possible use of contemplation: war. "[T]he power developed through deep contemplation can be put to bad ends, not only good ends. For example, an army commander who wants his solders to become single-mindedly focused on their hatred and desire to destroy the enemy will use meditative methods of conditioning to cultivate their intense and unquestioning engagement" (236). So it looks like this kind of Buddhism is well aware of the possible unconscious or deliberate forms of abuse for which contemplation might be used.

To ward off these dangerous possibilities certain preparations are practiced, such as "meditations," which are "time-tested techniques for analyzing old thought-habits and developing new thought-habits and new behaviors" (39). These preparatory techniques are based on the so-called "transcendent virtues," the *pārāmitas*, through which in "the last two thousand years [...] many millions of individuals in many civilizations have transformed their lives from quiet desperation into happiness" (38). The recommended practices promise to enable transformative insights and conclusions. Each practice starts with one specific preparatory practice "from an ancient tradition known for optimizing your opportunity for success in the subsequent practices" (41). This practice is basically a variation of *taking refuge*. Central to this visualization practice is the "spiritual, intellectual, and moral mentor," who can be, in the words of Thurman, visualized "with a body made of light like Obi-Wan Kenobi's after he died in the last *Star Wars* film" (42). Taking refuge is the central act of connecting with one's mentor, who himself stands in an unbroken line of transmission reaching back to Lord Buddha himself. In this manner it is assured that every practice takes place in a sphere of holy congregation. The refuge, the *pārāmita* training and the crowning contemplation of the thoughtless blissful self leads to the point where one becomes not only the transmitter of the force of redemption but redemption itself. It is about becoming able to save all sentient beings from suffering—the famous undertaking of the *bodhisattva*. And with Obi-Wan Kenobi in the refuge tree, Thurman's time-tested technique is complemented by brand new components from the late 20th century to gain the age-old goal of incarnating the savior.

In the words of Herbert Guenther, the *pārāmitas* lay out a plan of ethical development and are, as a central part of Mahayana culture, a shift from "representational thinking to existential awareness." They "comprise sociocultural actions that themselves are already expressions of the individual's awareness of his being ethically embedded in a social context, as well as mental activities aimed at breaking the impasse of one's everyday mentation" (Guenther, 1989, 141). This takes for granted that an individual undertaking the *pārāmita*-training must himself already be aware of being part of a society and that he is being formed by it. Furthermore, Guenther comments that the Tibetan term for *pārāmita* (*pha-rol-tu phyin-pa*) literally translates as "having gone to the other (opposite) shore" (142). With this, we can conclude that Thurman is over there on the other shore. Otherwise, he couldn't write a book about going there. He himself is in "the infinite realms of beings [and] engage[s] in the infinite evolutionary actions of fortunate buddhas that discipline and mature beings" (Thurman, 257). This should be a guarantee that his program and his assertion about the enlightened blissful Tibetan culture is true. But is this so? Does Thurman's Buddhism really hold up to the promise that it can educate unenlightened beings; and has Tibet really been the morally most developed country on earth?

The problem with Thurman's Buddhism is that at no point does it ask what it is to be *ethically embedded in a social context*. It takes for granted that there are no hidden variables that might influence either this noble undertaking of saving the world or any other analysis of what we are. It takes for granted, in a naïve way, that everything that comprises us is open to us via introspection. Introspection in this case does not mean only the first person view, the perspective from one's own experience. Introspection here also means the uncritical observation of the culture we live in, the view from within this culture. This kind of introspection takes for granted that everything visible to consciousness in itself provides us with the essential tools to analyze consciousness. It does not realize that the very consciousness that observes is to a large extent dependent on what it observes. Such introspection is an individual and social "autoepistemic closure"— to use a term coined by Thomas Metzinger here—and becomes visible when Thurman speaks of Obi-Wan Kenobi as a model of the spiritual mentor. In mentioning the *Star Wars* saga, he evokes an important part of the socialization of the baby boomers and, with it, one of the central identification figures in it— Luke Skywalker. At the same time, he evokes the entire lineage of western European narratives centering on the theme of good fighting evil. It remains unquestioned whether such a reliance on a certain narrative structure brings with it a dependence on that structure. For example, we might ask about the history of the terrorist in one's head. Why such strong language, especially after 9/11? And with the true self, pure consciousness, etc., it could be asked whether it is really a Buddhist concept at all or if this ultimate goodness, rather, is a reincarnation of the savior. Luke Skywalker hears Obi-Wan Kenobi's voice. Obi-Wan, who became one with *the force* after his physical death, leads his disciple through his dangerous adventures. Is this Buddhism, a voice in my head?

Thurman sets a certain tone when he invokes Obi-Wan. He invites the reader implicitly to imagine himself as Luke Skywalker. To identify with this contemporary hero is to see oneself as the chosen one. It concerns the fantasy that we, in our small, little accidental lives, could be a superhero—like Clark Kent ripping off his shirt, flying right out of the window or like Bruce Wayne keeping a watchful eye on Gotham City. This is Hollywood providing us with hours of blissful escape from the dread-mill of daily routine. When Thurman mentions Obi-Wan Kenobi in the context of becoming a *bodhisattva*, he is laying out a subtle piece of bait. The *Star Wars* saga is not an attempt to make visible the hidden variables constituting ourselves. On the contrary it is entertainment that conceals these variables. Here, the very structure of this Buddhism begins to look flimsy. It seems more like we are getting hooked on *Hollywood*, on the literal dream-machine that provides us with an escape from ordinary life. No such escape can engender insight into what, exactly, structures subjectivity.

It becomes even more dubious when we see how Thurman himself is longing to be the superhero. He likens himself to Morpheus, the character in *The Matrix* who represents no one less than John the Baptist, who similarly baptizes the world savior. Again,the narrative that drives the film is that of the young hero, the chosen one who will save the world. Thurman himself becomes an Obi-Wan Kenobi figure when he addresses the reader in the role of Morpheus: "In inviting you to shift your perspective, I am similar to the rebel leader Morpheus in the popular movie *The Matrix*, when he offers Neo, his latest recruit in the battle to free humanity, a new perspective on life. Neo must choose between a red pill, which will allow him to discover the truth, or a blue pill, which will return him to his ignorant, imprisoning, yet familiar reality" (21). Again unspoken, it resonates with this metaphor that the reader is the chosen one—Neo—and that Thurman knows a secret, ancient and mysterious truth, one that will transform the mind of the seeker once and for all. *Choose the right pill, submit yourself to the true faith!* This is the dream. But in reality, again, the reader is not addressed as the savior: he is addressed as the one dreaming about being a superhero while being coached safely in a comfortable lounge chair in an air-conditioned cinema—in one hand a coke, in the other an ice-cream. What is really addressed here is a narcissistic individual dreaming megalomaniacal stories about freeing humanity. It is a dream about becoming the savior. In this way, this kind of Buddhism tops evangelic Christian fantasies. While the latter only asks the follower to submit himself to the Lord, the former asks him to entertain fantasies about becoming the lordly savior incarnate. This is the *bodhisattva* as Lord Jesus Christ. Is this what Buddhism offers, an omnipotence fantasy?

It is ironic that *The Matrix*, at first sight, deals with the hidden truth that, namely, humans are not what they seem to be. Thurman's Buddhism, on the other hand, which uses Neo and Morpheus as role models, does not see *how* it uses these role-models—namely, as fantasies to flee reality. Can this kind of Buddhism really be so unaware of its structuring elements? After all, Buddhism centers on "awakening." Awakening means, at a minimum, becoming aware of the defining structures of consciousness, or, for instance, narratives that we employ to explore our situatedness, and of our blind spots, and of new vistas to bypass them. This being the case, Thurman's Buddhism fails in any attempt to awaken. Let us call this "Neo-Buddhism" in remembrance of Neo, the Lord-Savior of *The Matrix*.

Maybe some review is in order. It's the old story about the bad boys vs. the good guys. And, of course, the latter do not hesitate for an instant to use utmost murderous brutality to reach their goal. The main—and timeless—delusion that the story of Neo transmits to the consumer is as follows. The one absolute truth about the dark side of reality is that if it can be battled and exterminated once and for all it will no longer prevent the resplendent light of truth from shining forth. In other words, the true self has to defeat the terrorist. To conceal its simplistic, naïve structure, the story gets cluttered with numerous profound sounding hints which, on closer inspection, lead nowhere. In this regard, it is, as we might expect, just like Neo-Buddhism. We will see this similarity again when we look at Thurman's *holidays in the sun* (as Johnny Rotten exclaims in the old song: "I wanna see some history").

If, then, *The Matrix*—Morpheus and Neo mimicking the saviors—is a template for Neo-Buddhism, what then is *The Matrix* about? On one reading, it is a kind of conspiracy theory, one involving, moreover, a false ontology. It is about entities—localizable as atomized individual self-contained beings that sit at the controls somewhere or another and manipulate us. In light of modern theories of subjectivity, this conspiracy theory—suggesting as it does the easy solution of sending the enemy to hell, preferably through a remote controlled drone—becomes absurd. The conspiracy theory of being that is put forward by Neo-Buddhism suggests that with the elimination of the bad self—the terrorist in my mind—a true self arises. Prior to this, the true self was suppressed, fallen from grace, expelled from paradise. But in fact, if we take the self as a dependently arising entity, socially and biologically dependent, we are never able to simply kill off the bad self: there is nothing but this dependently arisen self of which the terrorist is a part. If we accept dependent co-arising as a human truth then the dualistic separation of a good and a bad side leads us nowhere. In a modern theory of subjectivity, dominion is a function of interaction and not a function of atomized entities that are able to make decisions independently from their social habitat. It follows then that change means change in interaction *and not execution*. It is exactly this latter problematic solution that is offered using *The Matrix*, a.k.a. *The Neo-Buddhism à la Thurman, et al.*

If we think in terms of interdependency, contingency, or of dependent co-arising, an interesting question comes up: how might we understand the origination of the dark side of *The Matrix*? As a dream of the dream machine, what is it about? What is so fascinating about the dark side that Neo-Buddhism utilizes a Hollywood fantasy to make its case? Could it be that the dark side of the force, the world of machines, is a repressed part of the *goodfellas*? At least one can say that the stomach-wrenching cruelty in parts of the film is an indication that something has to be killed with uttermost urgency.[2] We have to consider this violence in the context of the *bodhisattva* vow and Tibet's endless vacation, which Morpheus/Thurman boasts to the aspiring Neo-Buddhist. In one of the significant final sequences of the film, Neo becomes a mass murderer. With mask-like faces he and his companion Trinity (sic!) perform a ballet of slaughter. Trinity dressed in shiny black latex, a sexed up merciless killing machine and her lover-to-be, Neo, the chosen one, a gun in each hand, both killing real people (every avatar they run down is connected to a real, physical human body that is kept somewhere for harvesting its bioelectrical power, and dies if its avatar is killed). Neo, the role-model we are invited to accept as a blueprint for our development to become a *bodhisattva*, looks very much like an emotionally disconnected madman ignoring any other solution except total extermination of the terrorist in the brain in which they both are situated—that of *The Matrix*.

Of course, before it comes to this massacre, the dream machine emotionally logs us into this persona: before Neo the Neo-Buddhist enters into mass-murder, we are programmed by the dream machine into the establishment of a passionate link with Neo. In one of the opening scenes of the film, Neo is approached by Trinity. They meet in a club. Erotic bodies pulsing to hot rhythmic music, she whispers in his ear: "I know why you're here, Neo. I know what you've been doing." Her lips are brushing his ear. "I know why you hardly sleep, why you live alone and why night after night you sit at your computer." Her voice is seductive: "You're looking for him. I know because I was once looking for the same thing. And when he found me he told me I wasn't really looking for him. I was looking for an answer." Their cheeks touch. "It's the question that drives us mad. It's the question that brought you here… You know the question, just as I did: What is the matrix? The answer is out there, Neo. It's looking for you. And it will find you… if you want it to." On one level Trinity addresses Neo as one who is looking for a more accurate description of the reality he lives (in). At the same time she insinuates that there is a *mystery* out there, one that he himself speculates about. This is the enigma that Neo senses and so urgently desires to resolve. At the same

---

2   One could muse here, too, about the fact that bloody hard core splatter movie violence in films and video games is a widely accepted norm in our society, and that a Buddhist like Thurman finds such violence totally acceptable. In the direct neighborhood of Hollywood's latest *Die Hard* incarnation and first-person shooters in which killing humans in highly realistic representations is just another nice pastime, and down into the pits of torture porn like the *Hostel* films, the violence and killing in *The Matrix* and *Star Wars* is plain entertainment. Have a good laugh while the terrorist is tortured. The question has to be asked: what kind of Buddhism puts infantile fantasies of violent omnipotence in its refuge tree?

time, Trinity addresses him as somebody who is being sought. She tells him that he is a VIP—*it is looking for you, you are important, you are not just another lame human being biding his time*. And on top of that, the scene is loaded with eroticism. A wet dream for every male. The cinema becomes a hallucinatory flight into another reality: I am highly intelligent, finding out about the biggest mystery ever, I am the chosen one and there is this gorgeous, hot woman whose heart I hear pounding in the pulsing music of *The Prodigy,* and it feels like I am floating away with this rhythmic arousal, two bodies interact, most intimate: Identify! And get logged in! Now we are Neo at last—and we are him in his quest to establish ultimate truth by whatever means necessary. We, as Neo-Buddhists, even say "yes" to murder—and, as we will see later in the text, war is nothing new to a blissful vacation, neither in cinema nor in Tibet. But what is Neo aiming to kill? What must we aim to kill if we accept him as our role-model? As Thurman himself says, we have a terrorist in our head. Why such strong language? A "terrorist" after 9/11 is nothing but the worst kind of being imaginable, indeed, one that is no longer even human, an unlawful combatant who is denied any right s/he might have previously had. A terrorist put under imperial ban. Anybody is allowed to kill him.

Why not see the dark side of the force as our dark side? Not in cinema, but in real life? The machines keep humans for generating energy. In *The Matrix* huge towers harbor countless bodies, each one neatly separated from the others. Why not interpret these humans as a dream symbol for the repressed knowledge that we in the developed world, in fact, harvest energy to the disadvantage of billions of people? Why not interpret Agent Smith as our own face reflected in a mirror-cinemascope? *Agent Smith.* Among all the arbitrary name-dropping in this film, at least this is a revealing name. Revealing, that is, in its no-nameness: Mr. Smith, an everyday man with an everyday face, nothing special. Come to think of it, aren't we Mr. Smith and not Neo? Purely average, normal, faceless? And aren't we the ones who use up most of the energy we can find? A U.S. citizen uses roughly thirty times the energy of an African. We are, as a collective, repressing the knowledge that we are exploiting the world's energy resources in a ridiculously shameful manner and to our own ends. At the same time we are constantly confronted with this truth via the media, which give us intimate access to the situations in which terrorists live. Could it be that Mr. Smith comes back now to haunt us, our bad conscience still not dead? In *Matrix Reloaded,* Neo fights against Mr. Smith. Mr. Smith becomes a multitude. It's like a nightmare, ever more Mr. Smiths show up to fight Neo the savior. Only at the last moment does Neo flee, flying away, mutating into Superman. Why doesn't he do so at once, in the very beginning, when Mr. Smith first shows up? He could have spared his energy. Is this simply film logic, which is required to show us a lengthy, boring fighting scene? No, it is dream logic. It is the bad dream of the good guy who *has* to fight the truth. The truth that he is in reality part of the machine that exploits human resources on a massive scale. The truth that he is at last the vampire-like terrorist who suppresses his fellow beings by sucking out their life force. Neo begins to look like the terrorist—and while he and Trinity are shooting their way into the building in cold blood with faces made from stone, Agent Smith, somewhere on an upper floor, shows *emotions*. Speaking to Morpheus, he accuses humans of being like a virus, spreading regardless of any constraints that its biotope may impose. And he tells Morpheus: "I hate this place! This zoo, this prison, this reality—however you want to call it. I can't stand it any longer." He can't stand the stink any longer, he fears being infected, he finds it repulsive, and imploringly says: "I must get out of here. I must get free!" In a strange twist the computer program Agent Smith becomes a sentient being begging Morpheus to give away the code he needs in order to become free. Ironically, Agent Smith, the bad guy, sees it as it is. Humans are a plague. Things become shaky at this point. Agent Smith is addressing the person who thinks he is holding the key to salvation—Morpheus, with whom Thurman identifies—confusing the matter of who is good and who is bad. Why is the robot emotional? And why does Neo, the human, behave like a machine? In the logic of a dream, this is no big question. For Thurman the Neo-Buddhist, though, it looms large.

Slicing

There is a repressive force at work here which presents to us a sanitized Neo-Buddhist mirror image of ourselves. Nowhere in its presentation does Neo-Buddhism ask about the basic structures and powers that form individuality and society. Never does it venture to explore the history of "individuality," or the evolution of our present economic system and what repercussions it has on our ecological habitat. Repressed, too, is the knowledge that we live by robbing energy, and that those whom we rob have to be violently suppressed. The Neo-

Buddhist refusal to see this violence in contemporary narratives, such as *The Matrix*, is paralleled by its denial of Tibetan Buddhism's violent heritage.

Thurman's program for building a moral being is based on the assumption that the program has been successfully used to this end by an "ancient tradition." This tradition, together with its program, moreover, has helped in the last two thousand years "many millions of individuals in many civilizations to transform their lives from quiet desperation into happiness" (cf. Thurman, 2004, 38). Specifically, this claim is made for Tibetan Buddhism, for Thurman asserts that the home of this Buddhism was for many centuries, from 1409 to 1959, "the closest any human society so far ever came to experience the delightful quality of life that the Buddha tells us is our birthright, our destiny" (xxi). This "destiny" is the fulfillment of the so called third noble truth, the end of suffering, peace – nirvana. This, then, is the claim on which Thurman's program rests: Tibet, the major and most visible exponent of Buddhist awakening in the West, realized for hundreds of years real peace. The point that I want to make, however, is that Thurman's foundational claim is, to put it succinctly, *utterly false*. Let's look at one brief episode in Tibet's history.

To achieve its aim of being a shining model of peaceful living and friendly social interaction, the rule of the Dalai Lamas was accompanied, hand in hand throughout its history, by violent force. "The rise of the Dalai Lamas, however, culminating in the foundation of the Ganden Palace, the seat of the Fifth Dalai Lama, as the government of Tibet, occurred in tandem with the emergence of sharp sectarian rivalries" (Kapstein, 2006, 128). In 1642, the Great Fifth (*Ngapa Chenpo*), as he is respectfully called, achieved "the historic reunification of Tibet under a single regime after some two centuries of intermittent civil war" (137). Modern historiography teaches us that the first two centuries of what Thurman calls "the experience [of] the delightful quality of life that the Buddha tells us is our birthright" has been one of an intermittent civil war. On the side of the Gelugpa this war was fought with the help of a close relationship with Mongol tribal leaders, with whom they had a long-lasting relationship. The conversion of these Mongols themselves in the latter part of the sixteenth century from their traditional shamanistic religion to Tibetan Gelugpa Buddhism was in its own a forced and violent transformation. It was a forceful replacement of Shamanism with Buddhism as a state religion under the auspices of the third Dalai Lama, Sonam Gyatso. In 1578, he arrived at the lake Kokonor, in the far north-eastern region of the Tibetan ethnic region, to forge a strong priest-patron relationship with Altan Khan, a foremost Mongol leader. The fourth Dalai Lama (1589-1617) was the son of a Tümed prince, the Tümeds being the clan to which also the Altan Khan belonged. This means that the Gelugpa where directly involved in the development of a civil code that inflicted harsh punishments on those who did not obey the religious ordinances of the Mongol leaders. "Those who demonstrated irreverence for Buddhist monks or who continued to perform the native funerary practices of blood sacrifice, to sponsor shamanic performances, or to make shamanic blood offerings on the first, eighth, and fifteenth days of the month were subject to brutal punishments or executed" (Wallace, 2010, 91). The priest-patron system between Mongol tribal leaders and Gelugpa priests led to the involvement of the former in the civil war, which culminated in the establishment of the rule of Ganden Palace. "The Gelukpa, once victorious, proved themselves no more magnanimous than their predecessors had been [mainly the Kajupa]. The monasteries of rival orders were in many cases forcibly converted and their possessions expropriated... On the political front, the Fifth Dalai Lama and his partisans decided that the surviving adherents of the Tsangpa regime [military supporters of the forces opposing the Gelukpa] where to be systematically annihilated, to eliminate any further possibility of rebellion" (Kapstein, 137-138). Despite the remarkable achievements of Tibetans in literature, arts, philosophy and spiritual discipline "sustained reflection on the basis of political organization itself was never part of traditional learning" (138). This lack of a kind of political theory has been a constant throughout the centuries up until 1959.

Fighting here means nothing but brute force. It literally means to murder one's opponent with one's own hands. With the enthronement of the Seventh Dalai Lama, Kelzang Gyatso, in 1720, a government-reform took place in Lhasa. The head of this government was a council of four (later five) ministers. In 1727, dissension in the council had grown to a point of open aggression. The dissent arose mainly from different interests of the council members concerning how and with which ally to pursue their personal business. On August 6th, during a meeting in the Jokhang temple, three members of the council—Ngabo, Lumpa and Jaranas—stabbed the council's chairman—Kangchennas—to death. Assassins were sent to the chairman's house where his two wives, his secretary and a steward were killed, too. Two other governors who had sided with the chairman were also killed. In the ensuing civil war a surviving member of the council—Miwang Pholha (Mighty Pholha)—defeated the three dreadful ministers. In September 1728, the three ministers and fourteen of their closest supporters where convicted of rebellion (cf. Shakabpa, 1988, 140-144). "On the first of November, all seventeen were executed at the foot of the Bamari hill, half a mile from the Potala. The three ministers were executed by the excruciating process of slicing. Hereby the victims are literally sliced into small pieces while being still alive. This slow, torturous means of execution was carried out in public to cow the Lhasa populace. Two lamas in the group were strangled, and the rest were decapitated. The families of the men were also executed, with the exception of Jarana's family members, who were deported into slavery in China" (144). The Dalai Lama had nothing to say in all this. Worse, his father was a strong supporter of the three ministers, and even intrigued in Lhasa on their behalf. The Dalai Lama, together with his father, was sent to exile in eastern Tibet.

This is the Tibet of Neo-Buddhism. The political Tibet of the Dalai Lamas—of which only the Fifth, the Thirteenth and the current one had any influence at all—throughout the time Thurman indicates indeed was a place of violence, bloodshed, inhumane punishment, intrigue and brutal conspiracy in forms that would make Richard III look pale. Matthew Kapstein comes to the conclusion that the "fundamental structures of Tibetan political life remained much as they had been over the centuries, defined by the incessant competition among local strongmen seeking regional dominance. In the political universe thus understood, the essential rule was: to live oneself, one's enemies must die" (138).

On May 20, 1934, Dorje Tsegyal Lungshar, a high ranking government official, received his punishment in retaliation for a *coup d'état* he had staged. Originally, he was sentenced to death. But it was feared that his willful mind might become a vengeful ghost. So he received the next most serious punishment: mutilation—in this case, the removal of both eyeballs. "The method involved the placement of a smooth, round yak's knucklebone on each of the temples of the prisoner. These were then tied by leather thongs around the head until the eyeballs popped out" (Goldstein, 1989, 208). The highest government official at the time, the Fifth Reting, "could clearly have blocked the mutilation on religious grounds if he had wanted to do so" (208). He did not.

Neo-Buddism is definable by, among other features, its ability to rationalize away contradictions, or, in other words, it develops discourses to generate the necessary forms of truths required to uphold a certain form of power. This is the case with Thurman and *The Matrix*, as it is with the Fifth Dalai Lama. In 1642, the Gelugpa order was victorious over the Kajupa order. In the *Song of the Queen of Spring*, a text composed after the war, the Great Fifth conceptualizes a picture in which the victorious forces, the Gelugpa and their military arm, the Mongols under Gushri Khan, are carefully colored in a light that justifies the war and the newly established supremacy of the Dalai Lama. Gushri Khan is depicted as an emanation of Vajrapāni, who came for help to settle a conflict between rival Mongolian factions. Songtsen Gampo—a Superhero of Tibetan Buddhism—is quoted as having made a prophesy about the coming of Gushri Khan (cf. Maher, 2010, 81-82). All this is a rearrangement of historical facts for the purpose of justifying power. This narrative about *How I Won the War* by the so called Great Fifth is to this day a powerful feature of the Neo-Buddhist discourse on the great savior—the Dalai Lama. It is a discourse that comprises one part of a totality of practices—a *dispositive*—which consists of forms of knowledge, rules and institutions, whose goal it is to govern and control the behavior and thoughts of humans in order to guide them into an ostensibly useful direction (cf. Agamben, 2008, 24).

Thurman's project constitutes such a part of a totality of practices, a project which exemplifies the useful direction toward which the Neo-Buddhist is to be manipulated. These examples from Tibet are not singular events or an aberration in an otherwise smoothly functioning tradition of the wise teachers of mankind, the Dalai Lamas. That Tibetan Buddhism wasn't able to develop a more ethical political system can be generalized up to a certain degree. "As far as we can tell, Buddhism has always been closely associated with rulers, even if the Indian context gave the Indian monks more autonomy than their Chinese and Japanese counterparts had. From the start, Buddhism was seen in these countries as an instrument of power. The same is also true in Tibet and Southeast Asia" (Faure, 2010, 217). Tibet's Buddhism in the West is a microcosmic example of an autistic biotope making itself comfortable in a much larger, equally autistic, biotope living off the resources of the great majority of the planet. As such, the structure of Neo-Buddhism should be taken as an example to test any other Buddhism. Is any kind of given Buddhism using false dichotomies, like the terrorist vs. the savior? Is it using silly idols like Obi-Wan Kenobi in the refuge tree? Is it idealizing its past?

But it would be an error to point our finger exclusively at Tibetan Buddhism, saying, "see, they are violent, too. No use." Violence and religiosity go hand in hand in Tibet, as in so many other cultures. The important point here is that both extremes—the childish fairytale about Shangri-La and the violent political struggles—do not tell us much about the overall culture. When regarded as isolated characteristics, these two extremes become oscillations in a fantasmatic land-scape reflecting the fantasies of the observer, and not any realistic approach to the people of Tibet. The reception of Tibet in the West has been much like that of other "primitive" cultures. It is simultaneously filthy, uneducated, godless, wick-ed *and* pure, natural, down to earth, uncorrupted, and heavenly. Both extremes are simplifications that serve more to construct *useful* descriptions vis-à-vis a certain other as part of a dispositive, rather than providing the human with clear anthropological insights about his development.

When Joseph Conrad diagnosed the *Heart of Darkness* in the Belgian Congo, he described how *useful* the filthy aboriginal inhabitants where for the white man. They were, for instance, a cheap workforce to collect ivory and rubber. If, at the end of the day, an insufficient amount of the valuable natural latex has been collected for the newly invented cars with their fine rubber tires in Europe, hands would be chopped off—literally. At the same time, Paul Gauguin fled from France to the Caribbean and later to Polynesia in search of an exotic paradise in the midst of the same "primitives" that were, in other places, despised and exploited by his very countrymen. Gauguin was looking for an uncorrupted, non-colonized past. He was on the outlook for a pure and untainted existence. Back home in the Paris of the early twentieth century, these extremes—*the nigger* and the *noble savage*—would then seamlessly merge into each other. A piano with ivory keys from the Belgian Congo in a beautiful salon with a Gauguin painting hang-ing on the wall (along with other progressive artists) and down on the road the new car of Madam, a shiny dream machine, black rubber tires, *with the pistons a'pumpin' and the hubcaps all gleam*. In such a way, horrors and dreams became integral parts of the domesticated mundane everyday world with its various shades of grey until everything looked innocent and natural. It is not different today.

The horrors of colonial exploitation and the idealizations of exotic landscapes as refuges of purity became useful accessories of edification. And it is no differ-ent today: a vast geographical region on the roof of the world is idealized as the last refuge of true goodness while other people with the poor karma of having masses of exploitable valuables under their feet get ripped off. In an uncanny reincarnation, the filthy nigger finally becomes the terrorist in your brain and the noble savage brings pure consciousness like a present by the Magi from the ori-ent. Somehow, Robert Thurman, though unintentionally, seems to be right on target when he locates the terrorist right in the heart of our being. *We* are the heart of darkness. *We* make the decisions. *We* produce the weapons of mass destruction. And we do so within our collective being and brain for the terrorist to hit back, haunting us in a disguised persona that, paradoxically, looks just like us, the intelligent young Arab guiding the plane into the tower, the repressed truth, the specter of the past that is now.

Marketing emphasizes the shiny part of this bipolar disorder. In the case of Neo-Buddhism, the fantasy of becoming a truly good being, of attaining a clear conscience, is the value sold to the consumer. It functions like an auto-absolution: I absolve myself from my sins in the name of the Buddha, and of the Dharma, and of the Holy Sangha. *Om Mani Peme Hung.* The filthy nigger-terrorist becomes invisible. What remains is the fantasy about the most important truly good self-image. The noble savage has become the high priest of pure consciousness.

The Thaumaturge

It is important to see how Neo-Buddhism emerges from popular culture by using elements of the well-known to establish a view on the unknown, thereby domesticating and rendering it unknowingly into something that has been there all along. The whole process of this kind of social construction is oblivious to its own work of construction. It is still a kind of orientalism, and, as such, a delusion—it is that which makes Buddhism Neo-Buddhism. But the pit holes and traps do not end here. Social construction has another side which reaches back into our phylogenetic heritage. In an amalgam that is even more difficult to see than the weaving of the strange tapestry of western pop-culture and eastern religious thought, these kinds of religious behaviors are also influenced by cognitive functions humans bring with them from thousands of generations of evolution. Sometimes certain functions of organisms developing in evolutionary adaptation come to meet environments in which they "accidentally" begin to fulfill new functions, ones for which they had not adapted originally. A much used example for this process are feathers, which, originally might have developed for heat regulation but then became what everybody knows them to be today, the means for birds to fly. A similar "exaptation," as the process is called, is supposed by evolutionary psychologists to exist for cognitive functions. The results suggest that religious behavior, like the belief in supernatural abilities, can be explained in a way that makes it clear that the emperor not only wears no clothes when seen as a social construction, but also when seen from an evolutionary point of view. There are certainly difficulties involved in accepting this point of view. First, for instance, like all evolutionary processes, the exaptation hypothesis cannot be tested in real time. It can only be inducted. A second difficulty is that the cognitive functions in question cannot be observed phenomenologically. The functions in question underlie consciousness as basic structures that are not observable by introspection. The second point particularly makes it difficult to come to terms with the outlook opening here because we are still deeply suffused with the belief that we can solve every conundrum by phenomenological inquiry and induction from our own first person experience. The outlook opening here is one in which the grand hierophant of the holy congregation of true believers, the thaumaturgical superman, the guru-lama-shaman, the leader of the Neo-Buddhist church, becomes deconstructed in a way that no longer leaves him room to retreat, back into his shelter of last resort, that he is endowed with the special gift because he feels it and everybody else seems to confirm it. As it turns out, the ontology we regard as natural, what is and what is not, might be dependent to some extent on cognitive functions that developed during the evolution of the hominidae and that are now, since symbol-manipulating social evolution emerged, reformatted and used in ways alien to their original context. The difficult outlook opening here means that what we think within these old cognitive functions in an environment reformatting them might be misleading in regard to what is really there. The difficulty here is that we are used to thinking that what we think is that which *is*, while the difficult outlook might teach us that what we think is, *is not*.

A distinguishing element of modern Buddhism in the West is the emergence of a certain kind of community—the "charismatic congregation" centered on the "charismatic leader," as described by Max Weber. Weber's model can help provide an explanation for why religious groups function so well without critical thinking, which would expose contradiction. Weber describes charisma as "a non-ordinary quality of a person," because of which s/he is seen as endowed with supernatural, superhuman powers, differentiating her from ordinary persons and making her god-like, god-sent or at least exceptional, and therefore predestined as a leader (cf. Weber, 1922, III § 10). The approval of this leader is, from a psychological point of view, "a personal religious devotion based on enthusiasm or predicament and hope" (III § 10.1), whereby the "congregation," which gives the approval, is an "emotional community" (III § 10.3). Importantly, the approval is an "obligation" of those who feel the vocation or destiny to testify in favor of the leader (III § 10.1). This means that the charisma of the leader is not based on the approval of the congregation, it is there in the first place, and therefore it is an obligation to approve it for those who feel a vocation to follow a given leader. The vocation comes with an obligation. And with this, a strong affective link between disciple and leader is established at once. The charisma of the leader, however, is in no way dependent on approval. Thus, both—the disciple and the leader—come into the relationship with a strong conviction about their respective roles and how each serves the other.

Regarding the succession of a charismatic leader, Weber gives different examples of how it is managed. The Dalai Lama, interestingly, is Weber's example of a "rather pure type" (III § 11) of succession. In this type of succession, the successor is chosen and educated according to a set of characteristic features based on tradition, while the personal characteristics of the candidate recede into relative unimportance. Indeed, as we now know, the Tibetan tulku-system is able to produce impressive charismatic leaders, although it has always been prone to corruption and misuse. But besides this, the point here is that since the 1970s a strong upsurge of charismatic congregations centered on Buddhist teachers from various schools, not only Tibetan ones, can be observed in the West. Of course, the Dalai Lama is the primary example here again, filling whole football arenas with his disciples. But there are also hundreds, if not thousands, of less visible Buddhist charismatic leaders who serve their parishioners by constantly traveling from one parish to the next. The degree of devotion of the disciples may vary, but we should nonetheless question the *real* basis of this devotion in each and every case.

A central question is: why do so many people tend to believe such hair-raising assertions like the ones Robert Thurman makes about the Tibetan Garden of Eden? As we saw with the examples of *The Matrix* and *Start Wars,* and how their role-models have been incorporated into Neo-Buddhism, part of the answer is that the culture industry and its marketing forces are able to sell the consumer a certificate of indulgence marked *nirvana*. Another part of the answer is that Thurman himself partakes of the charismatic energy of the Dalai Lama; therefore, he himself stands within the charismatic lineage. This lineage descends through Thurman to the last and least Tibetan Buddhist practitioner, fueling the *vocation* of the latter. Since the practitioner has an obligation toward the leader, but neither the right nor emotional ability to doubt his assertions, Shangri-La and every other fairy tale goes unquestioned. This system is auto-immunizing. Not only does it contain all sorts of rhetorical trickery, it protects itself via an impregnable closed circuit emotional feedback system. To see it at work one need only visit any Buddhist group and observe or test for himself to what extent critical thinking and uncovering contradictions is valued, encouraged or hindered by the charismatic leaders.[3]

A question that remains unclear is exactly how—on a cognitive level—the strong affective bond between leader and disciple works. How is the impression of being an exceptional, if not superhuman or godlike, charismatic leader created in the interaction of leader and disciple? Charisma (leader) and devotion (disciple) are still descriptions that operate on a phenomenological level. Weber's analysis describes a functional coherence that makes plausible the robustness of the charismatic congregation when it interacts with adverse social structures. But this is still a descriptive, sociological model, one that posits no hypotheses concerning possible cognitive mechanisms that might be inherited phylogenetically.

To draw a picture of the role that human evolution might play here, let's consider for a moment how the charismatic congregation looks and feels in real life, from the perspective of the individuals involved. To accomplish this, we can turn to Swiss journalist Christian Schmidt's account of a meeting with the Dalai Lama. Schmidt, together with his colleague, the photographer Manuel Bauer, published a photo-book about the great man from Tibet. Schmidt describes an interview they conducted. He begins by drawing a picture of the holy man as a relaxed and easygoing guy, making jokes about his "boss," the Buddha, while talking to the wife of the French president, Mitterand. He recounts the funny story of the young Dalai Lama driving around in Lhasa with the car of his predecessor, hitting a tree. And he relates how the "Kundun" recites prayers while working out on a tread mill every morning. Schmidt closes his introduction by asking, "is this the conduct of an enlightened being;" and he answers: "Why

---

3   It is important to remark that, although in this context the charismatic congregation is identified as a delusional Neo-Buddhist institution, Weber is not qualifying "features of charismatic rule" in any positive or negative way. He emphasizes that "charisma is *the* revolutionary power in traditionally bounded eras... [C]harisma *can* be a transformation from within, which, born from enthusiasm or misery, could mean a change of central convictions and actions paralleling a total reorientation of all attitudes in regard to all individual forms of life and in regard to the 'world' as such" (III § 10.5, his emphasis). Thus, he identifies "charismatic rule" as a powerful and in itself neutral social force that can be used to any ends.

not?" Then he describes what he and his colleague experience when nearing the quarters of the Kundun for the interview. They leave the elevator, and "suddenly everything is quiet and instantly the tension rises." He asks himself if this is an illusion or if they really feel the presence of the Dalai Lama. At the crossroads of the long corridors in the grand hotel, bodyguards are standing "rigidly and silent." Everybody is "whispering." It seems a long way, like in a "labyrinth," until they finally reach the door to the Dalai Lama's room. An attendant whispers: "Here!" The door opens, and they are met by His Holiness. Beginning the interview, they ask him about "this charisma," and whether they might have really felt his presence over a distance. The Kundun plays down the issue. Yet, he offers, sometimes his appearance does have "consequences," a "rainbow," for example, might appear at an "initiation." But, of course, these are "coincidences," although, nonetheless, the Dalai Lama calls them "local spirits." Then, he goes on to relate a little story about an initiation that he was to give when suddenly a small cyclone appeared and disturbed him. It was an "unhappy spirit" that, in the last moment, went in another direction—away from the gathering. He closes by noting that he knows what they mean by "charisma" since he himself was once attracted magnetically to a charismatic leader. "That was in 1954. In Peking. The magnet's name was Mao Tse-tung" (cf. Nordman, 43f.).

This excerpt does not, perhaps, look exceptional. But considered in detail it reveals that a certain atmosphere was already generated in the first sentences. The short introduction and first section of the interview is certainly not neutral journalism. Leaving an elevator in a first class hotel and walking down the corridor, one wouldn't expect anything other than a quiet area. Hotels are like that. The tension that rises is surely not owed to some paraphysical influence—it already signals the mood of *the visitors*. Whispering people in hotel corridors—why mention them at all? The labyrinthine hallways with silent motionless guards—after all, they are guarding a VIP. What is the function of this paragraph? Would any journalist mention walking the silent hallways of a hotel on his way to a famous person he is about to interview? Probably not. But in this case it is significant, for it sets the tone of what is to come. In the presence of the Dalai Lama silence is somehow different. It is profound. Consequently, beginning the interview, the Dalai Lama is asked about "this charisma" that the visitors just perceived on their way. He replies in a "modest" manner, declining the suggestion that he might be special. He does so, however, not without relating that his appearance "sometimes has consequences"—indeed supernatural ones. He talks about "local spirits" reacting to his rituals, and even mentions a small cyclone making room for his initiation ceremony. The stage-setting description of the walk through the magical labyrinth is complemented by the confirmation that supernatural powers are real. Indirectly, it is thus confirmed that the Dalai Lama's presence could be felt. And, again, only the chosen ones are able to enter. Whispering guardians would chase away any unlawful entrant. The gateway opens only to a few happy ones. It is an atmosphere of rainbows, spirits, holiness. Everything is in place to fuel the imagination of the reader. At the same time, the great man is very undemanding. He's just a little monk—as he loves to call himself. Besides his supernatural claims, touched quite *en passant*, he is so utterly unassuming. *This*, above all, is really exceptional: he is just so unassuming. We shouldn't think bad thoughts about such a nice guy. And we certainly shouldn't deconstruct him.

But in fact, of course, what we have here is a being endowed with supernatural power and special insight. Who else could tell just another whirlwind from one of Ariel's relatives? Rejecting his very exceptionality, he becomes all the more exceptional. In denying his charisma he is supporting it, and in mentioning his own experience with a charismatic leader he admits to know very well what charisma is and how it works. Mao introduced him to it. With this reference, he fully acknowledges that he is aware of what is going on, and that his visitors see in him a charismatic leader. Otherwise, he wouldn't feed the expectations of his visitors with anecdotes about something like Prospero's faithful servant—for what is a ghostly whirlwind other than a Shakespearean persona? Furthermore, the first paragraph, particularly the way the labyrinth leading to the mythical creature is described, evokes a certain mood, one resembling the obligation of those with a vocation to testify on behalf of their charismatic leader. The necessity to transform otherwise ordinary hotel architecture into the prelude for a meeting with a trans-human being is nothing but the compulsion to convince the reader that, indeed, here is somebody extraordinary. The whole event represents a charismatic congregation in miniature.

One hundred years after Weber, Pascal Boyer, an anthropologist, adds more insight to the question of the charismatic congregation. While Weber analyzes the phenomenon from the social side, this time it is seen from the biological side of the human: "What happens in religion can be explained in terms of human propensities that would be there, religion or not" (Boyer, 2004, 27). These propensities are based on structures developed during evolutionary adaptations of the hominid. And with evolutionary psychology religious demeanor becomes apparent as a function of cognitive structures that are there regardless of what specific religious attitude one has. Boyer's approach helps to decenter even more religious hubris and the stale doxa of metaphysical hallucinations. Boyer's argument is powerful in regard to our biological and phylogenetical heritage and how they plausibly explain religious performance. Boyer's main hypothesis regarding religion is that "the way we acquire, store, organize religious concepts is to a large extent inaccessible to conscious inspection" (30).[4] This is to be understood in the way we understand other cognitive features without being able to observe them on a phenomenological level. In the processing of sense impressions, for example, the development of a visual impression from the retina to a conscious visual impression is invisible to phenomenological consciousness.

The conscious impression of the Dalai Lama talking about a rainbow is only the last step in a sequence of neurological processing. Boyer: "[W]e do not know or experience the processes whereby we attribute agency to unobserved agents or moral judgments to those same imagined agents" (30). The power of the Dalai Lama influencing natural events is such an unobserved agent. The attribution of the peculiar silence in the corridor to the Dalai Lama is an attribution of a real event to an imagined agent. Boyer gets more specific with his next tenet: "Most religious concepts are parasitic upon mental systems that would be there, religion or not" (30). In contrast to other human abilities such as vision, language recognition or understanding other people's emotions, religion does not require any specific cognitive mechanisms. It is parasitic in the same sense as aesthetic pleasure is dependent on cognitive systems that developed during human evolution. Vision and hearing did not evolve for a romantic dream about the *Blue Flower.*

Regarding interaction with the Dalai Lama and his blessings, Boyer formulates the following: "Interaction with religious agents is parasitic upon cognitive systems for social interaction" (31). Sociality, understood in its widest sense, coordinated behavior in groups of animals, developed long before any religion. Group behavior in mammals, the behavior of the great apes, and, finally, of humans, is highly organized, and we can therefore infer that there are phylogenetically evolved complex cognitive systems that regulate interaction. But "these mental systems are largely inaccessible, only their output is consciously

---

4   I give here Boyer's results without further discussion. For his inductive derivations, see Boyer, 2001. For a critique of Boyer's by-product theory of religion see, for example, Slyke, 2011.

represented" (32). Now, following Boyer, every interaction with supernatural agents is framed by those mental systems that developed originally to detect intentions, trustworthiness, cheating, who is an ally, who not, and so on. The highly artificial cultural rituals, prayers, costumes and customs sit on top of these eon-old structures like a blue flower. The feeling tone of being with a supernatural being like the Dalai Lama (or Obi-Wan Kenobi) comes with costumes and customs, but it only triggers a phylogenetically old cognitive system that would be there regardless of this specific setting. Moreover, morals aren't safe either. They, too, are not a genuine religious effect: "Religious morality is parasitic upon non-religious moral intuitions" (32). Boyer points to developmental research that shows the early appearance and systematic organization of moral intuitions, and points out that "[moral intuitions] appear in the same way in cultures where no one is much interested in supernatural agents" (32).

We are moral beings regardless of religion. "Religious concepts do not change people's moral intuitions but frame these intuitions in terms that make them easier to think about" (32). No way out. Immanence means we already have it all. But to be precise, Boyer speaks about *moral intuitions*. This is not about specific explicit moral rules. Boyer differentiates *moral reasoning* and *moral feeling* (cf. Boyer, 2001, 174f.). Moral reasoning is a general template like "thou shalt not kill" (Exodus, 20:13) plus the attachment of a particular value, the name of a specific type of person that should not be killed. This is necessary because there are exceptions: "And he that curseth his father, or his mother, shall surely be put to death" (Exodus, 21:17). Thus, *moral reasoning* is a social construct that puts people in categories. *Moral feeling* is the fact that we do know that certain decisions we enact entail certain feelings, like guilt or outrage. Boyer makes the very important point that *moral reasoning* and *moral feeling* are entangled, and that reasoning and feeling are not as clearly separated as we often would like to have it. Indeed, he concludes that "emotions themselves are principled," and that our "*explicit* moral principles are optional."

Now, this looks like the opposite of what Boyer originally said, namely that—"morality is parasitic upon non-religious moral intuitions," that morality is principled, i.e., socially formed. He states, "an abstract moral code, with principles and deduction, may well be a cultural artifact" (Boyer, 2001, 175). So, de facto, he does not assert at all that all morality is biological. But it would be equally problematic the other way around: it makes no sense to say that all morality is socially formed. In fact, this assertion is falsified by the observation that there are sociopaths who know perfectly well that harming or killing people without reason (self-defense for example) is against moral reasoning, but who have no moral feeling that hinders them from doing so (cf. 176). So, neither *moral reasoning* nor *moral feeling* suffice to explain each other. This is where *moral intuition* comes in. Boyer tries to show that "there is an [ontogenetically] early-developed specific inference system, a specialized moral sense underlying ethical intuitions" (179). In short, Boyer asserts that humans bring with them what I would call a basic propensity to differentiate action in a given situation via feeling; for instance whether it is appropriate to harm or kill in a given situation (for evidence, cf. 176ff: *Early Morality*). Only later in onto-genetical development do humans learn specific rules about who and when to harm and kill, and only then—and this is the crux of it all—are feelings attached to explicit *reasons* for doing so. These feelings, then, seem to be the true affective ground of morality.

Thus, in Boyer's view, (religious) morality builds on a basic propensity of the human, which, of course, has a phylogenetic history. Confusion might arise because this *basic propensity to differentiate via feeling* is still coupled with the term "moral" in the notion of *moral intuition*. In fact, we have three components to differentiate: a) the basic propensity or moral intuition; b) social rules; and c) what Boyer calls *moral feeling*. In a nutshell A + B = C, whereby phenomenologically only B and C are observable.[5] Only through analyzing the historicity of social rules and biologically based propensities does C come into view as not being given by nature, and thereby inevitable, but dependent on social history. This, then, leads to the last of Boyer's tenets that should be mentioned in this context.

"Notions of ritual specialists are based on non-religious notions of causal essence" (2004, 33). The ritual specialist, in our example, is the Dalai Lama. He is the specialist to be found in many religious human groups, the one who is able to interact with supernatural agents or forces. The shaman, the high priest, the magician, the seer, the medium—they are all similar in that they journey beyond the natural realm, and offer their services as intermediaries to the otherworld. The felt presence of the Dalai Lama is an indication of his alleged internal capacity, called causal essence, which alone authenticates him as such an intermediary.

---

5 Apart from the three main terms *moral intuition, moral reasoning* and *moral feeling*, Boyer operates with a couple of other semantic compounds that make use of the term "moral:" in the relevant passage of *Religion Explained*, pp. 174-180, we find moral *judgment, principle, concept, tag, dimension, code, rule, sentiment, norm, standard, understandings, development, transgressions, violations, attitudes, sense, imperative* and finally "what philosophers call *moral realism*"—all in all, that makes for some fun reading while deciphering what he is up to.

Learning rites or reciting appropriate mantras is not crucial for this authentication. What counts is the assumption that he has this little special something extra that makes him what he so obviously is. The question is, on what is this assumption based? The answer of evolutionary psychology is sobering. It is not only that we produce these feelings all by ourselves, of course, but that their origin is below the conscious threshold of individual phenomenological access. What Boyer refers to with the notion of "causal essence" is, in his terms, a "domain of competence" corresponding to problems arising during evolution. That is, it is an adaptation to certain problems of evolutionary fitness, as in, for example, the ability of offspring to recognize its kin. What looks quite ordinary to us is in fact a complex cognitive task in which the domain of competence is identifying certain *aspects* as objects. For example *who is that?* or *in what mood is he?* etc.

This visually operating system developed adaptively in evolution and was originally used only in recognizing kin, prey, predators, attractive mates, and so on. The same system today is used by specialized people, for example, to identify cars, birds, stamps or whatever somebody might have an expertise in. Thus, a domain of competence that originally developed over a long evolutionary haul is adapted today for uses which were originally impossible. The same goes for music, ballet, and to be general, for everything that we today call "aesthetics." The different domains of competence result in an "intuitive ontology." This ontology comprises classes of objects that must not automatically correspond to classes we develop as humans in a certain social setting. Intuitive ontology together with its objects is not a product of deliberate reflection: it is a result of adaptation in a natural environment, and is phylogenetically older than *semantic knowledge*. It is also older than any religion and any other cognitive *tool* the human has developed over time.

Semantic knowledge is not to be meant as a declarative database. Semantic knowledge is coupled with tacit inferential principles specific to certain domain competences and the field of meaning, the connotation, can vary widely. Now, the domain of competence is not to be seen as a one way precursor to or determinant of knowledge systems, and it is also not descriptive of neurological correlates of perception and agency. Rather, it is a *model* induced empirically from, for example, anthropology and developmental psychology. The important point is that the domains of competence have to be seen as neither the result nor the cause of biology or culture but rather as the ongoing adaptability of a biological organism. This organism, moreover, developed symbolic interaction, whereby the symbolic interaction leads to accelerated adaptability of the domain of competence that nonetheless remains bound to its physical correlates, the actual cognitive systems. In other words there are *proper* (evolutionary) and *actual* domains of a system—face recognition being a proper one and the ability to identify cars of all variety by an enthusiast, an actual one (cf. for the foregoing Boyer, 2005, 96 - 101).

Although this description of Boyer's theory is necessarily simplified, it may nonetheless suffice to understand better the underlying empirical findings, and the assumptions that follow from them. This is particularly helpful when it comes to explaining the status of the Dalai Lama as a charismatic leader, for which the "causal essence" is most important. As Boyer puts it, "developmental and cognitive evidence suggests" that humans make profound differentiations between the domain of living beings on one side and the domain of man-made objects on the other. Man-made objects are construed in terms of their function. Children and adults seem to construe functional features in teleological terms and/or in terms of the intention of the designer. *This* is used to do *that*, scissors are used to cut, a car is for a ride to school, etc. Now, animal species, in contrast, are "intuitively construed in terms of species-specific *causal essences*. That is, their typical features and behavior are interpreted as consequences of possession of an undefined, yet causally relevant, quality particular to each identified species."[6] The causal essence is not about function but about an undefined, yet causally relevant, quality that distinguishes each species from another. An individual of a species is not this individual because of her perceivable features. And neither is she identified by them.

The individual is what it is only by power of this assumed inner essence. Children "regard the 'insides' a crucial feature of identity for animals even though they use only the 'outside' for identification criteria" (102). So, causal essence is a kind of place holder for an assumption. Possibly, it appeared in evolutionary adaptation because it enabled individuals to have instant assumptions about other animals or humanoids. It is, for example, of utmost importance to identify instantly whether another being is prey or predator. For a frog it makes all the difference if it has before it a fly or a stork. But we have to be clear that what we call "assumption" comes into play only when the proper domain enters an envi-

---

6 Cf. Atran, 1998, for the coinage of the term *causal essence*.

ronment in which it could be actualized through symbolic interaction, i.e., it is "kidnapped," as Boyer puts it—a kidnapping otherwise called "exaptation." Humanoids and humans also depend on instant recognition of the state or mode of their conspecifics, and this instant ability to judge seems to be based on the same causal essence. This crucial feature is older than any religion and older than any symbolic system, yet it is still with us today when it comes to interacting with certain species of people—for example, with priests and shamans and the like. Their customs and costumes, their environment and behavior, all classify them as special in some way. As Boyer says, "People think of such ritual specialists as having some internal, vaguely defined quality that sets them apart from the common folk" (Boyer, 2004, 33). And that is exactly where we are when we sit with the Dalai Lama—or, for that matter, when we sit with any other meditation leader. Causal essence proper, hundreds of thousands of generations old, becomes actual causal essence when we hear the sound of the conch trumpet.

Jimi's No-self

Human thinking separates the development of sociality from all other evolutionary processes. The human is an animal. But his thinking distinguishes him from other animals, and it leads to disruptive processes in contrast to mostly smooth adaptive natural evolution. Human development has not occurred along a smooth and calculable path. It is at times interrupted by revolutionary instability, the dismantling of established patterns leading to new equilibria or to times of continual experimentation. Revolutionary processes open up sudden new vistas, flipping possibilities from potentiality to actuality. This, in turn, forces complex systems into new configurations, while multiple new solutions have to be developed under stress, time constraints, and the pressure of competing factions in a process of ad hoc invention. Human history isn't a smooth process of adaptation. Often enough, it is led by contingent development. But still, history is often seen from a privileged standpoint—especially by the Neo-Buddhist. It is seen as a teleological process looked at from a point of view detached from the process itself. History, then, is described as seen from the endpoint, from the now, whereby all meaning is given in the frame of reference of the ruling power structure. And all meaning is then projected backwards. This optical illusion makes history look like a linear development that leads of necessity to a certain endpoint.

A typical example from Buddhism for this kind of historiography is the process of framing that was initiated after the end of two hundred years of civil war in Tibet in 1642. As Derek Maher puts it in his *Sacralized Warfare*: "In the wake of these bloody battles, members of the dGe lugs pa alliance were compelled to develop a discourse that configured events in a meaningful way, in order to satisfy public opinion and to contribute to a stable new social organization...The approach that evolved over the period of decades consisted of a new symbolic system, with the institution of the Dalai Lama at its apex. In its mature form, it had historical, ritual, narrative, architectural, and biographical components" (Maher, 2010, 80-81). What we are seeing here is Michel Foucault's "production of truth to exercise power." In a text on Nietzsche's genealogy, Foucault describes the process of interpretation and reinterpretation as "the usurpation of a system of rules, which in itself has no essential meaning, with violence and cunning, to put it into operation for a new will, to put it into play in a different way and to subject it to new rules" (Foucault, 2002, 178, my translation). Neo-Buddhism's subjugating itself to pop culture narratives is such a subjugation to a new rule. Dreaming on in its new-found cozy dungeon about its superiority, its sufficiency, its omnipotence, it fantasizes, in the words of Foucault, "a trans-historical perspective" that tries to "gather the already reduced multitude of a time in a self-contained totality" (178). Neo-Buddhism is hallucinating a "history which enables us to recognize ourselves everywhere we look," a history that takes its viewpoint from beyond time, a delusional objectivity enabled only by assuming "an eternal truth, an immortal soul and a consciousness which always remains the same" (178).

But there is, of course, no natural or divine law as a guiding principle. History is a disruptive and disturbing process in which, often enough, the flip of a coin determines which way is taken at any given crossroad. The presidential election in the U.S. in 2000 was won by George W. Bush by an extremely small margin—probably much smaller than statistical random noise. What would history after 9/11 have looked like with Al Gore as president and without the *Project for the New American Century?* The example of the GDR, the former East Germany, shows that political forces often do not see how near a disruptive sudden change could be. It was becoming increasingly clear by 1985, with Mikhail Gorbachev as the General Secretary of the Communist Party of the Soviet Union, that the cold war was nearing its end. Yet nobody in West Germany would have thought, in the spring of 1989, how near to the end the GDR was. Even knowing about its bankrupt economy, the ruling Socialist Unity Party of East Germany (SED) remained absolutely clueless about what to do. And even with growing civil unrest in the East, nobody in West Germany would speculate that the end of the SED was near at hand. From Alexander to Napoleon, and on to Hitler and Stalin, powerful personalities influence the historical process in a way that is totally alien to the natural realm of the animal. It is not evolution. Evolution is blind: it decides nothing.

The different developmental processes in history are not to be understood as different gestalts, each following the other as formations of one meaning. This would mean the unearthing of one concealed, original interpretation, something that could only be an undertaking of metaphysics. This would mean to look from a privileged viewpoint, to interpret from the end backwards, to take for granted what is, to absolutize the now and what we are now. This is exactly the dream world Neo-Buddhists act in: *"The Buddha said"* is this ghostly axiom of the original meaning. Obi-Wan Kenobi in the refuge tree is exactly this privileged view of history. Contrary to this view,"the progress of mankind is a succession of interpretations. And genealogy is their history: history of morality, of ideals, of metaphysical concepts, the concept of freedom or that of the ascetic life, in each case as a formation of a different interpretation" (cf. Foucault, 177-178).

This view, formulated by Nietzsche, developed by Foucault, and expanded in multiple fields in the last half century has turned around everything humans thought about their role in history up until the nineteenth century, and it shows us—yet again—how shaky the ground we live on is. In its most generalized form, this view reverses the relationship of the *event* and *continuity*. The event is not embedded in a continual necessity—the human searching for enlightenment, for example. "A whole tradition of (theological and rational) historiography tries to inscribe the single event into an ideal continuum—either in a teleological development or in a natural causal chain... Thereby, an event is not a single verdict, a contract, a reign or a battle. It is the complete change of a relative strength, the loss of power, the taking over of a vocabulary which is now used against its former user" (180). This point applies to any text in any context in any language. The "former user" could be a person falling in love, being totally transformed by the event. The text could be the reading and interpretation of the movements of the planets, totally transformed by Kepler, in contrast to its former interpretation by

Ptolemy. The event is any radical change of rules in which a given material is set to behave in a certain predicable way, to the extent that it becomes something unrecognizable. Stravinsky's scandalous "Rite of Spring" or Warhol's "Campbell's Soup Cans" are examples—vocabulary used against established rules.

Jimi Hendrix on stage one early Monday morning in August 1969 playing the "Star Spangled Banner." The hymn becomes, in one frightening moment, in *the dawn's early light*, a text with its meaning turned upside down. In the middle of the hymn of *what so proudly we hailed*, suddenly we hear the screaming engines of the fighter jets coming in, carrying their napalm death to the killing fields. Suddenly, *the perilous fight* is real. The horrific howling of incoming mortars, bombs, brutal detonations, shock waves, shrieking shrapnel, the smell of burning human flesh tortured by Dow chemicals, and a naked young girl, running, crying, scared to death, skin singed and set on fire by the heavenly terror from overseas—*and the rockets' red glare, the bombs bursting in air*—this all in a moment of truth to be heard in the hymn of *the land of the free and the home of the brave*.

Machines, techniques, gestures, traditions, sciences, architecture, music, literature, art, cooking, clothing, speaking—in one word: languages—fall apart and reconfigure in a permanent process of struggle, connecting in unforeseen accidental patterns, thus permanently formulating new thought. Much of the technical equipment for the production and redistribution of music, from playing (vacuum tubes), to recording (magnetophon), to broadcasting (VHF) was developed and optimized in World War II for the purpose of conducting war (cf. Kittler, 1986, 163-173). The ancestor of Hendrix's antiwar version of the *Star Spangled Banner* is war. The Beatles' *All You Need Is Love* was produced on a BTR3, a tape recorder that was a direct descendant of the AEG/BASF Magnetophon K7, built in Nazi-Germany. "The tape recorder of the world war opened the musical-acoustic present" (164, my translation). "The powers at work in history obey neither a destiny nor a mechanism, they are nothing but accidents of the fight" (Foucault, 180).

This is not a statement about evolution. This is "the production of truth to exercise power." The becoming visible of the monstrosities of the Vietnam War in the middle of the national anthem is a production of a truth. It is a reinterpretation that renders the symbol unrecognizable to the former user. It is a sudden dependent unveiling, a myriad of causes crashing into each other, forming a new gestalt—a moment in history, a historical moment. It is an appearance not as a logical development of a rational and predictable causal chain of events. Rather, it is a net of objects *becoming* interdependent despite never intended to be the cause for the appearance of a certain truth. Obviously, at times something becomes apparent although it has not existed until the very moment it appeared. The vacuum tubes in the Marshall amplifier, the wah-wah pedal, lysergic acid diethylamide, Hendrix's longing to play the guitar from early on, all who taught him the blues, Presley, the history of the Second World War seamlessly blending over into the Indochina wars, the Dharma Bums in San Francisco, the Beat Generation, sex and drugs and rock 'n roll, Zen from overseas, thirty years in jail for a bit of dope and Leary at large, the president in Dallas, Black Panthers, men on the moon, the Weather Underground, Malcolm X, Martin Luther King Jr., and, finally, Helter Skelter—written in blood. Hendrix was dead a year later. It was all nothing but a flare. But nonetheless a truth became visible. America, namely, is lying. It is possible to live differently. The Summer of Love was the antithesis to the mass-murderous first half of a century of hitherto unseen human suffering. Its synthesis was capitalism and its ability to embrace its most dangerous criticism.

Capitalism did not only see the risks that were accumulating in the sixties, but also found ways to channel the dangerous new forms of living. Perhaps the assault of the brave, erupting from the anthem, was already in itself the foreboding of what would soon become the capitalist *non-plus-ultra*: sell the critique of capitalism to the protesters! Ever since, no protest has occurred without being subject to commercialization. If punk rock was the negation of the hippy movement's dreaming about a *stairway to heaven*, punk was itself, by 1977, when the Sex Pistols presented their album *Never Mind the Bollocks*, negated by consumerism. The jet set celebrated stylish punk parties in Paris, the punkish razor blades became golden, and instead of cheap beer it was lots of coke and cognac. The monster riff of "Purple Haze" erupting from Hendrix's agonizing anthem already fuses the ecstasy of the new freedom from the fifties and sixties with the normalizing powers of marketing. The *raw power* of the Hendrix experience was already domesticated via the selling power of the record companies who took the artist under contract in the first place. In pop today, we see a bewildering merger of the filthy nigger and the noble savage in the incarnation of stars who rap about rape, murder, drugs, pornography, and violence, and who venture, at the same time, into all sorts of businesses, from body sprays to condoms, hip clothing and creepy sweet energy drinks. Anything goes for 50 Cent.

This move, this combination, the merger of *the good, the bad and the ugly,* the filthy and the noble, the terrorist in the pure lands, the beauty and the beast, His Holiness the Dalai Lama shaking hands with George W. Bush—marketing is able to integrate it all. Auschwitz in the time of Facebook? There is but one possibility: Like! The only other possibility is to ignore. But then it ceases to exist, and, as such, an unpleasant truth has not even to be ignored. Market economy truly creates a peculiar ontology: All that exists is good. Everything else is non-existent. Neo-Buddhism is the perfect corollary to this ontology. It sells the fairy tale story of Shangri-La as a true account of so called enlightenment, representing the dream about being saved finally from all the hassles of life, and merges it with omnipotent fantasies from Hollywood about being a superman. Thereby, it effectively excludes every critical stance toward the circumstances one is living in, and instead creates a subject who sees itself as omniscient and in possession of the ultimate truth.

This offsets the fact that life is to a great extent dependent on mere dumb luck—"accidents of the fight." So what about the subject in this fight? There are two thresholds we cannot cross merely by thinking about them from a phenomenological first person perspective. Hendrix's bombing of the auditorium with his take on the dominant 7#9 chord, a purple hazed monster unleashed against the hypocrisy of the good white man perfumed with agent orange, spraying bullets, praying the true gospel of consummate consumption: who was he, apart from tubes and tapes, six strings, and the blues of his forefathers, *and* blood, hormones and nerve cells composing an age-old hyper-complex system capable of tasks still dwarfing anything thinkable in technology today? Who was Hendrix? Who was that animal playing a guitar? If there is a term from the world of nature for this exaltation, then it would be "symbiosis," ecstatic symbiosis. It would be the fluid ecstatic symbiosis of blood and electricity, 110 volts and 60 Hertz in a deliberate Hofmanesque distortion of neural oscillations incarnated in a lineage merging the *heart of darkness* with the American dream. Indeed, everything is one. Colonel Kurtz meets the Voodoo Child.

There is no true self or any ugly ego that is suppressing it. The subject is subject to the same relationship that the event is to continual necessity, to, that is, the historical process as such. There is here no teleology, no natural causal chain embedding anything. "Exactly at the point where the soul demands its unity, where the I is inventing its identity or coherence, there the genealogist begins his search for the beginning" (Foucault, 172). The beginning is the event which does not fall back any more on a fantasized historical continuity. It is the point in time where tubes and tapes and chords form a subject. Genealogy is the science of making visible this subject—which, by the same token, can no longer be seen as a singular entity. The subject is now seen, rather, as a non-localizable effect only coming into being as an interface. "The subject" is multiple brains communicating—with other brains, tubes, tapes and strings, with Nazis, savages, adrenalin, and fire bombs, with the Dalai Lama, blood, sweat and tears.

History as genealogy becomes a great carnival, and our human face becomes visible as a mask, a tool, an attempt. Nietzsche speaking through Foucault—Foucault also nothing but blood and electricity, Nietzsche nothing but blood and typewriter—makes it clear: Genealogy is concerned with "a usage of history that is forever free from metaphysical and anthropological models of memory" (186). We are neither grounded in an idealized past nor do we have a destiny. We are just potential. History becomes a parody, and with this comes the "systematic dissolving of identity" (187). Identity was once a hypothesis that is no longer viable and nothing more than a "complex system of a multitude of different elements that are not held together by any synthetic power" (187).

Then, the last step is a dangerous but inevitable move, "the sacrifice of the subject of knowledge" (188): "knowledge does not free itself step by step from its empiricist roots... to become pure speculation, subject only to reason; its development does not lead to a free subject; rather the fury grows and compulsive violence accelerates" (189). This is the deconstruction of history as a process of finding identity—what if I am really nothing but tubes and electricity with a bit of acid to open my eyes to the truth of emptiness?—making room for an unstoppable race for knowledge which destroys, in the event of realizing there *being no one*, every "orientation towards truth" (190).

So, we have to sacrifice ourselves, our fantasies about our identities, as reliable loci of truth, and we inherit along with this truth a difficult problem: nobody tells us in this crystal clear light of insight what to do—the wise men went overboard. Truth is no individual domain. Whoever wants to be a Buddhist: beware of the truth of no-self!

Norm

Consider the following example from real life today. A team is working together at, let's say, a big car rental station at a busy airport. Ten or fifteen people, men and women, are working the desk, the back office, the car maintenance, etc. The head of the group is working at all stations. He is on good terms with his colleagues, and he keeps everything coordinated, from vacations to network management. He is responsible to someone at the headquarters. But he rarely sees this person, although they talk regularly on the phone. The phone is ever-present. He has an earphone and talks to everybody everywhere in every situation. Regular working hours are eight hours a day, five days a week. But in reality it is much more. Our manager begins checking his phone at breakfast before leaving home. And he is available until late in the evening no matter where he is. Colleagues call because they need advice with sudden problems that have to be handled immediately. If he turned off his phone his colleagues would be the first to complain.

Does this have anything to do with Woodstock? It might not seem so, but in fact it has. What we find realized in modern management culture has its roots, in part, in the upheaval of the sixties—a time when it became possible to live and speak differently. The collective and the commune provided laboratories beyond structures of family, school, factory, barracks, spaces where non-hierarchical interaction could be experimented with. Arthur Rimbaud was one of the early poet-shamans sensing the possible transformation of rigid social structures. He, as one of the grandfathers of Woodstock, also formulated attempts to break and bend the rules and to read out from an old vocabulary new messages. His *Dérèlgement de tous sens* practices what later would transform a whole generation. It was the negation of the teleological, mechanistic thought. It was the annihilation of the rigid self. *Auteur, créateur, poète, cet homme n'a jamais existé!* Instead he realizes *si le cuivre s'éveille clairon, il n'y a rien de sa faute*—if the brass awakes as a trumpet that's not its fault. This, alas, is a sentence the Neo-Buddhist will never understand. A sentence maybe much more revealing than the famous one that precedes it: *Je est un autre* (cf. Rimbaud's *Second Letter of the Seer*). If the tape recorder wakes up recording *Come Together*, it's not its fault— *Come Together*, beginning and end of a social experiment. This is the beginning as *dérèglement* of the discipline forming a human who is pressed into the environment of developed capitalism in the nineteenth century. It is the human of the factories reduced to a mechanical part of uncontrollable machinery. It is the human being disciplined in "environments of enclosure, particularly visible within the factory: to concentrate; to distribute in space; to order in time; to compose a productive force within the dimension of space-time whose effect will be greater than the sum of its component forces" (Deleuze, 1992, 3). Rimbaud marks the beginning of a time in which the poet, "the seer," came to realize that the historical process is not calculable. Instead, what happens in certain intense times are experiments and wars of opposing ideas: the realization that family, fabric and battlefield were not God-given, that one could live differently, and that the time opened a window of time within which it was possible to change. The end, with *Come Together*, again 1969, marks the falling apart of the experiment, the point when marketing finally took over—*the end of our elaborate plans, a funeral pyre, the end my beautiful friend.* The war machine selling revolution to the consumer.

In the sixties the society of discipline was decomposed to a degree that for the first time in history, propelled through an electronic revolution, psychoactive drugs, free anarchic revolutionary political thinkers and the backing of Zarathustra, the experiment of *a living community*, no longer being fragmented in cubicles, became not only thinkable, but possible. The power of demanding the destruction of the environments of enclosure became so mighty that it became possible to reject the so-called natural laws of being held captive by family, school, factory, hospital, prison, asylum, hierarchy, your place at the desk, your place at the assembly line, your rank, color, ethnic group, religion and even gender. It culminated in 1968, and then control returned. The year 1968 saw the birth of the subject of control. A subject no longer subjected to obvious oppressive forces, but a subject controlled by an invisible power structure that results in a sociality operating properly on its own without any apparent supervision. The manager at the car rental service cannot demand his contractual rights to work just the eight hours per day he is paid for because his colleagues, not his bosses, would object. Perfect teamwork results in forcing each other into maximum workload instead of solidarity in opposition to an employer who is able to bypass contracts by using, among other things, modern technology—the mobile phone.

What does this have to do with Buddhism? First, Neo-Buddhism in the West hasn't any insight into the historical development of society. The multiple dependencies of a historical formation are lost to it. Such a formation is taken as a given without further consideration. Second, Neo-Buddhism has no theory of subject formation. No-self, *anatta*, or whatever they call it, is an empty word devoid of significance. If anything, the Neo-Buddhist view of subject formation is the opposite from what we see in reality: Neo-Buddhism sees *anatta* as an idealized, pure entity in opposition to a dark and dirty devil who has to be eliminated. Thereby it creates a vision about a detached, pure and uncompounded self which effectively is still a self, albeit one which simply denies that it always can only exist as a compounded structure. Third, Neo-Buddhism as an institution isn't aware of being part of the game. It sets itself apart as if it were an ahistoric independent entity. We see all this at work in a paradigmatic way in the understanding of Tibetan Buddhism in the West. Thurman's never-ending *holidays in the sun* of Tibet are only the latest instance of a development beginning in the era of Woodstock.

In 1970, Chögyam Trungpa arrived in the U.S. and began lecturing. From these first lectures the book *Cutting through Spiritual Materialism* was compiled. Originally, Chögyam Trungpa came from Tibet, via India, to England, in 1963. He studied comparative religion for a short time, renounced his monastic vows after he crashed his car, got married to a young girl, tried out everything the free West offered to a young man from one of the most remote areas of the world, delved into the arts—and began boozing. His drinking would eventually bring him to the grave at age forty-eight. *Sex and drugs and rock 'n' roll*—this lama surely had it all. When he began pursuing the American dream, he had already had quite a bit of experience with life in the West. It wasn't alien to him anymore, and therefore the question must be asked: Did he recognize, in one way or another, the situation? Did he establish an explicit opinion about the social and political situation? Did he have any picture at all about what was happening during the sixties? The time he spent to the U.S. was a critical one, and one would think that everybody coming to this place and time, particularly a great teacher and charismatic leader, would have great interest in what is happening. Reading his book, one can say that he really had a good sense of the expectations of his audience. Everybody wanted *instant karma*, enlightenment now and a finger pointing to the right thing to do. He seemed to have known perfectly well that a lot of people coming to his retreats were looking for an easy way out of the difficult situation the U.S. was in at the time. Two years before, the country seemed on the brink of civil war with the whole spectrum of political action from militancy to resignation. King and Kennedy had both been killed in one year and Iggy Pop, the early punk, sang: "Well it's 1969 okay / We've got a war across the

USA / There's nothing here for me and you / We're just sitting here with nothing to do" (The Stooges, 1969). Chögyam Trungpa warns his reader repeatedly throughout the book not to use spirituality as a means to escape this ordinary life, not to buy into enlightenment. But he never addresses the political or social circumstances he finds himself and his growing sangha in. This seems strange because one would think that he would have to analyze the causes and conditions that lead people to their erroneous pursuit of "spiritual materialism." It is, however, not difficult to see why he isn't interested in an explicit analysis of the situation he finds himself in. It is because of the principle of sufficient Buddhism, which, in short, means that he holds the magic key to answer every question solely from a Buddhist position.

The only example one finds in this book where he make an explicit reference to something beyond Buddhism is when he is asked about "the function of the sort of things people do in psychotherapy" (88). Although he tells his audience again and again not to flee the world they live in, he provides them with the key of all phantasmagoric escapes by playing the role of the omniscient magus who knows it all. In a tone of complete certainty, he tells his audience about his absolutely naïve general conception of "psychotherapy"—not even discriminating between the latter and psychoanalysis. He is making fun of the whole topic in asserting the cliché that "[b]ecause something went wrong in your relationship with your father and mother, you have the unhealthy tendency to ... [sic!] Once you begin to deal with a person's whole case history, trying to make it relevant to the present, the person begins to feel that he has no escape, that his situation is hopeless, because he cannot undo his past" (88). Instead of interrogating the building blocks of history and biography of an accidental self, his solution is to say "[e]verything is right here, so we do not have to go any further than this to prove who we were or are or might be. As soon as we try to unravel the past, then we are involved with ambition and struggle in the present, not being able to accept the present moment as it is" (89). There is no need to analyze anything. It is necessary to work with oneself and it is, indeed, hard and painful work but it is not necessary to fall back on anything other than just what is right *here and now* in the mode of seeing *as it is*. No dependent arising, no construction of dispersed subjectivity, no question of historical situatedness. This is the mantra that runs through the text; and it is indeed the blueprint for all Buddhism to this very day.

What Chögyam Trungpa says in the short answer about psychotherapy represents the "principle of sufficient Buddhism" in pop-culture and in Neo-Buddhism as it developed from his first teachings. We meet the "Ego." The bad guy in the game. The one who has to be eliminated. As it is for Thurman, the ego is a neurotic entity that somehow usurps a good core. "Generally, all religious traditions deal with this material, speaking variously of *alaya-vijnana* or original sin or the fall of man or the basis of ego." Then, in regard to salvation, "our most fundamental state of mind, before the creation of ego, is such that there is basic openness, basic freedom, a spacious quality; and we have now and have always had this openness" (122). What Chögyam Trungpa presents here is not only sufficient Buddhism in times of war across the USA, denying the dependent origination of the situation, it is already a presentation of Buddhism in terms of a perennial philosophy written in Christian terms. He teaches a Christian salvation; and either he is unaware what terms like "original sin" mean or he doesn't know the teachings of his own tradition.

The "space" metaphor Chögyam Trungpa uses is a central one in the mahāmudrā and dzogchen teachings in which he was educated. The problem is that in these traditions the idea of original sin is unknown. As Herbert Guenther explains in great detail in *From Reductionism to Creativity,* in these Tibetan traditions there is nothing resembling the breach of the law of a transcendent entity such as the Christian God. Instead, the initial problem is ignorance, the simple lack of understanding. "This missing-out on realizing one's full potential is known as a going astray, an errancy mode (Tib. *'khrul-pa*), which in itself is a lack of understanding (Tib. *ma-rtogs*), a not-knowing-better or plain low-level (cognitive) intensity (Tib. *ma-rig-pa*)" (199). This means it is not a process of original purity, fall, and redemption but one in which the beginning is an ignorance concerning our situation. We are not aware of being dependent on circumstances, on blood, electricity, tapes, films, hormones, wars, scripture, etc. Once we learn about dependent origination, we are in what Guenther calls "an emancipatory mode" summed up by a symbol called Kun-tu bzang-po. A symbol which, in the Buddhist context, corresponds to the idea of the teacher and, in the western context, indeed, to the idea of God (cf. 195)—with the crucial difference that this symbol, representing the "emancipatory mode," is nothing substantial apart from the sheer immanence of a process termed *gzhi-snang*, which Guenther translates, borrowing a term coined by David Bohm, as "holomovement" (190). This "emancipatory mode" is the realization of potentialities and possibilities through understanding (Tib. *rtogs*): It is about learning, plain and simple.

Chögyam Trungpa's "basic openness and freedom" looks like an absurd sim-
plification of parts of a Tibetan philosophical approach taken out of context.
Whatever his intention was, he rephrased his tradition in foreign terms in a manner that changed the meaning in a dramatic way and gave the uninitiated a
wrong idea. It is not much different in his *Shambhala: The Sacred Path of the Warrior,* published in 1984. He mentions some socio-economical problems, but only
in passing. He declares, for example, that the "Great Eastern Sun vision is a very
ecological approach" (44), and that this ecological approach goes back—of
course—all the way to the Buddha, and has been handed down to this day orally
in an unbroken line (cf. 26). What will save the world is an "innate wakefulness of
human beings" (44) in "a world which is clean and pure" (45). All we have to do is
to restore our "basic goodness"—a theme that runs throughout all his teachings.

Again what he does is embed a speculative essence of purity and goodness in
a fictional history of the world as originating from a primordial purity. Again, he
takes a chunk of a Tibetan philosophical tradition, suppressing a far more complex system in favor of a dangerous oversimplification. And again one wonders if
he simply doesn't know his own tradition, and if he thought that the primordial
pure paradise he dreams about in his Shambhala-vision was really the same as
the Christian Garden of Eden, as his mention of primordial sin would suggest.[7] In
any case, resorting to plain and simple openness or basic goodness, without any
claim to understand the situation in the West of 1970, Chögyam Trungpa turns
his disciples into willing victims of consumer capitalism by making them believe
they don't have to understand how their personality is constructed by the culture they live in.

What we see here is the blueprint of all that is to follow in Neo-Buddhism:
just look inside and the rest will follow. In reality his disciples and followers to
this day, in their multitude of forms from reactionary conservative Tibetan Buddhists to pseudo-modern MBSR aficionados, learn nothing about the structures
they live in. Not being aware of the structures and historical originations of the
autonomous, self-regulating subject that begins to form in the sixties and seventies as a social experiment makes this subject prey to the capitalist subject and

---

7   Apart from the problem of rendering notions of one culture in terms of another, Nestorian Christians and
    Buddhists, not only from Tibet, had many contacts, and it is quite possible that mythologies crossed over; cf.
    for example the so called "Jesus Sutras" from Dunhuang. Jenkins (2008, 92) gives an account of the rich but
    mostly unknown history of Christianity in the East and its contacts with the respective cultures there. In any
    case, Shambhala, or the *Kalachakratantra,* is more likely to come from a Hindu myth and, more importantly, is
    embedded in western esoteric lore at least since H.P. Blavatsky, the founder of the theosophical society.

its mode of super-optimization. Relaxing in just what is, keeps the autonomous, self-regulating subject unaware of how the capitalist subject is using its abilities to guide it into a slavery which feels like nirvana. For the sixteen-hours-a-day-manager of the car rental service, just seeing as it is, letting-go, learning to relax fast and efficiently by "meditation" means to regain mental and physical fitness more quickly in a strenuous schedule. Nothing else. The autonomous self learns to reload its own batteries. It feels good. Together with sports activity and healthy food, the modern human becomes more efficient and creative at the workplace—i.e. more profitable. What go undetected are the invisible social forces framing the norms we live by. Thus meditation, which originally looked like a panacea for the modern human to understand finally her reason and meaning of life, became just another tool to enhance individual auto-regulation with an agenda not set by the meditator. Meditation becomes a Trojan Horse to control the mind from within. Seen from today, what Chögyam Trungpa brought to the West is the *going astray*, the *errancy mode*, the total *lack of understanding, not-knowing-better, plain low-level cognitive intensity.* In plain Tibetan: *ma-rig-pa!*

After the Second World War, significant changes in the social structures took place that allowed large portions of society for the first time to demand more flexibility in individual development. Woodstock, for example, is illustrating a huge increase in individualism compared to what was possible or even thinkable one or two generations earlier. This is not to say that this change did not occur in other areas of western society. But here we see how the arts as a breeding ground for ideas of change are domesticated and neutralized by the society of control, namely, in keeping at bay dangerous new thinking or, more often, to render it useless by selling it back to the marketplace. Capitalism is itself exaptive in enabling itself to commodify any thought by transforming it into a sellable product.

A sociological prognosis done in 1976 went as follows: The cultural upheaval ensuing from the student revolts in the sixties produced a new hedonistic morality, one that would be increasingly incompatible with the economic requirements of capitalism. Aesthetic creativity and sensual impulsiveness, formerly only enacted by avant-garde movements of artistic subcultures, gained wider acceptance among the population. This would increasingly prevent the forming of an ethics of labor, which ethics would be necessary to maintain economic efficiency.[8] But as it happened, this prognosis was wrong. It is true that the individual character is much more hedonistic today than fifty years ago. The subject of consumer capitalism has a wider variety of careers to pursue, but this doesn't lead to an anarchic, uncontrolled situation diminishing the ability of capitalism to function properly. On the contrary, the desire to be whatever is possible is the means to unleash powerful new forms of productivity. How is this possible? First, since the Second World War, certain developments have laid the groundwork for these changes. We have seen, for example, a strong increase in income accompanied by more leisure time, leading to more individual flexibility and diminishing influence of the social milieu. The build-up of the service industry in the western capitalist societies, too, provided the opportunity for advancement for a large segment of the population. This segment increased so dramatically, in fact, that that a broader process of upward mobility could be initiated, through which one's quality of life could be further diversified. Furthermore, the expansion of the educational system after World War II brought with it increased diversity of career options.

These are some of the influences at work at the time of the student unrests in the sixties, indicating that there was already a much more pluralistic picture regarding personal development and social forms of existence than ten years earlier. The effect was that in the short time frame of roughly twenty years up to 1970, available forms of existence where strongly individualized: "For the sake of their futures, the members of western societies were forced, urged, or encouraged to make central their own life plans and life styles" (Honneth, 2010, 70). That is the difference between the society of control and the society of discipline. Instead of control from the outside—family, school, barracks, factory— now each individual must decide on her own what life to live, and learn to control herself from within. The society of control is actually a society of *self*-control.

But the increase in wealth, individual freedom, flexibility and possibilities to choose would not in itself lead to the specific form of individualism we see today—individualism as a process of experimental self-actualization linked to highly emotionalized experiences. Why is individualism coupled so strongly to emotion? It seems that there is neither a natural innate disposition for such behavior nor adequate modern economic theories like the *theory of marginal utility*

---

8   For the following socio-historical sketch cf. Honneth, 2010; direct citations are my translations.

to explain this (cf. Campbell 2005, 39f.). Investigation into the reason for this link leads us all the way back into the origins of the modern notion of self, its formation, the parallel emergence of an inner emotionality and the developing capability to arouse comfortable, positive emotions—happiness—via hedonistic experiences or via pure imagination. In short, it was a cultural learning process that linked our individualism today to emotionality, to exaltation and a refinement and differentiation of feelings. Individualism is a matter to experience whatever one wants and having the means to generate certain feelings. Only then can wealth and freedom function as the fuel for the production of a specific form of self-disciplining subject. While auto-arousal of happiness and self-experimentation was available before World War II to only relatively small groups, the sociocultural processes after the war made them available to wider portions of the population. What became widely possible in the sixties was the search for an "authentic" self via the multiple possible models for one's own life. Authenticity was found through highly emotional experiences that gave life meaning. The important change of individuality is the emotional sense of inner fulfillment in a highly flexible social setting in contrast to the hierarchically cemented and emotionally muted position one would have in the society of discipline.

Theodor Fontane's *Effi Briest*, written in the late nineteenth century, is a detailed image of social discipline. Neglected by her husband, who is mostly immersed in working for his place in the political hierarchy, Effi has a love affair. Years later her husband learns about this and gets divorced at once. She is ostracized even by her parents for her adultery, separated from her daughter for years, and develops a nervous illness. Fontane gives a detailed picture of an environment in which all those involved feel and know that their harsh judgment of Effi's adultery is emotionally not justified, knowing at the same time that the social code of conduct has to be obeyed.

Three generations later, in the sixties, Herman Hesse's *Steppenwolf* helped to ignite and illuminate consciousness of the multiple possibilities sociality provided in the sixties and seventies. Written only thirty years apart, Fontane's and Hesse's novels make visible the drastic changes taking place in regard to what individuality could be. In the sixties and seventies Hesse's novel helped to teach a whole generation how to fill the "normative gaps and new degrees of freedom that opened with the structural changes in sociality" (Honneth, 71). Of course, *Steppenwolf* leans more toward the dark and difficult side of the new possibilities. Sex and drugs and the vanishing demarcations of what separates reality and imagination make for a difficult and dangerous way to enlightenment. Somebody like Chögyam Trungpa seems like a perfect fit here: crazy wisdom, Padmasambhava riding the pregnant tigress, drinking, sex, being stoned, and getting enlightened—it is possible to have it all. The *dérèlegement* now is for everybody, and everybody can be as she likes.

This kind of process, which was not restricted to the Neo-Buddhists (far from it), threatened capitalism to a point where it became possible to demand hitherto unseen changes. The anti-capitalist critic in the West became very powerful. Unlike earlier times of upheaval, critique in this period can be understood to take two distinct forms: a) social critique and b) artistic critique. While the former was much more organized, elaborated and supported by marxist analysis, which provided the major thrust for the pressure on the capitalist economy in the late sixties, the artists' critique had for the first time an opportunity to articulate itself in a manner that would be more widely heard. In a differentiation developed by the French sociologists Boltanski and Chiapello, social criticism "underlines inequality, poverty, exploitation and egoism in a world which encourages individualism instead of solidarity" (Boltanski and Chiapello, 29). The artists' critique emphasizes "the domination of the market, of discipline, of the factory, uniformity in the mass society and the transformation of all objects into commodities. It does so, furthermore, while it fosters the *ideal of individual autonomy* and freedom, holding in high esteem uniqueness and authenticity" (29, my emphasis, my translation).

The German Joseph Beuys can be seen as a famous example of a political and critical social-activist artist promoting the unique expression of the individual. He proclaimed, "every human is an artist!" and enacted this vision in what he called the "social sculpture." Beuys can be seen as a descendent of Romantic artists like Novalis. He was also influenced by the anthroposophical doctrine of Rudolf Steiner. In the seventies, Beuys was one of the founding members of the Green Party in Germany. He was highly successful in the art market, too, and can thus be seen as an exemplar of the critical *and* successful artist—which leads to the important point Boltanski and Chiapello are making: radical critique of capitalism in the sixties was highly threatening. The critique is expressed not only verbally, "it is articulated through strikes and violence, which result in a disorganization of production, falling quality of products and rising wage cost... For the persons responsible in the capitalistic institutions, mainly the employers, the situation is alarming" (28). How did the capitalistic institutions cope with this crisis? Boltanski and Chiapello come to the conclusion that, in an incident of dark irony, but one already foreshadowed by the financially successful critical artist, it was the artistic critique that provided the key to the solution. Beginning in the eighties, "claims for autonomy were integrated into new corporate strategies. In this way, it was again possible to integrate the employees into the production process while reducing the costs of control by replacing them through self-control. Furthermore, it was possible to link autonomy and responsibility directly to customer demand" (30). This is it in a nutshell. In the eighties and nineties, creativity and the striving for authenticity and autonomy is finally integrated into the work process.

And as the role of the employee changes so changes the whole infrastructure of production and services. "The model of the hierarchical and integrated company has broken down in favor of a conception based on the metaphor of the network" (31). Flat hierarchies, team autonomy an "autonomous" control of work processes are the answer to the desire of the post-68 employee for self-actualization. The working individual is no longer a dependent employee but a creative employer whose initiative and intellectual competence becomes as important an asset for himself as for the company of which he is now an integral part, and no longer just an interchangeable object. At least, *he should feel like this*, because work now has to be *vocation*.

The search for authenticity becomes realizable on a broad basis through labor, especially with the changes manufacturing and service industries have gone through from the seventies on. But self-actualization is no longer an idea of freedom and experimentation: the will for self-actualization is now a prerequisite for getting the job. To work for the good of the company is now an intrinsic desire of the creative worker. "Over the run of twenty years a new system of demands has been established which makes it possible to predicate employment on the convincing presentation of the will for self-actualization in the job" (Honneth, 75). As with Hendrix's tubes and electricity, this isn't exactly an intentional process. It is the result of a linkage of different processes, each having its own history. On one side are, for example, the Romantic ideal of authenticity, higher income, more free time, better education, the vision of an autonomous life, technological development in telecommunications, computing and transportation which lead to a new and different lifestyle. On the other side, the marketing industry developed, which sells along with its products the means to live that new aesthetically appealing life. It provides the products to improve the originality of one's own personal life. Finally, self-actualization thereby becomes the central energizer of an ideology of endless production of more necessities.

The artistic critique made all this possible. It provided the capitalist system of reproduction with the means to master the crisis. It's all about "authenticity." The visions of the artist, his vocation, plays a major role here. Everything has to be a vocation. Furthermore, we find that the artist and the shaman fulfill overlapping functions. The search for a true vocation is the point of intersection where they both meet. Both Joseph Beuys and Chögyam Trungpa want to empower the individual to find his true vocation. For Beuys, every single act of life is of utter importance. Beuys's vision is the "social sculpture" in which each human finds self- and co-determination in each area of life. Similarly, Chögyam Trungpa's vision of Shambhala is a vision of a society of enlightened citizens in which each and every one finds her unique mode of existence. As such, artist and shaman become indistinguishable. Beuys is explicitly referring to the shaman who makes possible the view that there are "totally different dimensions" vis-à-vis the materialistic natural sciences (Krueger, 51:40) and Chögyam Trungpa, in his quest for artistic expression, finds hitherto unknown forms of expression for a Tibetan lama.

Finally, we find today's amalgam of both, the shaman and the artist, in Marina Abramović. Her *The Artist is Present* is an example. Ninety days at the Museum of Modern Art in New York, in 2010, from March to May, from the time the museum opens until it closes, the performing artist celebrates one of the most basic forms of human communication: looking into the eyes of the other. Huge crowds wait for long hours in lines to sit four or five feet from Marina. With her eyes closed, she will wait for somebody to sit down; and when the visitor is seated, she will look up, her calm gaze meeting the eyes of the person facing her. Her expression is neutral and relaxed, neither openly friendly nor reserved or withdrawn. Her assistant tries to explain what she is doing between two visitors: "She's sort of cleaning the thing, and then: boom! It reconnects and is only for use for each and every one and like a clean, unique and personal contact with Marina" (1:10:00). Somebody else explains, "for most masterpieces people stand in front of it for thirty seconds. *Mona Lisa* thirty seconds. People come here and sit all day." Finally it is here. The greatest piece of art, fascinating people, no need for scholarly explanation, literally moving people, making them spellbound, making them cry, giving them profound spiritual experience—two humans looking into each other's eyes. Presence. Authenticity. Creativity. Art. Behind walls of glass and concrete. The greatest and most simple. The Holy Communion of true being administered by the artist-shaman at the Church of Modern Art. The most dangerous human abilities are confined to the museum. Finally.

Discord

What the artist does in her performance does not seem so difficult or extraordinary. She turns towards the other. She devotes her gaze to the other. Regardless of name, gender, color, age. Without name and without precondition. She turns towards a singular being. Her gaze is with that being as being there right now. Each individual, unnamed, is the human. In their gaze, two humans exchange their *you are*. They free themselves from the burden of loving each other because of a because.

This performance is shocking. The unconditional *turning towards* is open to each human. But now it is confined to the museum. We see how the human condition, the recognition of being, is turned into a commodity. Food, water, shelter and sex, and now sheer being itself, the unconditional recognition of the being of the other itself, is turned into a product, a kind of performance for which we have to stand in line.

Such is the corollary for the Buddhist telling me not to look at the disturbing realities in the James Nachtwey photographs from Sudan and Somalia—the most horrible sights we are confronted with when we follow him down into the *Inferno*. Skeleton-like humans, heads like skulls but still alive, on hands and knees, creeping through the dust of some eastern African desert. They are beyond the point where they could be resuscitated, and, as such, beyond the point where any unconditional human gaze could reach them in their sheer being. Creeping, leaving a trail in the sand. Falling over on the side. Finally dying. A bundle of skin and bones wrapped in dirty rags.

The being-recognizing gaze is confined to the gated community. The filthy nigger still has to die in some *waste land*. That corpse that you planted last year in your garden, has it begun to sprout? I will show you fear in a handful of dust, a rattle of bones, and chuckle from ear to ear.

We turn away, turning it into surplus value. And the artist isn't critic anymore. The lament about the commodification of everything under the sun is turned into an asset. Do we have to resign? What kind of critique is left to us? And what does Buddhism have to do with it? Certainly, we can put aside the kitsch of Neo-Buddhism. But is there something left in Buddhism that we could use to get out of this catch-22?

What the Buddhist couldn't know, what I saw in *Inferno* was not depression. It was, rather, the opposite. The sudden discord shifted my perception and intensified it. Depression dampens thought. This didn't.

The event culture seeks to thrill. Discord is foreclosed. Alteration by discord is a subtle move, a touch, resulting from conflict. Excitement is thrill: Jump out of a plane. Surf a monster wave. Have kinky sex. Eat vegan. Sit Zen for eighteen hours. Get enlightened. Whatever it is, it is not discord. It is always the same.

Humans have no destiny, no essence, no vocation, nor a biological determination. Therefore, there cannot be any decision. But something can happen. We can look at each other differently. That's the other shocking consequence: We own the art.

We have to take it back.

Works Cited

Agamben, Giorgio. *Die kommende Gemeinschaft*. Berlin: Merve, 2003. Print.

Akers, Matthew. *Marina Abramivić. The Artist is Present*. Chicago: Music Box Films, 2012. Film.

Atran, S. A. *Folk Biology and the Anthropology of Science: Cognitive Universals and Cultural Particulars*. In *Behavioral and Brain Sciences, 21*. Cambridge: 1998. Print.

Boltanski, Luc & Chiapello Ève. *Die Arbeit der Kritik und der normative Wandel*. In *Kreation und Depression. Freiheit im gegenwärtigen Kapitalismus*, Ed. by Honneth, Axel. Berlin: Kadmos, 2010. Print.

Boyer, Pascal. *Religion Explained: The Evolutionary Origins of Religious Thought*. New York: Basic Books, 2001. Print.

—. *Out of Africa: Lessons from a By-Product of Evolution*. In *Religion as a Human Capacity*, Ed. by Light, Timothy and Wilson, Brian C. Leiden: Brill, 2004. Print.

Boyer, Pascal and Barrett, H. Clark. *Domain Specificity and Intuitive Ontology*. In *The Handbook of Evolutionary Psychology*. Ed. by Buss, David M. Hoboken: Wiley, 2005. Print.

Campbell, Colin. *The Romantic Ethic and the Spirit of Modern Consumerism*. Great Britain: Alcuin Academics, 2005. Print.

Chögyam Trungpa. *Cutting Through Spiritual Materialism*. Boston & London: Shambala, 2002. Print.

—. *Shambala. The Secret Path of the Warrior*. Boston: Shambala, 1984. Print.

Conze, Edward. *Buddhism, its Essence and Development*. New York: Philosophical Library, 1951. Print.

Deleuze, Gilles. *Postscript on the Societies of Control*. In *October*, Vol. 59, pp. 3-7, 1992. Print.

Ehrenberg, Alain. *Das Unbehagen in der Gesellschaft*. Berlin: Suhrkamp, 2011. Print.

Eliot, T.S. *The Waste Land*. Frankfurt am Main: Suhrkamp, 2008. Print.

Faure, Bernhard. *Afterthoughts*. In *Buddhist Warfare*, Ed. by Jerryson, Michael K. and Juergensmeyer, Mark. Oxford: Oxford Universitiy Press, 2010. Print.

Foucault, Michel. *Schriften in vier Bänden, Dits et Ecrits, Bd. II*, Frankfurt am Main: Suhrkamp, 2002. Print.

Goldstein, Melvyn C. *A History of Modern Tibet, Vol. 1*. Berkeley: University of California Press, 1989. Print.

Guenther, Herbert V. *From Reductionism to Creativity. rDzogs-chen and the new sciences of mind*. Boston: Shambala, 1989. Print.

Honneth, Axel. *Organisierte Selbstverwirklichung. Paradoxien der Individualisierung*. In *Kreation und Depression. Freiheit im gegenwärtigen Kapitalismus*, Ed. by Honneth, Axel. Berlin: Kadmos, 2010. Print.

Jenkins, Philip. *The Lost History of Christianity*. New York: HarperCollins, 2008. Print.

Kapstein, Matthew. *The Tibetans*. Malden: Blackwell Publishing, 2006. Print.

Karmay, Samten Gyaltsen. *The Great Perfection (rDzogs chen). A Philosophical and Meditative Teaching of Tibetan Buddhism*. Leiden: Brill, 2007. Print.

Kittler, Friedrich. *Grammophon, Film, Typewriter*. Berlin: Brinkmann & Bose, 1986. Print.

Krueger, Werner. *Joseph Beuys – Jeder Mensch ist ein Kuenstler*. 1979. http://www.youtube.com/watch?v=JjkHYQnxZTE&feature=relmfu, retrieved 11/9/2012. Film.

Maher, Derek F. *Sacralized Warfare: The Fifth Dala Lama and the Discourse of Religious Violence*. In *Buddhist Warfare*, Ed. by Jerryson, Michael K. and Juergensmeyer, Mark. New York: Oxford University Press, 2010. Print.

Nordmann, Koni (Ed.). *Unterwegs für den Frieden*. Muenchen: Deutsche Verlagsanstalt, 2005. Print.

Shakabpa, Tsepon W. D. *Tibet. A Political History*. New York: Potala Publications, 1988. Print.

Slyke, James A. Van. *The Cognitive Science of Religion*. Burlington: Ashgate, 2011

Sogyal Rinpoche. *The Tibetan Book of Living and Dying*. Ed. by Gaffney, Patrick and Harvey, Andrew! London: Rider, 2002. Print.

Stooges, The. *1969*. Performed by *The Stooges*. Elektra, 1969. Album record.

Thurman, Robert. *Infinite Life. Seven Virtues for Living Well*. New York: Riverhead Books, 2004. Print.

Wachowski, Andrew and Larry. *The Matrix*. United States: Warner Bros. Pictures, 1999. Film.

—. *The Matrix Reloaded*. United States: Warner Bros. Pictures, 2003. Film.

Wallace, Vesna A. *Legalized Violence: Punitive Measures of Buddhist Khans in Mongolia*. In *Buddhist Warfare* , Ed. by Jerryson, Michael K. & Juergensmeyer, Mark. New York: Oxford University Press, 2010. Print.

Weber, Max. *Wirtschaft und Gesellschaft, Grundriss der verstehenden Soziologie.* § 10. Merkmale der charismatischen Herrschaft. In *Textlog.de Historische Texte und Wörterbücher*. http://www.textlog.de/7415.html, Retrieved 11/14/12. Print/Internet.

CPSIA information can be obtained at www.ICGtesting.com
Printed in the USA
LVOW11s1022231013

358230LV00001B/37/P